THE *EAGLE* AND THE *DOVE*

Essays in Seventeenth-Century Literature, 1

University of Missouri Press
Columbia, 1986

THE *EAGLE*
AND THE *DOVE*
Reassessing John Donne

Edited by Claude J. Summers
and Ted-Larry Pebworth

Library of Congress Cataloging-in-Publication Data
Main entry under title:

The Eagle and the dove.

  Bibliography: p.
  Includes index.
  1. Donne, John, 1572–1631–Criticism and inter-
pretation–Addresses, essays, lectures. I. Summers,
Claude J. II. Pebworth, Ted-Larry.
PR2248.E24 1986   821'.3   85–20874
ISBN 0-8262-0489-9 (alk. paper)

∞™ This paper meets the minimum requirements of the American
National Standard for Permanence of Paper for Printed Library Materials,
Z39.48, 1984.

FOR *JOHN R. ROBERTS*
AND *GARY A. STRINGER*

CONTENTS

SOULES EXHAL'D WITH WHAT THEY DO NOT SEE

AND HOW POSTERITY SHALL KNOW IT TOO

A NOTE ON TEXTS AND CITATIONS

Unless otherwise noted, all quotations from Donne's poems follow the text of John T. Shawcross, ed., *The Complete Poetry of John Donne*, The Anchor Seventeenth-Century Series (Garden City, N.Y.: Doubleday, 1967). The use of *i, j, u, v, vv,* and *w* has been silently modernized in all quotations, including those from works other than Donne's. The following abbreviations are used:

DAI	*Dissertation Abstracts International*
EA	*Etudes Anglaises*
EIC	*Essays in Criticism*
ELH	*Journal of English Literary History*
ELN	*English Language Notes*
ELR	*English Literary Renaissance*
HLQ	*Huntington Library Quarterly*
JEGP	*Journal of English and Germanic Philology*
MLN	*Modern Language Notes*
MP	*Modern Philology*
OED	*Oxford English Dictionary*
PLL	*Papers on Language and Literature*
PMLA	*Publications of the Modern Language Association of America*
PQ	*Philological Quarterly*
RES	*Review of English Studies*
SCN	*Seventeenth-Century News*
SEL	*Studies in English Literature, 1500–1900*
SP	*Studies in Philology*
UTQ	*University of Toronto Quarterly*

INTRODUCTION
THE EAGLE AND THE DOVE
Reassessing John Donne

CLAUDE J. SUMMERS AND TED-LARRY PEBWORTH

John Donne is a poet of dichotomies. Dualities of love and death, the sacred and the profane, the idealistic and the cynical, the delicate and the coarse are juxtaposed within individual works and throughout the canon, including the prose. Donne's dichotomous vision may even be said to predicate his choice of a dramatic mode and a style characterized by oxymoron and pun and paradox. The opposed postures and attitudes that he assumes create a nervous tension in his work, energizing the poetry and complicating such issues as persona and tone. At the same time, however, the dualities typically strain toward reconciliation or at least resolution. In fact, this impulse toward completeness is as much a hallmark of Donne's work as the dichotomous way of thinking that gives it urgency. Thus the recurrent patterns of separation and individual assertiveness are usually countered by equally insistent images of return and union. In "The Canonization," for instance, the persona defines the mystery of love in terms that are at once immanent and transcendent, but above all comprehensive:

> Call us what you will, wee'are made such by love;
>> Call her one, mee another flye,
> We'are Tapers too, and at our owne cost die,
>> And wee in us finde the'Eagle and the dove. (19–22)

Donne's tendency to reconcile opposites by conflating them into self-contained, internally compatible wholes is apparent throughout Songs and Sonets, where he frequently strives to "forget the Hee and Shee" ("The undertaking," 20) and achieve a "dialogue of one" ("The Extasie," 73). The goal of the idealistic Donnean lovers is "a way more liberall, / Then changing hearts, to joyne them, so wee shall / Be one, and one anothers All" ("Loves infinitenesse," 31–33). For them, the power of love is that it "all love of other sights controules, / And makes one little room, an every where" ("The good-morrow," 10–11). Even the famous images of contraction can be seen, from another perspective, as images of expansion, as when in "The Sunne Rising" the world is contracted to the lovers' bed, so the lovers' absorption in each other is simultaneously expanded into a whole new world impervious to the scientific laws that govern the natural one. If the love lyrics characteristically acknowledge the obstacles to love, they also often chronicle the successful discovery of a love that transcends all worldly impediments.

But despite the unambiguous triumph of idealistic love in some poems, and despite the straining toward reconciliation that is characteristic of Donne's poetry, an uneasy irresolution remains. This irresolution is related to Donne's habitual sense of conflict, which accounts for much of the poetry's power and tension. Not only is this sense of conflict indicative of the dichotomous vision that divides the world into opposed entities, it also manifests itself in all the familiar dichotomies on which the poems of Songs and Sonets pivot, including especially the body-soul duality. Donne frequently attempts to reconcile this duality, as in "Loves growth," where he observes,

> Love's not so pure, and abstract, as they use
> To say, which have no Mistresse but their Muse,
> But as all else, being elemented too,
> Love sometimes would contemplate, sometimes do. (11–14)

The fullest resolution of the dichotomy is, of course, in "The Extasie," which vigorously defends physical love even as it celebrates a transcendent, spiritual union: "Loves mysteries in soules doe grow, / But yet the body is his booke" (71–72).

Donne's rejection of neoplatonic asceticism is a crucial aspect of his attitudes toward love, as is the concomitant tendency toward reconciling the body-soul duality. But for all the resolutions in particular poems, the dichotomy remains, a potent force in the canon as a whole as well as in the individual works that express contradictory perspectives on love. Indeed, Donne poses not only as the rakish seducer and the idealistic lover but also as the victim of postcoital tristesse, who denounces the very delights on which he has surfeited. "Farewell to love," like Shakespeare's Sonnet 129, "Th' expense of spirit in a waste of shame," and Jonson's *Underwood* 88, "Doing a filthy pleasure is, and short," realistically acknowledges the complexity of human responses to sexuality. The disgust with physicality articulated in "Farewell to love" is no more authentically Donnean than the different attitudes, themselves expressed in strikingly opposed ways, in, for example, "The Extasie" and "The Indifferent"; but that repulsion is also no less Donnean than those attitudes sounded more frequently in the canon.

Donne's contradictoriness is among the ways in which he is a difficult poet and a fascinating one. The struggle of contraries in individual poems and throughout the canon makes it impossible to saddle Donne with settled attitudes. One function of the dichotomous vision is to be constantly aware of contradictory points of view, and this awareness gives the poetry extraordinary resilience as well as restlessness. The poems remain fresh because they invite so many different approaches and yield so many different perspectives. In their characteristic instability, the poems reflect the contradictions on which they are built, even as they frequently strain to reconcile those oppositions. By habitually juxtaposing the eagle and the dove, Donne creates restless poems of remarkable suggestiveness and power, fashioning from his dichotomous vision a highly individualized style of contradictoriness.

The essays collected here originated as submissions to the fifth Biennial Renaissance Conference at the University of Michigan–Dearborn, "The Eagle and the Dove: Reassessing John Donne," held on 15–16 October 1982.[1] The original versions of

---

1. Selected papers from the first four Dearborn conferences have been published: those from the 1974

nearly all the essays were presented there, some in abbreviated form. The collection reflects the aims of the conference: to reassess a major literary figure by exploring the critical assumptions on which his reputation rests, by reevaluating his most celebrated work, and by focusing on relatively neglected areas of the canon. As John R. Roberts has observed, the daunting bulk of Donne criticism confines itself primarily to less than one-half of the canon, concentrating almost exclusively on a handful of secular love poems, the Holy Sonnets and a few other religious poems, and the *Anniversaries*.[2] The reassessment offered here hopes to extend the range of critical inquiry. Taken together, the essays yield no glib consensus as to the precise nature of Donne's achievement. Rather, they witness to the continuing claim of Donne's work on twentieth-century readers, while defining that claim in terms somewhat different from those that led to Donne's popularity earlier in this century. If Donne no longer seems quite the exciting innovator who energized English and American poetry of the 1920s, he emerges here as a complex and individualistic product of the late Renaissance. Placed in a variety of biographical and intellectual and generic contexts and seen from a number of vantage points, Donne and his work continue to inspire admiration and interest.

Fascination with Donne's life has been an important factor in his reputation. Several essays collected here explore his biography and consider the implications of biographical knowledge for the study of his work. Presenting the poet as a "survivor" rather than an "apostate," Dennis Flynn argues the importance of the Elizabethan persecution of Catholics as a factor in shaping Donne's personality. Ilona Bell reassesses the central emotional relationship of the poet's life by focusing on three letters that she believes he wrote to Ann More during their courtship. In the process, Bell sheds light on the love poetry and carefully examines the elusive Burley manuscript. Biographical issues in criticism are discussed by John Shawcross, who explores the tricky question of "personal and impersonal" in Donne's poetry. He insists on the primacy of poetry as literature rather than autobiography or philosophy, but defends the efficacy of biographical contexts in helping determine an author's point of view in particular works.

Perhaps no aspect of Donne's artistry has attracted more critical comment than the felt presence of an individual voice in the poems. In an exciting essay that explores this voice, Judith Scherer Herz challenges a widespread notion, contending that in fact Donne is rarely a presence in his poems: "the urgent speaking voice we think we

---

conference on Robert Herrick as *"Trust to Good Verses": Herrick Tercentenary Essays*, ed. Roger B. Rollin and J. Max Patrick (Pittsburgh: University of Pittsburgh Press, 1978); those from the 1976 conference on seventeenth-century prose as a special issue of *Studies in the Literary Imagination* 10, no. 2 (1977), ed. William A. Sessions and James S. Tillman; those from the 1978 celebration of Herbert as *"Too Rich to Clothe the Sunne": Essays on George Herbert*, ed. Claude J. Summers and Ted-Larry Pebworth (Pittsburgh: University of Pittsburgh Press, 1980); and those from the 1980 conference on Jonson and Sons as *Classic and Cavalier: Essays on Jonson and the Sons of Ben*, ed. Claude J. Summers and Ted-Larry Pebworth (Pittsburgh: University of Pittsburgh Press, 1982).

2. John R. Roberts, "John Donne's Poetry: An Assessment of Modern Criticism," *John Donne Journal* 1 (1982), 62.

hear in the poems is a calculated illusion, the consequence of the collision of an unstable poem and a dislocated reader." Herz describes Donne's poems as "self-animating tropes" and outlines his mastery of a baroque "poetics of concealment."

One essay focuses exclusively on the Songs and Sonets. Stella Revard argues that the major model for Donne's conception of the lover in his amorous verse is not Ovid but Propertius, in whose elegies she discovers "the very prototype of the self-examining lover: neurotic; intelligent; witty but eccentric; learned but difficult in his learning; cold and sensual at the same time; forever defining and redefining his feelings and those of his mistress."

Four essays consider neglected works—the epigrams, the satires, the epithalamia, and "La Corona"—and explore Donne's complex responses to generic issues. M. Thomas Hester finds that the epigrams "offer an instructive example of [Donne's] poetic achievement *in parvo*," particularly of his characteristic "play with the problematics of signification." James Baumlin traces the influence of Persius's public voice and protreptic zeal in "Satyre III" and "Satyre V," emphasizing the way Donne both imitates and transforms his classical model. By focusing on the epithalamium for Princess Elizabeth and the Elector Palatine, Heather Dubrow demonstrates Donne's imaginative manipulation of generic norms to accommodate his individualistic talent. Revising the conventional critical estimate of "La Corona," Patrick O'Connell presents the sequence as paradigmatic of the entire body of Donne's religious poetry in its concern with the possibility and difficulty of self-transcendence.

Roger Rollin, Kathleen Kelly, Anna Nardo, and Walter Davis also contribute to the reassessment of Donne's religious works. Rollin approaches the Holy Sonnets from the vantage points of seventeenth- and twentieth-century psychology. Describing them as "sick poems in the service of preventive medicine," Rollin contends that "they constitute powerful dramatizations of how deeply rooted melancholy is in human nature and in the human condition." Kelly demonstrates how the speaker of the "Anatomy of the World" converts the reader to his world, forcing us to "play the role of the biblical prophet's audience." Examining the sermons as well as the lyrics, Nardo discusses Donne's almost obsessive playfulness, finding that he played "because play is always in between—the precise location his poetic speakers and his preaching persona need to occupy." In a long and richly illustrated essay, Davis demonstrates the structural functions of typology and meditation in the sermons.

The final contributions are concerned with aspects of Donne's reputation. In a fascinating study of the elegies occasioned by Donne's death, Michael Parker discusses the opposed responses of Thomas Carew and Henry King to the legacy of Donne and reveals a hitherto unnoticed relationship between Carew's elegy and King's. In the final essay, Paul Gaston observes that seventeenth-century composers were unable to cope successfully with the challenges posed by Donne's poetry, but that twentieth-century composers, on the other hand, have developed a musical idiom capable of accommodating Donne. Gaston finds especially impressive Benjamin Britten's setting of nine of the Holy Sonnets.

The essays collected here were written without consultation among the authors. The studies did however profit from the exchange of ideas afforded by the Dearborn conference, and, despite their diversity in subject matter and approach, they intersect and reinforce each other in significant ways. If these essays reassessing Donne achieve no coherent consensus, they do illustrate the seventeenth-century poet's continuing vitality. The susceptibility of his work to historical, generic, psychological, reader-response, and structural and formalistic analyses witnesses to his enduring presence in the critical imagination.

This book and the conference from which it grew have benefited from the generous advice and unstinting effort of the conference steering committee: Robert B. Hinman, William B. Hunter, Jr., Frank L. Huntley, Leah S. Marcus, David Novarr, John R. Roberts, John T. Shawcross, and Gary A. Stringer. Their suggestions have been invaluable, and we join the authors in expressing gratitude to them. We also gratefully acknowledge the support of the Campus Grants Committee and the following administrators at the University of Michigan–Dearborn: Sidney Warschausky, former Chairman, Department of Humanities; Eugene F. Grewe, former Interim Dean, College of Arts, Sciences, and Letters; and Eugene Arden, Vice-Chancellor for Academic Affairs.

THENCE WRITE OUR ANNALS

1. "AN EXCELLENT EXERCISE OF WIT THAT SPEAKS SO WELL OF ILL"
Donne and the Poetics of Concealment

JUDITH SCHERER HERZ

One speaks of Donne as a constant presence in his poems, an actor of the self, always there, always busy, self-advancing, self-promoting. I am going to claim the contrary, that Donne is rarely there, indeed in some poems never there, that the urgent speaking voice we think we hear in the poems is a calculated illusion, the consequence of the collision of an unstable poem and a dislocated reader. What sounds like confession is concealment, what sounds like the speaking voice is, like Don Quixote's enchanted head, masterful and duplicitous ventriloquism.

Unlike Jonson, whose poems, despite an amazing and as yet not entirely charted subtlety, remain pretty much unchanging objects the while we become their better "understanders / take-in-handers"; unlike Herbert, whose poems equivocate, their conclusions belying their beginnings, but on the assumption that there exists a stable poem that can yet be written even if each effort breaks down before that promise is achieved ("thy word is all / if we could spell"); unlike these, Donne wrote poems that are self-animating tropes, poetry as theater. Their subject, like Pozzo's ceilings or much of Bernini's oeuvre, is the nature of illusionism itself. Even though some saints may be glorified along the way—that is to say, there may be content—it is the resources of the medium itself, miracle as sleight of hand, transubstantiation as trompe l'oeil, that primarily engage the reader / spectator and artist.[1]

To a large degree this is familiar, another version of the elevation of insincerity, of lying as high art. But there is another aspect to it, to which Cervantes may provide a useful perspective. Older than Donne by a quarter-century, Cervantes was writing *Don Quixote* during the period of both the Songs and Sonets and the verse letters. Although the material is vastly different, there is a curious intersection of result, especially concerning the status of the author in his fiction. For Cervantes, authors are liars—Cide Hamete Benengeli—not to be trusted. They hide behind pseudonyms; they are confounded by unreliable translations. Although they claim to be historians, even moralists, they remain uncertain of the reality of their own creations. And this apparent debunking project contains yet another one, for, as we all know, the osten-

---

1. Pozzo's San Ignazio ceiling and false cupola provide the most obvious examples. Yet even Bernini, an infinitely more complex and accomplished artist, directs the spectator's gaze to his subject via the amazement the sculptor elicits as a result of his defiance of his materials. He sculpts marble that becomes silk, soft enough to button, to feel the flesh through. However, material is not merely defied, it is not technique alone that startles, for the marble seems transformed, made immaterial in such sculptures as the ecstatically enraptured Saint Teresa of the Cornaro chapel (Santa Maria della Vittoria), or the Mary Magdalen of the Siena Cathedral, or, the most physically provocative of all, Ludovica Albertoni of San Francesco a Ripa in Rome. Bernini was the master of the rhetorically heightened, theatrically elaborated gesture. A technician of light and stone, he made every moment dramatic, even creating "boxes" from which sculpted members of the Cornaro family, as if in a theater, could watch the spectacle of his swooning Teresa.

3

sible aim of *Don Quixote* is to discredit the romances of chivalry, to prove all their writers liars! Thus, if the author of *Don Quixote* is, like the author of the Songs and Sonets, daring us to find him, taunting us to believe him to the extent that he "proves" to us that we cannot believe him, the fictions themselves, novel and poems, share a further similarity: they are primarily about themselves. What pieces of plot there are in *Don Quixote* exist primarily as illustrations of the theoretical propositions on which the whole fiction is based. They are finally less interesting as story than as theory; indeed that seems to be, in part, the novel's point. It is the telling that we must attend to more than the tale, a truth that Sancho painstakingly demonstrates when he breaks off his narration of the shepherd, Lope Ruiz, pursued by the shepherdess, Torralba, at the very moment when Don Quixote stops keeping count of (that is, telling) the number of goats that have been ferried across the stream.[2]

To be sure content often seems to take over; that is, we begin to attend to events. But it is usually by virtue of their parodic function as they challenge notions about heroism, idealism, fantasy, reality. One cannot discuss here how Cervantes managed to create so magnificent a triumph of the human spirit in a construct so totally self-generating that, as Borges brilliantly demonstrated, it could be written word for word as new, or at least two chapters of it could be, by his Pierre Menard—but create it he did.[3] I do not believe, however, that there is any similar example in the whole repertoire of baroque art.[4] And Donne is no exception to this generalization, for his brilliance is closer to Pozzo's or Bernini's. The reader is baffled by, often excluded from the poems, notwithstanding marvelous lines, even magically moving lines: "Nor houres, dayes, moneths, which are the rags of time" ("The Sunne Rising," 10), or "I scarce beleeve my love to be so pure / As I had thought it was, / Because it doth endure / Vicissitude, and season, as the grasse" ("Loves growth," 1–4), or "Heaven is as neare, and present to her face, / As colours are, and objects, in a roome / Where darkness

2. Cervantes, *Don Quixote*, trans. J. M. Cohen (Harmondsworth, Eng.: Penguin Books, 1959), pp. 152–54.

3. Jorge Luis Borges, "Pierre Menard, Author of the Quixote," in *Labyrinths* (New York: New Directions, 1964), pp. 36–44. Borges also provides a wonderful description of the baroque in his "Preface to the 1954 Edition" of *The Universal History of Infamy* (London: Alan Lane, 1972): "I should define as baroque that style which deliberately exhausts (or tries to exhaust) all its possibilities and which borders on its own parody. . . . I would say that the final stage of all styles is baroque when that style . . . exhibits or overdoes its own tricks. The baroque is intellectual, and Bernard Shaw has stated that all intellectual labor is essentially humorous. Such humor is not deliberate in the work of Baltasar Gracián, but is deliberate, or self-conscious, in John Donne's" (p. 11).

4. All discussions of baroque art, both painting and poetry, emphasize in varying degree the qualities of illusion, play, distortion, the artificial. These are all aspects of the strategy I am here identifying as "the poetics of concealment." There have been several studies of baroque poetry and Donne's relation to the baroque tradition. See especially: Murray Roston, *The Soul of Wit: A Study of John Donne* (Oxford: Oxford University Press, 1974); F. J. Warnke, "Marino and the English Metaphysicals," *Journal of Aesthetics and Art Criticism* 22 (1964), 160–75; F. J. Warnke, *Versions of Baroque: European Literature in the Seventeenth Century* (New Haven: Yale University Press, 1972); Lowry Nelson, *Baroque Lyric Poetry* (New Haven: Yale University Press, 1961); J. H. Hagstrum, *The Sister Arts* (Chicago: University of Chicago Press, 1958); J. M. Cohen, *The Baroque Lyric* (London: Hutchinson University Library, 1963); Harold B. Segal, *The Baroque Poem* (New York: E. P. Dutton, 1974); and Odette de Morgues, *Metaphysical, Baroque and Précieux Poetry* (Oxford: Clarendon Press, 1953).

was before, when Tapers come ("The Second Anniversarie," 216–18). One takes one's solace in the fragment, for the poems as a whole do not often create that resting place for the imagination, that space between poet and poem where something happens to the reader. For Donne, the artist remains the conjurer who disappears into his own illusions, whose art, therefore, runs the risk of emptiness in proportion as its content is largely a mirror reflecting its own devices.

But *pace* William Empson, this is no debunking campaign.[5] What I have described I by no means deplore. On the contrary, such Escher-like virtuosity is its own excuse for being. Only I think we have become somewhat unwilling to trust our own responses to Donne's poetry, to acknowledge uneasiness, as if anything less than total assent would somehow diminish him. We are eager to subscribe to readings that chart macro-processes both in the poetry and in the poet's life, readings that seek to explain the poems by importing full-scale ideological systems that often ignore the individual poem in the interest of the comprehensive theory.[6] We have learned a great deal about sixteenth- and seventeenth-century poetics, rhetoric, theology, and politics in the process, much of which we can use as we read, but I am arguing for a redress of emphasis, a modest, albeit impertinent, program. For at the same time that we have radically expanded our sense of context we have come close to losing Donne as pretext or, more accurately, to losing our sense of engagement with Donne as the master of complex, unsettling, prickly poems, poems that simply will not resolve. Thus, if we do not look for consistency beyond the boundaries of any single poem, indeed not even necessarily within those boundaries, if we are willing to entertain continuous revisions of our readings, we may possibly begin to recover the Donne who, I have been suggesting, is in some danger of disappearing, the Donne of linguistic surprise, of ventriloquist virtuosity, of theological and philosophical inconsistency, the Donne who will say anything if the poem seems to need it.[7] This Donne hardly speaks at all *in propria persona*; rather, marvelously crafted, self-propeling, self-generating poems speak out of their own rhetorical systems, the putative speaker in each disappearing into his own rhetorical excesses. Thus the reader's bafflement becomes as much a part

5. See William Empson, "There Is No Penance Due to Innocence," *New York Review of Books*, 3 December 1981, pp. 42–50.
6. In very different ways both Barbara Lewalski and John Carey do this. The latter, himself the object of Empson's attack in the review just cited, reads much of Donne's poetry in terms of the trauma of his apostasy. The emphasis is on how "Donne's mind worked," the poems offering their evidence but taking second place to this putatively retrievable mind. John Carey, *John Donne: Life, Mind and Art* (New York: Oxford University Press, 1981). All students of seventeenth-century literature are indebted to Lewalski for her investigation of the literary and theological contexts for Donne's epideictic poetry. Yet the individual poems she discusses blend dangerously one with the other as they, too, are made to offer their evidence to the overriding theory. Barbara K. Lewalski, *Donne's "Anniversaries" and the Poetry of Praise: The Creation of a Symbolic Mode* (Princeton: Princeton University Press, 1973).
7. A. C. Partridge makes this point very nicely: "Any student who seeks to explicate the writings of Donne must be prepared to amend his judgements repeatedly." *John Donne: Language and Style* (London: André Deutsch, 1978), p. 11. Brian Vickers in somewhat different terms reaches a similar conclusion in his discussion of Donne as performer, wit, and clown. "'The Songs and Sonnets' and the Rhetoric of Hyperbole," in *John Donne: Essays in Celebration*, ed. A. J. Smith (London: Methuen, 1972), p. 160.

of a Donne poem as his clarification / edification is a part of Jonson's. Instability and dislocation are not accidents, they are ends.

In many poems the speaking voice makes claims about the world it has created that the experience of the reader with the poem contradicts; a break occurs between what the "I" asserts and what the reader knows. But it is not a simple duality. In the most interesting of the poems the reader's knowledge itself is not a constant. It is, rather, subjected to a continuous process of reinterpretation. At moments his experience may merge with the speaker's, but since he is given no reason to trust the speaker's version any more than another, he is thrust back onto his own resources once more.

If, for example, the speaker of a poem is presumably our guide through the poem, then who is he, what is he saying in "The Canonization"? Cleanth Brooks's famous response to such questions, however compellingly argued, seems finally not to stand up, for it requires the reader to impose upon the poem from the outset a dramatic fiction, essentially a dramatic character, which is the creation of the resolved paradox of the poem's conclusion. The entire poem, then, save for the last stanza, becomes this character's speech, its subject the totality of his experience of love, its tone constant, although variously nuanced ("the poem opens dramatically on a note of exasperation . . . and closes . . . on one of triumphant achievement").[8] But the reader of the poem does not have the advantage of this hindsight even on successive readings, since each stanza is entirely enclosed in its own voice and specified by its own vocabulary and rhetorical conventions.

Neither the gruff and colloquial voice of the first stanza nor the high literary voice and its successor, the world-weary voice, of the second, is even echoed in the hermetic, private voice of the third. Certainly after the mysterious transformations of the third stanza, one expects a different kind of assertion in the fourth. Yet the "pretty roomes" that are offered as the appropriate literary form for this new, mysterious love are indeed those sonnets, however well wrought, whose typical language is one of sighs, tears, colds, heats, the language that the second stanza so readily discarded.

Furthermore, the burden of the poem's argument has up to this point been on the discontinuity between the world's claims and the lovers' desires, but by the final stanza this boundary is blurred and the lovers, now *out* of the world (and, in a sense, out of the poem, for they no longer speak but are spoken to), would like to imagine their continuing efficacy within that world. In its rhetorical modes the poem has moved through satire, love lyric, hermetic, coterie poetry, and hymn, but it has not offered the reader any stable perspective for ordering these modes and their distinctive voices, just as, by the poem's conclusion, inside and outside are no longer clearly fixed points, nor subject and object fixed relationships.

---

8. Cleanth Brooks, *The Well Wrought Urn* (New York: Reynal & Hitchcock, 1947), pp. 11, 14. There is an interesting refutation of Brooks's reading by William J. Rooney, "'The Canonization'—The Language of Paradox Reconsidered," in *Essential Articles for the Study of John Donne's Poetry*, ed. John R. Roberts (Hamden, Conn.: Archon Books, 1975), pp. 271–78.

Indeed the only stabilizing element in the poem is provided by the rhyme scheme, particularly the reiterated rhyme on "love," that encloses each of the stanzas. Set against metrical constancy, however, is rhetorical discontinuity, but there is yet another challenge to stable meaning, and that derives from the reader's potential unease with the governing notion of canonization. Brooks's answer here is that Donne can make such a claim precisely because he "takes both love and religion seriously."[9] But *seriously* seems to me the directly problematic word. Why is Donne more "serious" here than in the elegy beginning "Come, Madame, come"? And what religion is he taking seriously? Certainly from a Protestant point of view all such cults, rituals, and hymns are irrelevant if not outright false. This is a version of the problem that is raised more pointedly in "The Relique." For there the argument based on miracle depends directly on our accepting the veneration of relics, a practice specifically identified as "misdevotion" in stanza 2. Does this undermine the final assertion of miracle? If miracles are nonsense, what happens to the lovers' miraculousness? Finally the poem rests its case on the other side of poetry, indeed of language itself ("All measure, and all language, I should passe, / Should I tell what a miracle shee was," 32–33), but the reader must simply take this as a given. Left to his own devices the reader may still be negotiating the odd leap from cynical worldliness ("For graves have learn'd that womanhead / To be to more then one a Bed," 3–4), to joking blasphemy ("Thou shalt be a Mary Magdalen, and I / A something else thereby," 17–18), to the glorification of the saints of love.

The reader cannot even depend on the accumulated experience of reading other poems of Donne to help him out. If he looks to "The Funerall," for example, he discovers the same problem in reverse. Nothing in the opening statements of that poem prepares for the brutal reversal of imagery and meaning that occurs suddenly in line 14. The "subtile wreath" of line 3, apparently resonant with the mystery of their souls' love, becomes abruptly a manacle and the very act of relic worshiping denounced as idolatry. The poem translates its images in a quite arbitrary fashion, valuing and devaluing at whim:

> As 'twas humility
> To'afford to it all that a Soule can doe,
>   So, 'tis some bravery,
> That since you would save none of mee, I bury some of you. (11–14)

In many poems whole clusters of lines defy direct translation. If we were asked to identify the poem from which the statement "all is wither'd, shrunke, and dri'd" comes, we would reply without much hesitation, "A nocturnall upon S. Lucies day," although we might not be able to place the line in its stanza; possibly the "First Anniversarie," especially if we read the following two lines: "All Vertues ebb'd out to a dead low tyde, / All the worlds frame being crumbled into sand." But we would be

---

9. Brooks, *The Well Wrought Urn*, p. 14.

twice wrong, our first mistake perhaps the more instructive. We assume that we hear sorrow, gloom, and despair, but what we are listening to, in fact, is pure courtly compliment. For these lines, addressed to the Countess of Salisbury, are part of an extraordinary conceit that rehearses nearly the entire repertoire of Donne's images and metaphors (the sun is stale, but your beauty shines; his light is for frivolous sonnets, your's to repair the book of god's creatures) at the same time that it devalues all other instances of this conceit's use as it attempts (for what seems to be the last time) a reinstatement of this claim for the Countess of Salisbury alone: "And if things like these, have been said by mee / Of others; call not that Idolatrie" ("To the Countesse of Salisbury," 37–38). For, the poet goes on to argue, my study of other great ladies whom I have praised "Enabled me to profit, and take forth / This new great lesson, thus to study you" (68–69).

The problem of how to assess the poem's language, of what to hear in a line, is particularly vexing in the verse letters, and I will return to this point later; in varying degrees, however, it runs through the entire canon. Sometimes we cannot even tell who is speaking. In "Womans constancy," for example, there are simultaneously two voices, two orders of experience. One can either describe the poem as one in which a man is speaking to a woman, ventriloquizing the woman's voice speaking back to him, then rebutting in his own voice the woman's position he has both created and reported, or as one that moves in precisely the opposite direction, in which the male poet creates a woman speaker who paraphrases his evasive quibbles and syllogisms in her voice, but then asserts her own inconstancy as the poem's conclusion and the situation's only constant. Indeed we have no way of knowing who is speaking, who is spoken to. We, no more than the voices, have any point of constancy. What is even more interesting about these voices is the way they are contained within one another. Present in one voice is the other; disengagement, the poem's subject on a social level, is both enacted within the poem and describes the reader's activity in the poem. Inside the poem someone speaks, someone listens, but the listener subtly inhabits the speaker's voice so as to deflect it from its purpose, to turn it into the opposite of what it claimed for itself at the start.

In terms of its content, "Womans constancy" is a slight and fashionable piece, cleverly and elegantly cynical, but at the same time it provides a complex and suggestive structure for the manipulation of voice through the creation of a typically Donnean double presence. It is a presence that is half in, half outside the poem, a listening voice that simultaneously speaks and hears. This double voice occurs in poems as diverse as "The Flea" and "The Extasie," but particularly in those poems whose aims are to ingratiate, and to claim the deserving of patronage, Donne developed a strategy whereby he could disappear altogether into the poems, so manipulating the "I" that it became a discardable fiction by the poem's end, thus enabling the poem to accomplish its social transactions without implicating him directly. What I would thus like to do is look at three such poems, all of which share the common ground of a relationship with Lucy, the Countess of Bedford,[10] that assume, in varying degrees of explicitness, modes of social transaction, and that also share certain similarities of language and forms of discourse.

The three poems, "Twicknam garden," "A nocturnall upon S. Lucies day, Being the shortest day," and "To the Countesse of Bedford. On New-yeares day," have for the most part been held to illustrate three different aspects of Donne's poetic. "Twicknam garden" has been seen as essentially literary play, "A nocturnall" as a profound expression of real loss, and the verse letter as an instructive document that is both socially real and philosophically (or theologically) true. These, however, are differences of ostensible content, of what the poems claim to be about (unrequited love, the death of the beloved, the worthiness of a patron). As forms of discourse they are strikingly similar. All three block ready access to themselves at the same time as they make an external presence, the implied audience for whose benefit the poem is being written, part of the materials of the poetic fiction. All challenge us from the start to identify what we are doing as readers, since the poet refuses to disclose the terms on which he wishes to engage us with the poems.

The two lyrics I will consider are both poems of hidden center, poems that use the declarative mode to elicit the interrogative, that entertain a wide range of possible readings but that leave all possibilities as merely provisional. Their most striking qualities are their veiling of the center, the dissolution of the "I," and the consequent engagement of the reader in a continuous process of revision.

What do we do with the very first line of "Twicknam garden," for example, a line of Carrollian excess with a speaker, Alice-like in his pool of tears, worked upon rather than working, the object of his own passions—"blasted," "surrounded"—the auditor of his own exhortations, and with no apparent control over the rhythms of his speech? Do we laugh at the speaker? Is he laughing at himself? Is this the stock figure of the Petrarchan lover or the anti-Petrarchan parody of that lover (who is also a part of that same convention)?[11] Is the "spring" of line 2 the healing season or the well of grief? If the latter, does it intensify or alleviate the speaker's sorrow? If the former, is he immune to its solace and cure?

To be sure, a recovery of sorts does begin to take place in the stanza—from object

10. Of course for two of these poems there is no clear proof that the countess is an implied presence. In several manuscripts of "Twicknam garden," for example, the title is omitted. Furthermore, "A nocturnall" is associated with her chiefly on the strength of the Saint's name and, by circular argument, the poem's similarity to "Twicknam garden." Although the argument that follows sees similarities between these poems independent of their relationship to Lucy, it is useful to assume the traditional identification, especially for "Twicknam garden."

11. See Silvia Ruffo-Fiore, *Donne's Petrarchism: A Comparative View* (Florence: Grafica Toscana, 1976), p. 124. The role of Petrarchan elements in Donne's poetry has been variously assessed. Leonard Tourney, for example, merges the neo-Platonic and the Petrarchan, whereas A. J. Smith argues for their essential difference. Leonard D. Tourney, "Donne, the Countess of Bedford and the Petrarchan Manner," in *New Essays on Donne*, ed. Gary A. Stringer (Salzburg: Institut für Englische Sprache und Literatur, 1977), pp. 45–59; A. J. Smith, "The Dismissal of Love," in *John Donne: Essays in Celebration*, ed. Smith, pp. 89–131.

the speaker becomes subject, the passive "blasted" changes to "I come," "I do bring." The violent metrical disorder of line 1 becomes the lessening disorder of lines 2 and 3, the near order of 4 (the fourth foot can be either an iamb or a spondee), and finally the perfect order of 5. But thematically 5 is the most disruptive line, for here activity yields only paradox. The self is split and, no longer a mere unhappy lover, entertains visions of primal dislocation; he is the anti-Christ for whom transubstantiation is negation. If laughter were a response to line 1, a shudder should greet the stanza's close. And yet the speaker seems quite pleased with himself, even if we may wonder what kind of wholesomeness it is that depends on death ("a grave frost"), or why, if the garden has so little effect on him, did he come to it in the first place, especially if it exacerbates rather than lightens his grief.

All these questions, however, imply that there is some coherent and knowable center to the poem, an extractable "I." But if we rid ourselves of the notion of an "I" altogether, the poem becomes a set of talking tropes and figures that seem either self-generating or, possibly, set in motion by some identifiable other presence – the countess, for example – a presence that enters the poem to take over its voice and simultaneously to become its audience. This other presence both supplies the poem's rhetorical resources and is the judge of its accomplishment. We may imagine it demanding: describe grief, enact grief, resist grief, seek solace, describe solace, resist solace, love me, resist me, despise me, and so on. The poet happily complies, making "an excellent exercise of . . . wit which speaks so well of ill." The lamenting lover, however, is impervious to all games, all transactions. And he becomes so proud of his displays of wit that by the end of the poem he imagines their going on forever. It is not solace in solitude that he is after, no green thought in a green shade, but rather truth proclaiming her suffering in a crowd.

The phrase "an excellent exercise of your wit" comes from a letter that Donne wrote to the Countess of Bedford, describing a poem of hers that may well have been written in response to poems Donne wrote to her.[12] It epitomizes the transaction one senses at the center of the poem, a relationship that allows the poet to appear before the lady in every role imaginable and be safe in all roles, from the ludicrous to the blasphemous. Despite the extreme veerings of tone, the poem refuses to take itself seriously as it rather jauntily proclaims its own suffering, insisting upon it as its defining prerogative, indeed the prerogative of truth itself. Thus while we read the poem as a set of variations on a Petrarchan theme, we move it over to another frame in which it watches itself play out these variations as it engages in a conversation, on the other side of the poem's surface, with the poem's ostensible subject, who is indeed the subject as she supplies the language, the landscape, even the voice, for this "excellent exercise of wit."

---

12. In a letter to Lucy, Donne wrote: "It is for those your Ladiship did me the honour to see in Twicknam Garden. . . . I humbly beg then . . . with two such promises, as to any other of your compositions were threatenings: that I will not shew them, and that I will not beleeve them; and nothing should be so used that comes from your brain and heart." *Letters to Severall Persons of Honour* facsimile reprod., intro. by M. Thomas Hester (Delmar, N.Y.: Scholars' Facsimiles and Reprints, 1977), p. 67.

Although it would certainly be perverse to hear jauntiness in the frequent heavy stresses and long vowels of "A nocturnall," especially in the first stanza, I am not at all sure that we can hear something readily identifiable as real grief or real loss there either. As much as "Twicknam garden," "A nocturnall" develops as a theme (indeed as two fairly contradictory themes) and variations. Here, too, there is another presence that inhabits the speaker's voice, although it is a presence whose chief assertion is absence, not-being. If ever the phrase *presence of absence* applied, it is here. For the "I" of this poem hardly needs to disappear, since it claims not-being as its quintessence from the start. Yet this voice arrogates an extraordinary amount to itself, claiming as the "Twicknam garden" speaker did, but even more extravagantly, that only his experience is worth another's study. At the same time as this voice plays numerous changes on the notion of nothingness, he inflates himself to contain everything. All the rest of the world can be contained in the diminished image of life shrunk "to the beds-feet," but he is *"every* dead thing" (7, 12). There is thus a tension between what the poem imagines and what it claims: diminishment is expressed in a vocabulary of expansion. There is also an odd shift in the poem that is usually ignored in readings that support what I consider the highly unlikely proposition that the poem was written at the death of Donne's wife (or the countess's sickness for that matter), and that is the shift in subject from Love as the agent of death to *"her* death" in line 28.

Love—both the abstraction and the accumulated experience of him and her ("oft did we grow / to be two Chaosses," 24–25)—is the primary destructive element in the poem. The speaker is ruined by love, as he repeatedly says, and not by the death of the beloved. Lovers are asked to study him, not, as in "Twicknam garden," to test the truth of their mistresses, but rather to discover the devastating effect of love. Insofar as this poem works changes on the topoi it shares with "Twicknam garden," it is in the proposition that her death is the occasion for celebration not lamentation, that it is indeed a festival. The shortest day of the title and the first stanza thus becomes the long night of the poem's conclusion. As a result, the imagined death of the lady, far from generating the vocabulary of despair, sets up the celebratory part of the poem, which exists in a kind of uneasy proximity with the vehemently uttered denunciation of love and its destructive powers.

In terms of my argument here, what I wish to underline is how we as readers have been deprived of our bearings, asked continually to reedit our responses. We do not know whether we are overhearing lamentation and complaint or watching a futile exercise at multiplication with zero. Lucy, a somewhat close-lipped Eleanor of Aquitaine, sets her *questions d'amour*; her poet does the best he can.

For both these poems, however, one is working with the assumption and not the certainty that they were written to, for, at the command of, or at the suggestion of the Countess of Bedford. For the verse letters there is no such problem, but there are other quite tricky ones. For a long time dismissed as mechanical puffery, the verse letters have recently been reinstated as major work. But in the process their warts have been covered over, their differences one with the other ignored in the interest of theories that see them as a homogenous group, a group that, according to Lewalski, for example, reveals "the potentialities of the human soul as the image of God."[13] The assumption behind such an argument is that Donne is interested in "a particular person . . . as that person will reveal something about the nature of things." I am not arguing that Donne is not interested in the "nature of things," but I am convinced that the "incarnational" emphasis is misleading and that, on the contrary, Donne is interested in particular people precisely for their particularities, for their relationship to him and for the ways he can reconstitute both their reality and this relationship in his poetry. Margaret Maurer's study seems to me a major step in this direction as she emphasizes the *real* presence of the countess in an argument that never loses sight of the verse epistles' "impropriety," but rather uses it to discover how these poems "constitute a transaction between the lady and her poet" as they imitate her methods of courtly diplomacy to secure her patronage for himself.[14] Donne seems to have been completely aware of the transactional nature of his diplomatic maneuverings. In a 1614 letter to Gerrard concerning the Countess of Salisbury, he admits that he may not be believed when he claims that all his praises of all his other ladies were "but prophecy of her." But then he goes on to weigh their respective positions with a fine awareness of the poem's decorum as the bargaining counter in his relationship with his new patron: "I must use your favour in getting her pardon for having brought her into so narrow and low-roofed a room as my consideration, or for venturing to give any estimation of her; and when I see how much she can pardon, I shall the better discern how far further I may dare to offend in that kind."[15]

"On New-yeares day" is not an "offen[ce] in that kind," partly because the real relationship of Bedford and Donne both antedates and informs the poem. Yet it belongs with the other poems I have been discussing partly by virtue of its language and partly because more than any of the other verse letters it is a split text in which a second presence takes over the speaker's voice and the "I" that begins the poem totally disappears by the end. The first six stanzas constitute a complete structure that develops the topoi of the poet's incapacity, the transitoriness of fame, and the lady's worthiness to be praised. The seventh stanza is the "turn," from the perspective of which the poem starts to come undone, its attempts at praise becoming mere mis-sayings. The second speaker now takes over. It is a most audacious switch, this giving over of his voice to another, for in this case the other is God. The complete disappearance of the "I" at this point (line 33, exactly halfway through) is the more remarkable since the first thirty lines had been so busy establishing the speaker / subject relationship. Yet in those lines, despite all the expectedly encomiastic vocabulary, there has been an odd hanging back, an unwillingness by the poet to commit himself to the extremes of hy-

---

13. Lewalski, *Donne's Anniversaries*, p. 70.

14. Margaret Maurer, "The Real Presence of Lucy Russell, Countess of Bedford, and the Terms of John Donne's 'Honour is So Sublime Perfection,'" *ELH* 47 (1980), 205–34. See also Patricia Thomson, "Donne and the Poetry of Patronage," in *Essays in Celebration*, ed. Smith, pp. 308–23.

15. *Letters*, pp. 260–61.

perbole. The "I," although it goes through the gestures of attempting to "measure infinity" (30), seems finally more interested in its own incapacities and in its failures to complete the measure. Indeed, in the fourth stanza, where one might expect the various images of corruption and decay to be negated by some such line as "but you by virtue of the tincture of your name preserve these lines whilst they proclaim your fame," one finds instead "the tincture of your name / Creates in them, but dissipates as fast, / New spirits . . . / . . . no bodies last" (16–20).

Given the poet's acknowledged failure to rise to his subject, it is no wonder that he turns to God "To make it good" (35), "to mend my rhyme" as Herbert would say. That is, he would like his inadequate praises of her to be an act of prayer to God. But there is a wonderful ambiguity here:

> I cannot tell them, nor my self, nor you,
> But leave, lest truth b'endanger'd by my praise,
> And turne to God, who knowes I thinke this true,
> And useth oft, when such a heart mis-sayes,
> To make it good, for, such a praiser prayes. (31–35)

Who is to turn to God? I? You? Both, I think.[16] The speaker certainly, for his missayings need completing. But syntactically "turne" can be imperative as well as first-person present indicative. Thus God will make her good by teaching, causing and clearing doubt, engaging her in the activity of her salvation. Donne does not fudge here, for God has a remarkably clear view of her weaknesses and imperfections, and in his best didactic tones Donne, speaking from God's point of view, reveals the courtly preoccupations, the uncertain purse, the complex diplomacies that constitute her public life. This voice is developed in a nicely Jonsonian fashion, mingling correction and encomium. Indeed, in their play of opposites and neat turns of wit, the stanzas of the second half of the poem use Jonsonian epigrammatic strategies as well. But in all of this the speaker is totally absent, his voice replaced by the extraordinary compound of God and Ben! By the poem's end, however, both God and the poet have ceased speaking; in their place a grandly public "we" proclaims the private gospel of "our New Year" (64, 65). Impersonality cannot be taken much further than that.

For all the disappearing acts that Donne manages, he still remains in the verse letters a fairly stable presence in comparison with the artful dodges of his lyric poems. For there, as I have attempted to demonstrate, the aim was concealment rather than revelation. Or if that is too teleological a notion, one can substitute *result* for *aim*. Not the least of the paradoxes attending one's reading of Donne is one's growing

---

16. Milgate's gloss to line 35 ("Faltering or inadequate praise of God is regarded by Him as a prayer for forgiveness for this inadequacy and for grace to praise Him better") would seem to suggest that it is her inadequate praise that is at issue. But I think this misplaces the emphasis, for, from the poet's point of view, the truth that would be endangered by his praise is *her* truth. Thus who can fault him if he lets God take up the pen to make good his mis-sayings? *John Donne: The Satires, Epigrams and Verse Letters*, ed. W. Milgate (Oxford: Clarendon Press, 1967), p. 267.

awareness that Donne's reliance on rhetorical figure, instead of establishing a common ground of understanding between poet and reader, works in precisely the opposite direction. Since we have no stable point within the poem from which we can watch the heightening, embellishing, complicating functions of his rhetoric, we have to deduce statement from figure. But when we proceed in that fashion, we run up against the sorts of contradiction I have pointed to in the poems examined here.

Attempts to impose a unity, to make the poems yield single, albeit complex, readings, usually involve constructs external to the poem—a dramatic speaker, for example, whose varying moods are thus made responsible for the inconsistencies of statement and tone. But even if we describe the problem this way, we have not come closer to solving it; rather we have simply restated it at a second remove. For the questions remain: on what terms do we engage the poem? how do we hear the speaking voice? what determines pathos? comedy? what makes one statement true, another suppositious? That there are no ready answers to these questions does not make the poems less remarkable. But, from this perspective, the emphasis falls on process rather than on conclusion, on means rather than on ends. As we read we hear a voice speak but we cannot tell where it is coming from. We are dazzled by an extraordinary number of linguistic effects as we attempt to pursue that voice further into the recesses of the poem, but it evades us. There is so much to spare in a Donne poem, however, that it hardly matters if the speaker slips away. In its "excellent exercise of wit," the poem remains, happily talking itself—and taking itself—to its formally perfect conclusion.

2. *DONNE THE SURVIVOR*

DENNIS FLYNN

A surprising development in Donne studies is the emphasis by John Carey in his *John Donne: Life, Mind and Art* on what he calls Donne's "apostasy." One puzzling thing about Carey's emphasis is that it emerges out of what might be called the Oxford school of Donne studies, a school that generally declines to use this term. For example, the word *apostasy* is never used by R. C. Bald in *John Donne: A Life*. Catholic writers often call Donne an apostate, but the biographers, editors, and critics of the Oxford school naturally tend to avoid pejorative terms in describing a Protestantism most of them more or less tacitly approve. Carey goes out of his way to disassociate himself from the "primitive superstition" of one Catholic writer who thought Donne had damned himself by his apostasy.[1] But he does not scruple to depart from the Oxford school by making apostasy a central theme in his own interpretation of Donne.

This departure is evidently not intended as a concession to the Catholic point of view. Rather, Carey's use of *apostasy* reflects his stance *au-dessus de la mêlée*, as one who eschews the controversial wrangling of Protestant and Catholic Donne scholars. Not really agreeing that Donne was, after all, an apostate, Carey uses the word mainly in a metaphorical or ironical sense. For Carey *apostasy* could be used as well to describe any shifting or abandonment of principle or party. This usage is virtually a dead metaphor, deprived by skepticism and relativism of the horror and depth of feeling that the word has when used in a more traditional sense: the denial of God's revelation. Even though Carey does not use the word in this traditional sense, his usage retains enough of the original pejorative flavor to suggest a vague disapproval. One objection that can be made to Carey's use of the word *apostasy* is this vagueness or lack of the precision proper to what is in essence a theological term. And I am not merely urging subtle theological distinctions here, because Carey's lack of precision tends to obscure what, in a case like Donne's, is the vital core of the question.

A second and more helpful departure in Carey's book is his waiving of what has been a main tenet of the Oxford school over the years: that Donne was never in any lasting or fundamental way influenced by Catholicism. For example, Izaak Walton (appropriated as a sort of doyen by the Oxford school) laid down the basic premise suggesting both that in spite of maternal influence in childhood Donne himself had never been an actual Catholic, and that the influence of Catholicism practically disappeared from his life for good during his twentieth year. Carey argues to the contrary that Donne, "though he forsook the Roman church, . . . never, in a sense, escaped its grasp." To be sure, Carey's phrase *in a sense* is crucial to his argument. But there is no mistaking the radical tenor of Carey's book when we read such statements as that Donne "knew that his Catholic upbringing had marked him indelibly, and that his spirit could

---

1. John Carey, *John Donne: Life, Mind and Art* (Oxford: Oxford University Press, 1981), pp. 25–26.

not grow straight in any other direction."[2] One will search in vain among, say, the Oxford introductions and commentaries by Dame Helen Gardner and her colleagues for admissions that Donne's spirit was indelibly marked by his Catholicism.[3]

According to Carey, Donne's Catholicism left on him a number of striking psychological effects. For one, he remained sympathetic toward "persecuted Catholics, though he had joined their persecutors." Here Carey's ironical disapproval of Donne is expressed more clearly in directly psychological and political rather than theological terms. Similarly there may be a fine, clinical distaste for Donne expressed in Carey's further point that a sort of guilt over apostasy kept Catholicism always "close to [Donne's] mind as a reproach or a threat, or as an adversary with which he hoped he might finally be reconciled."[4] On the other hand, such a statement may express Carey's compassion as much as his distaste. In any case Carey is not at all conceding the point Catholics have made, that Donne felt a theological guilt for having rejected the revealed truth of God. The prospect of reconciliation with Catholicism is not one that Carey wishes Donne had seized. If he finds fault with or is pejorative about Donne, it is only that he is repelled somewhat by what he sees as a pathology of psychological or social rather than theological or spiritual origins.[5]

Carey's departures from the Oxford school may then be explained by his relative indifference to the theological conflicts that polarized Donne's England. Unrestrained in calling Donne an apostate, and apparently uninterested in Donne's salvation or dam-

---

2. Izaak Walton, *The Lives of John Donne, Sir Henry Wotton, Richard Hooker, George Herbert, and Robert Sanderson* (Oxford: Oxford University Press, 1956), esp. pp. 23, 61; Carey, *Life, Mind and Art*, p. 35.

3. Even in editing the satires (which several writers, including Inez Alfors, Howard Erskine-Hill, and M. Thomas Hester, have argued *are* thus marked with a Catholic spirit), Oxford editor Wesley Milgate found little to mention along these lines. His introduction does not even use the word *Catholic*, and in his commentary on the poems one finds only a scant sixteen (mainly obligatory) uses of the word, seven of them in contexts that actually try to distance Donne from the thought of any Catholic influence (*John Donne: The Satires, Epigrams and Verse Letters*, ed. W. Milgate [Oxford: Clarendon Press, 1967], pp. xvii–xxv and 151–71). Though one would think that in the satires if anywhere Donne's "apostasy" would somehow have urged forth in ironical expression, Carey in this area at least is true to the Oxford school. Only with regard to two of the satires does he mention Catholicism, and he maintains rather peculiarly that after 1597 Donne "dropped satire-writing" (*Life, Mind and Art*, p. 63). Perhaps this is the same sort of thinking to be found in Helen Peters's Oxford edition of Donne's minor prose, in which she excises Donne's Overburian satires from the canon.

4. Carey, *Life, Mind and Art*, p. 35.

5. It is worth contrasting Carey's attitude here to that of another Oxford man, Samuel Johnson, commenting not just on Donne's conversion but on conversions like Donne's: "A man who is converted from Protestantism to Popery, may be sincere: he parts with nothing: he is only superadding to what he already had. But a convert from Popery to Protestantism, gives up so much of what he has held as sacred as any thing that he retains; there is so much *laceration of mind* in such a conversion, that it can hardly be sincere and lasting" (James Boswell, *Life of Johnson* [London: Oxford University Press, 1969], p. 426). Dr. Johnson holds without any irony that the key question is still theological rather than psychological. The sincerity and soundness of the conversion are affected by theological content, the quality or quantity of doctrines believed. Johnson, like most eighteenth- and nineteenth-century English writers, believed that extirpation of the Catholic sacraments had been primary in the building of modern England. Retaining an expressly Protestant outlook, and still using the term *Popery* with its undertones of distaste if not contempt, Johnson felt a theological, not purely psychological, "laceration of mind" in cases like Donne's. But this is something Carey never addresses.

nation, Carey writes as if these things hardly matter. Nevertheless, he might well have considered the warning given years ago by William Empson about Catholics and Donne: "they are likely to damage him so much that he is no use to them when they have got him."[6] That is, calling Donne an apostate can cut with a double edge. In the same vein, reviewing *John Donne: Life, Mind and Art*, Empson deftly caricatures Carey's version of Donne's Catholicism: "He considers that the character of Donne, though bad to start with, got steadily worse because he felt intense shame at not having become a martyr. That is, he was always a papist and only denied it for ambition."[7] This is not entirely accurate, since Carey gives other motives for Donne's apostasy, among them that Catholicism was superstitious and thus impossible for an intellectual like Donne. But Empson is substantially correct in thinking the whole of Carey's theory rather a gratuitous attack. In contrast, Empson himself praises Donne as "heretical" or "blasphemous," thus having fun with other dead metaphors. However, my point is not to tangle with Empson but to show that Carey's departures from the Oxford school are not as useful as they might be. To be consistent he should have avoided the ironical, dead metaphor *apostasy* and dealt in phenomena and concepts more available to our common usage in this pluralist world.

I propose instead that we describe Donne not as an "apostate" or as a "blasphemer" but simply as a "survivor" of the Elizabethan persecution. This will have the advantage, it seems to me, of placing Donne among the vast majority of his compatriots of every persuasion and of allowing us then to approach the question of his Catholicism from a more historical rather than quasi-apologetic standpoint. And here we can cite Carey to good advantage, in sentences that perform an undoubted service for Donne scholars by calling attention to the importance of the Elizabethan persecution as a factor conditioning the formation and development of individuals: "It would be as reasonable to demand what the Nazi persecution of the Jews had to do with a young Jewish writer in Germany in the 1930s. Donne was born into a terror, and formed by it."[8] Of course, as Carey points out, the scale of the Elizabethan terror was small by twentieth-century standards. But then the very novelty of the thing—the unprecedented way a social structure, evolved to nurture and protect Catholic society, was systematically used by a government to persecute not "heresy" but Catholicism itself—may be thought to have impinged very sharply on the sensibilities of the English Catholics despite the relatively small number of executions. At least as pertinent as these executions were the pioneering ways in which bureaucracy and available technology were used for purposes of mass terror by a government intent on changing a nation's mind. Most Catholics started out in Elizabeth's reign as opponents of the religion established. Like many opponents of modern totalitarian ideology, they soon found themselves "in severe inner conflicts about whether to act in line with their convictions

6. William Empson, "Donne the Space Man," *Kenyon Review* 19 (1957), 395.
7. William Empson, "There Is No Penance Due to Innocence," *New York Review of Books*, 3 December 1981, p. 47.
8. Carey, *Life, Mind and Art*, p. 18.

and run the risks involved or to play it safe" and feel like cowards and betrayers of their cherished faith.[9]

But prescinding from the ultimate justice of Carey's likening Donne's England to Nazi Germany, we nevertheless may find his comparison useful in reassessing what actually happened to Donne. Carey does not contend that Elizabeth's government was totalitarian (though arguably it exhibited some early tendencies in this direction). Nor does he contend that Donne's Catholicism marked him for extinction as inevitably as did the Jewishness of Hitler's victims (though the Elizabethan government's intention to extinguish Catholicism in England seems clear). But Carey's comparison helps to place Donne's life and writings in a context emphasizing the effects of persecution on survivors—a context also to be found in a growing body of historical discussion about the experience of Catholic recusants, the "English Catholic community," as they have been called in various writings by John Bossy. Bossy's work focuses on the survival of the Catholics as an organized and separate community. One of his main points is that these survivors constituted not so much a continuing remnant of the Catholic Church before Elizabeth as a relatively new creation by Catholics responding after the Council of Trent to the government's success in destroying the medieval English Church. Bossy's theory has been challenged by Christopher Haigh, who argues that, although the English Jesuits and their supporters did bring the Catholicism of Trent to replace traditional English Catholicism, their efforts were hampered and modified by the resistance of other English Catholics, who regarded themselves as adherents of "the old religion."[10] In any case, these complexities regarding continuity and discontinuity in English Catholicism provide a basis for reinterpreting Donne's various anti-Catholic expressions, especially his anti-Jesuit writings. The point is that, apart from Bossy's new, post-Tridentine "sect," clearly there were a whole range of English Catholic responses to the persecution, different ways of surviving, and among these Donne's way deserves careful attention rather than consignment to some vaguely unsavory pigeonhole such as "apostasy," unexamined to the extent that it is not taken seriously.

As a starting point toward reassessing Donne as a survivor, consider the following sentence from an essay by Bruno Bettelheim: "Having to live for years under the immediate and continuous threat of being killed for no other reason than that one is a member of a group destined to be exterminated, and knowing that one's closest friends and relatives are indeed being killed—this is sufficient to leave one for the rest of one's life struggling with the unsolvable riddle of 'Why was I spared?,' and also with completely irrational guilt about having been spared."[11] As Carey vividly suggests, Donne

9. Bruno Bettelheim, "Remarks on the Psychological Appeal of Totalitarianism," in *Surviving and Other Essays* (New York: Vintage Books, 1980), p. 323. Bettelheim explains (pp. 324 and 327) how family and neighbors, the very structure of social life, become systemic elements of totalitarian repression.

10. John Bossy, *The English Catholic Community, 1570–1850* (London: Darton, Longman and Todd, 1975), pp. 11–76. For Haigh's critique of Bossy, see "The Fall of a Church or the Rise of a Sect?" *The Historical Journal* 21 (1978), 181–86; "The Continuity of Catholicism in the English Reformation," *Past and Present*, no. 93 (November 1981), 37–69; and "From Monopoly to Minority: Catholicism in Early Modern England," *Transactions of the Royal Historical Society*, 5th ser. 31 (1981), 129–47.

11. Bettelheim, "Trauma and Reintegration," in *Surviving and Other Essays*, p. 26.

lived for years under the immediate and continuous threat of being killed because he was a Catholic, and he knew that close friends and relatives were indeed being killed. According to Bettelheim, this would have been sufficient to pose a lifelong problem and inspire irrational guilt feelings in a survivor, even apart from any supposed guilt feelings attendant upon apostasy. Carey makes something of an ironical exposé of Donne's guilt over apostasy, but he misses the more interesting and useful idea of Bettelheim: that a man with Donne's experience would suffer disintegrating, irrational guilt merely for having survived the persecution.

Donne himself, in a famous passage from *Pseudo-Martyr*, his first published writing, all but tells us that this was the case: "I have beene ever kept awake in a meditation of Martyrdome, by being derived from such a stocke and race, as, I beleeve, no family, (which is not of farre larger extent, and greater branches,) hath endured and suffered more in their persons and fortunes, for obeying the Teachers of Romane Doctrine, than it hath done."[12] Donne's own brother, enrolled a class behind him at law school and living only a few streets away, had been arrested in his own room while making his confession to a priest and was purposely sent to die in a plaguey jail. For Donne, surviving had been experienced as a stroke of unmerited and inexplicable luck. But as Bettelheim has observed, the voice of conscience in such cases is apt to comment that "the reason you had the chance to survive was that some other"—for example, Henry Donne—"died in your stead." And then comes the more terrible accusation of conscience: "You rejoiced that it was some other who had died rather than you!"[13] Irrational and even inaccurate as such accusations may be, they can dominate a life. Precisely because of this they are mainly repressed and can be dealt with only on some deep emotional level.

Evidence that Donne had to deal with such feelings even years later can be seen in his poem "A Litanie," one stanza of which links the idea of surviving with Abel, the first brother and the type of martyrs. The stanza is addressed to God and invokes the blood of the martyrs in a prayer for patience to endure surviving:

> And since thou so desirously
> Did'st long to die, that long before thou could'st,
>   And long since thou no more couldst dye,
> Thou in thy scatter'd mystique body wouldst
>   In Abel dye, and ever since
>   In thine, let their blood come
> To begge for us, a discreet patience
> Of death, or of worse life: for Oh, to some
> Not to be Martyrs, is a martyrdome. (82–90)

This stanza has been thought by Gardner to rationalize Donne's apostasy, as if Donne meant to say that the "intransigence" of remaining a Catholic could somehow be understood as "a form of self-indulgence, an easy way out of the strain of conflicting

---

12. *Pseudo-Martyr* (London: for Walter Burre, 1610), "An Advertisement to the Reader."
13. Bettelheim, "Trauma and Reintegration," p. 27.

duties." Robert Silhol rejects Gardner's reading because he finds that the stanza is insincere and hence cynically calls into question the validity of the martyrs' sacrifice. Carey interprets the lines to signify a rather perverse thirst for martyrdom on Donne's part, as if having lived on were spoiled mainly by the fact that one had not been martyred.[14] But it seems tendentious to ridicule or blame Donne in these ways and so to rule out the validity of his pain as a survivor. The lines are surely more accurately interpreted as referring directly to the pain and guilt of surviving.

Bettelheim points out three possible psychological responses to the experience of trauma endured by persons like Donne: (1) one can be psychologically and even physically destroyed by the very effort to survive; (2) one can deny that the experience of having survived has had any lasting impact; and (3) one can engage in a lifelong struggle to remain aware, to recover from surviving, and to reintegrate one's personality on some new basis.[15] In Donne's life we can see traces of each of these varied responses to surviving.

In the first place, Donne himself often mentions—as, for example, in *Biathanatos*, a work focusing precisely on the plight of the English Catholics—that he has been infected by a "sickely inclination" toward suicide, toward giving up his role as a survivor in emotional exhaustion. He suggests in dramatic terms that the origin of this inclination is the fact that "I had my first breeding and conversation with men of a suppressed and afflicted Religion, accustom'd to the despite of death, and hungry of an imagin'd Martyrdome." More important is his further statement that "my Conscience assures me, that no rebellious grudging at Gods gifts, nor other sinfull concurrence accompanies these thoughts in me."[16] In other words, Donne does not indulge his "sickely inclination" in an overwhelming sense of the unfairness of it all. He has been able to deal somehow with that feeling and is not tortured by it to the point of giving up. On the other hand, it is and has been a pressure he is conscious of and can articulate.

More interesting and more characteristic of Donne is the second of Bettelheim's three responses: denial. In the aftermath of his brother's death, Donne seems to have tried to go on essentially as he had been before. We know from his 1591 portrait that Donne had fancied himself a swordsman. In the years after Henry Donne's death, this pose reemerged a reality when Donne joined the Cadiz expedition in 1596 and again sailed to the Azores with Essex in 1597. Such an effort to reintegrate oneself essentially as one had been before requires in a survivor the defenses of repression and denial, as well as a rather false exterior, a bravado.

Such a false exterior is characteristic of Donne's personae in various writings of

14. *John Donne: The Divine Poems*, ed. Helen Gardner (Oxford: Clarendon Press, 1952), p. xxv. Gardner herself reflected immediately, however, that her explanation may be "over-subtle"; Robert Silhol, "Réflexions sur les sources et la structure de *A Litanie* de John Donne," *EA* 15 (1962), 336 and n. 21; and Carey, *Life, Mind and Art*, p. 49.

15. Bettelheim, "Trauma and Reintegration," p. 28.

16. *Biathanatos* (New York: Facsimile Text Society, 1930), pp. 17–18. See also my "Irony in *Biathanatos* and *Pseudo-Martyr*," *Recusant History* 12 (1974), 49–69.

the 1590s. In the elegy "Here take my Picture," the speaker is leaving his mistress with a portrait of himself:

Here take my Picture, though I bid farewell,
Thine, in my heart, where my soule dwels, shall dwell.
'Tis like me now, but I dead, 'twill be more
When wee are shadowes both, then 'twas before. (1–4)

He suggests that his journey may lead to his death, and the implication is that she may never see him again. He is making her the conventional gift of a portrait to remember him by, but something in his speech is unconventional and even rather tactless. He not only refers explicitly to his prospective death (a topic better left unspecified on such occasions) but also anticipates that the picture will serve well after he dies as a sort of memento mori. His enthusiasm for this idea is puzzling; normally the gift of a memento at parting will be valued as a reminder of the living rather than for its resemblance to the dead. To vary this morbidity, he abruptly reconsiders that he will, after all, return. Yet the return he envisions is hardly more desirable from the standpoint of a mistress than the preceding prospect of death:

When weather-beaten I come backe; my hand,
Perhaps with rude oares torne, or Sun beams tann'd,
My face and brest of haircloth, and my head
With cares rash sodaine stormes, being o'rspread,
My body'a sack of bones, broken within,
And powders blew staines scatter'd on my skinne. . . . (5–10)

The graphic, preposterous accumulation of these repugnantly imagined deformities suggests that the speaker is poised between self-mockery and a real dread. About his physical appearance, even about physical death, he can afford to joke with bravado. But the real danger in his departure is the death of being abandoned, and this fear must be denied. In the second half of the poem, he fixes on his imagined disfigurement as if it alone could be the threat to her constancy, a threat to be rendered by the carping of his rivals. That a woman should be thus "taxed" for loving a wounded veteran, no matter how deformed, seems a singularly vicious social context. As a defense against it, the speaker offers the flattery that she will be strong enough not only to contemplate and brandish his portrait but also to regard his contrasting physical decay as the object of a higher form of love than any they have yet experienced.

Of course Donne's experience had provided occasion for such defensive bravado even before the 1590s. Certainly his 1591 portrait itself exemplifies such a spirit in its outrageous pose of the *ligueur* captain or gentleman volunteer. Above all, the motto of the portrait—*Antes muerto que mudado* ("Rather dead than changed")—strikes a note of histrionic defiance we might expect from a survivor denying the impact of his own experience. Especially poignant is the implication of the motto when we understand its context in the *Diana* of Montemayor, from which it is adapted. It is the oath of

Diana, a shepherd's mistress, recalled by the shepherd after her unfaithfulness. Thus the motto of the portrait has a hollow assurance, as if Donne knew unconsciously that his pose was only a pose.[17]

A related bravado may also be seen in Donne's second portrait, that sardonic parody of the melancholy lover in the shadows, painted in the later 1590s. This second portrait suits well with the fleering, self-assured insolence of the elegies and other love poems Donne wrote at this time. Bettelheim points out how, through denial, survivors may be relatively successful, in that their lives seem free of symptoms of disintegration, yet deep down they may be full of insecurity, living a "house-of-cards existence."[18] Though they do not admit the fact to full awareness, they are half conscious that any strong wind of serious trouble can collapse their integration and reveal their denial of the meaning and impact of the horrendous experience. For Donne, such a collapse seems to have coincided with the death of his friend and patron, Thomas Egerton the younger, and with the onset of his relationship with Ann More.

At any rate, he had no portraits painted for fifteen years. But in the three portraits he did commission between the time of his ordination and his death, none of that earlier bravado and brittle irony is seen. The 1616 portrait, by Isaac Oliver, shows us the husband and Horatian epistoler Wotton describes for Walton: "His melting eye, shewed that he had a soft heart, full of noble compassion; of too brave a soul to offer injuries and too much a Christian not to pardon them in others." Then in 1620 Donne was painted (probably by Cornelius Johnson) in a pose representing the successful diplomat described by Paul R. Sellin.[19] Finally, at the time of Donne's death, there is the famous portrait of him in his shroud, now lost like Donne's first portrait and, like the first, known to us only at the remove of a different medium. It is worth noting that in none of these three portraits dating after 1615 is Donne dressed as a preacher or minister. Comparison of Donne's portraits to those of his fellow members of the Anglican hierarchy suggests that, though he had taken orders, this did not form in his mind an identity to be symbolized by the customary clerical garb. Certainly Donne shows none of Herbert's care about this. On the other hand, there is at least about the 1616 and 1620 portraits a steady sobriety, especially in the frankness of Donne's gaze, suggesting that utter honesty about the self we sense also in the poem he wrote in 1624 after his near fatal illness—"A Hymne to God the Father."

This brings us to the most interesting of Bettelheim's three responses to surviving, the one I think most characteristic of Donne: his effort from about the time of his marriage to live with an existential predicament that could have no solution, the predicament of the survivor suffering the manifold effects of disintegration. It was in rela-

17. See my "Donne's First Portrait: Some Biographical Clues," *Bulletin of Research in the Humanities* 82 (1979), 7–17.

18. Bettelheim, "Trauma and Reintegration," p. 33.

19. Walton, *Lives*, p. 83; and Paul R. Sellin, "John Donne: The Poet as Diplomat and Divine," *HLQ* 39 (1976), 267–75; "The Proper Dating of John Donne's 'Satyre III,'" *HLQ* 43 (1980), 275–312; "John Donne and the Huygens Family, 1619–1621," *Dutch Quarterly Review of Anglo-American Letters* 12 (1982–1983), 193–204; and *John Donne and "Calvinist" Views of Grace* (Amsterdam: VU Boekhandel, 1983).

tion to Ann More that Donne moved out of mere repression and denial into a complete restructuring of his integration, in succeeding years giving full cognizance to the most tragic experiences of his life. Donne's most frank, least ironical references to his persecution as a Catholic (for example, those quoted above, and others from "A Litanie," *Biathanatos*, and *Pseudo-Martyr*) occur during these years.

A precondition of his new integration was the first full recognition of how severely this religious persecution had affected him. In the circumstances leading up to and following his wedding, we can discern Donne's difficult acknowledgment that he had been and in a peculiar sense still was a persecuted Catholic. Such a recognition can be seen, for instance, in his defensiveness about imputed Catholic sympathies in letters to Sir George More, his disapproving Puritan father-in-law; these contrast with his more confidential admissions to Lord Keeper Sir Thomas Egerton, a man who also had known what it meant to suffer as a Catholic during the reign of Queen Elizabeth.[20] Having lost his position in Egerton's service, Donne spent some years in partial seclusion, working out a recovery from the collapse of his fortunes—or "metaphorical death"—caused by his marriage. With this it became easier for Donne to accept and cope with his guilt and make the best of his life, even if still haunted by the question "Why was I spared?"

To this question, one partial answer Donne seems at least to have tried was that he was saved in order to love, in particular to love Ann More. Bettelheim has written that, in the reintegration of survivors, one of the most crucial factors of all is "the support they receive from those closest to them."[21] But erotic love was not the only answer Donne tried for the question "Why was I spared?" Besides (or building on the basis of) his marriage, we find him increasingly devoted to friendship. It is striking that, in the years after Henry Donne's death, Donne's two closest friends were also Henrys, Henry Wotton and Henry Goodyere, both of whom, like Donne, had come from families with branches that had suffered and still suffered from the persecution. It was in relation to these friends and others that Donne at length began seriously to prepare for trying a third answer to the question "Why was I spared?" This was his effort at the ministry of the only public religious forms his society would sanction.

It is beyond the scope of this essay, however, to attempt exploring any of these answers at length. My effort has been merely to suggest that, by labeling Donne an apostate, we may obscure rather than enhance our historical understanding of the man. And I have tried to show a few ways in which we can integrate to better effect our understanding of his life and writings under the rubric of the "survivor" in Bettelheim's sense. The main issue of Donne's formative years was, as Carey has noted, the memory of an experience commonly presented to all individuals who lived through the

20. The letters are those of 11 and 13 February and 1 March 1602 (printed in *The Losely Manuscripts*, ed. A. J. Kempe [London: John Murray, 1836], pp. 331–42). See my extended discussion of these passages in "Donne's Catholicism I," *Recusant History* 13 (1975–1976), 9–13.

21. Bettelheim, "Preface," in *Surviving and Other Essays*, p. xi.

Elizabethan persecution, regardless of how they reacted to it in their various religious developments. Moreover, as Bettelheim points out, "A survivor has every right to choose his very own way of trying to cope."[22] The threat of death and disintegration posed to the young Donne by the Elizabethan persecution now seems to me more arresting and important than the supposition that his reaction to this threat was "apostasy," whatever that means.

22. Bettelheim, "Trauma and Reintegration," p. 34.

3. "UNDER Y^E RAGE OF A HOTT SONN & Y^R EYES"
John Donne's Love Letters to Ann More

ILONA BELL

Compared to other great Renaissance writers, John Donne left to posterity an un-usual number of familiar letters. The Loseley manuscript contains letters to his father-in-law, Sir George More, and his employer, Sir Thomas Egerton, which allude to the dramatic events following his clandestine marriage. *Letters to Severall Persons of Honour* (1651) and *A Collection of Letters made by Sr Tobie Matthews Kt.* (1660) contain over two hundred letters that comment on his life and concerns after marriage.[1] Since there are so many letters about Donne's later years, and so few about the period before his marriage, it is tempting to analyze Donne the poet in terms of Donne the thwarted but undefeated professional. David Novarr presents the married Donne as an ambi-tious careerist who wrote only a few poems—all for sale and personal advancement. John Carey goes even further. Throughout the letters, sermons, religious poems, and love poems, Carey sees Donne as anxious to avoid the Catholic martyrdom of his brother Henry and determined to succeed at all costs.[2] Despite the wealth of evidence, I wonder whether this aggressive, calculating, self-seeking ambition pertains to the Songs and Sonets, where "All honor's mimique; All wealth alchimie" ("The Sunne Rising," 24) and where Donne places his love above all financial and professional con-siderations.

R. C. Bald's biography contains a long chapter on the years when Donne was secre-tary to the Lord Keeper but only a few scattered paragraphs on the courtship that took place during those years, even though falling in love with Ann was surely one of the shaping events of Donne's life.[3] Despite the multitude of Donne letters, schol-ars lament the complete absence of any correspondence with Ann More.[4] Since little fresh evidence has emerged, old, unexamined ideas about Donne's marriage have per-sisted. Many readers continue to assume that only "the simpler and purer, the more ideal and tender of Donne's love-poems"—to borrow Grierson's memorable phrase—are "the expression of his love for Ann More."[5] Yet, given the facts of the affair, I simply do not believe that either the young lady or the courtship could have been

---

1. *Letters to Severall Persons of Honour* (London: for Richard Marriot, 1651); *A Collection of Letters made by Sr Tobie Matthews Kt.* (London: for Henry Herringman, 1660).

2. David Novarr, *The Disinterred Muse: Donne's Texts and Contexts* (Ithaca and London: Cornell Uni-versity Press, 1980); John Carey, *John Donne: Life, Mind and Art* (New York: Oxford University Press, 1981).

3. R. C. Bald, *John Donne: A Life* (New York and Oxford: Oxford University Press, 1970), chap. 6, pp. 93–127. I rely on Bald throughout for biographical data.

4. Evelyn Simpson, in *A Study of the Prose Works of John Donne*, 2d ed. (Oxford: Clarendon Press, 1948), says "We would gladly have learnt something of the circumstances which gave rise to the earlier *Songs and Sonets*, but no letters in the published collections can be dated before 1601, and even the ear-lier letters in the Burley MS. contain but one explicit reference to the poems" (p. 295).

5. In his edition of *The Poems of John Donne*, 2 vols. (Oxford: Oxford University Press, 1912; rpt. 1963), Herbert J. C. Grierson says this "cannot of course be proved. . . . But the general thesis, that it was a great

as simple or pure as Grierson and others have so courteously assumed. Ann's elope-ment and Donne's imprisonment created such a scandal that seven years later the King still remembered the disgrace and doubted Donne's character. Donne replied that his "intemperate and hastie act" did not leave "anie dishonourable staine."[6] Moreover, in defending the actions of himself and Ann to Ann's irate father, Donne insisted "we adventurd equally . . . having these honest purposes in our harts."[7] In the Loseley let-ters, written to Sir George More and Sir Thomas Egerton after the hasty marriage, Donne repeatedly insists, "I can and wyll show myself very honest, though not so fortunate." Even though the couple's actions defied existing social conventions, Donne proclaims his own unconventional notions of honor and love, protesting "such affec-tion as *in my conscience* becomes an honest man" (emphasis supplied).[8]

The old-fashioned, idealized image of Donne's love for Ann More has not only limited our reading of his love poems but also obscured the significance of three ex-tremely revealing letters that, I believe, clarify the whole affair. They are among a group of letters discovered by Logan Pearsall Smith in the Burley manuscript and pub-lished by Evelyn Simpson in her 1924 *Study of the Prose Works of John Donne*, as Letters 16, 15, and 13, respectively.[9] These three letters have been generally neglected. Evelyn Simpson thought that Donne probably wrote one or two of them to his patron, Lucy Countess of Bedford, and the third to some unidentified party during the period of illness, misery, and imprisonment that followed his clandestine marriage. If we keep an open mind about Donne's love affair with Ann More, I think both the style and the content of the letters make it much more likely that these three letters were written by John Donne to Ann More over a year before their elopement. If so, they are the only known letters Donne wrote to Ann, and they contain the first substantive infor-mation about Donne's wooing of Ann, enabling us to examine a central moment in Donne's life (and poetry) that has remained unknown and undocumented until now. Beginning with expressions of intense passion and hints of consummated love, Donne

---

experience which purified and elevated Donne's poetry, receives a striking confirmation from the better-known history of his devotional poetry" (2:xlix).

6. In Toby Matthews's *Collection of Letters*, Donne writes to Lord Hay, "I have been told, that when your Lordship did me that extream favour, of presenting my name, his Majestie remembered me, by the worst part of my historie, which was my disorderlie proceedings, seaven years since, in my nonage . . . so I humblie beseech your Lordship to adde another to these, not to be too apprehensive of any suspicion, that there lies upon me anie dishonourable staine, or can make my King have anie prejudice against me, for that intemperate and hastie act of mine" (pp. 330–31).

7. *Manuscripts, and Other Rare Documents, Illustrative of Some of the More Minute Particulars of English History, Biography, and Manners, from the Reign of Henry VIII. to that of James I. at Loseley House in Surrey*, ed. Alfred John Kempe (London: John Murray, 1836), pp. 328–29.

8. *Loseley Manuscripts*, pp. 342, 335.

9. Logan Pearsall Smith describes his discovery of the Burley ms. in *The Life and Letters of Sir Henry Wotton*, 2 vols. (Oxford: Clarendon Press, 1907), 2:489–90. Evelyn Simpson printed the letters in *A Study of the Prose Works of John Donne*, 1st ed. (Oxford: Clarendon Press, 1924), pp. 271–320. The three letters that I will be discussing, referred to as S16, S15, and S13, appear on pp. 304–5, 302–3, and 300–301, respectively. Simpson altered the original manuscript order. Since she thought letters S15 and S13 were written to patrons, she assumed they were written later than S16.

in these three letters to Ann responds to a sequence of events that created great stress for them both and made him fear, desperately, that the affair might end. If, as these letters suggest, Donne's love affair with Ann entailed a much wider range of feelings than we have thought, it may well have inspired a much broader, more various group of poems than we have considered.

In the first letter Donne writes to Ann during a period of separation that interrupted one of glorious intimacy. Ann has written, announcing her arrival in London, and Donne responds, looking forward to their reunion. Here is the letter, both as it appears in the Burley manuscript and as I have transcribed it:

> Madam. I will haue leaue to speake like a lovor, I am not altogether one: for though I loue more then any yett my loue hath not ye same marke & end wth others. How charitably you deale wth vs of these parts? y^t at this tyme of ye yeare (when the suñ forsakes vs) y^o come to vs & suffer vs not (out of y^r mercy) to tast ye bitternes of a winter: but Madam you owe me this releif because in all that part of this someñr wch I spent in y^r presence y^o doubled ye heat and I liued vnder ye rage of a hott sonn & y^r eyes. that hart wch y^o melted then no winter shall freise but it shall ever keepe that equall temper wch you gaue it soft enough to receaue y^r impressions & hard enough to retayne them. it must not tast to y^o as a negligence or carelesnes y^t I haue not visited y^r Lad: in these dayes of y^r being here call it rather a devout humylyty y^t I thus aske leaue & bee content to beleeue from him y^t can as impossibly ly to y^o as hate y^o y^t by comãundment I am sodenly throwne out of ye towne so dayly and diversly are wee tempested y^t are not o^r owne. at my retourne (wch therfore I will hasten) I wilbee bold to kiss y^t fayre vertuous hand wch doth much in receaving this letter & may do easyly much more in sending another to him whose best honor is that hee is y^r leiuetenant of himself./ Anonimos. (f. 295)[10]

Evelyn Simpson thought that "if this letter is Donne's, it is probably addressed to the Countess of Bedford. The tone of devotion, which resembles that of a lover but is subtly differentiated from it, is the tone also of certain of Donne's poems addressed to that lady."[11] It is difficult to make distinctions of this sort, however, since in the Renaissance "the language of love, particularly of Petrarchanism, was exploited for the terms it had in common with the social and economic vocabulary of patronage." Most scholars agree, however, that the love language used by clients to patrons was elevated, generalized, distant, idealized, spiritualized, and quite undisturbed by the heat and rage of passion. "Complimentary love poetry," Arthur F. Marotti explains, "traditionally elevated love above the level of the body and the appetites to discourse about an experience that is spiritual and virtuous, if not angelic." Stephen J. Greenblatt notes

10. Since the Burley letters are neither signed nor preserved in Donne's handwriting, their authenticity is in dispute. For a more thorough discussion of this issue, consult the appendix to this article. In my discussions of the letters, I have silently expanded the abbreviations, ampersands, and brevigraphs and changed consonant u's to v's, but left the spelling otherwise intact. To avoid a host of awkward circumlocutions and to make my argument as clear as possible, I refer throughout to the writer of the three Burley letters as John Donne and to the recipient as Ann More, although the reader should remember that this is a hypothesis I hope to prove, not a matter of fact.

11. Simpson, *Prose Works*, 2d ed., p. 322.

Madam. I will have leave to speake like a lover, I am not altogether one: for though I love more then any yett my love hath not yᵉ same marke & end wᵗʰ others. Howe charitably you deale wᵗʰ vs of these partʒ: yᵗ at this tyme of yᵉ yeare (when the sunn. forsakes vs) yᵒ come to vs & suffer vs not out of yᵉ mercy) to tast yᵉ bitternʒ of a winter: but Madam you doe me this releif because in all that part of this somer wᶜʰ I spent in yᵉ presence yᵒ doubled yᵉ heat and I lived vnder yᵉ rage of a hott somer & yᵉ eyes. that hart wᶜʰ yᵒ melted then no winter shall freize but it shall ever keepe that equall temper wᶜʰ you gaue it soft enough to receaue yᵉ mipreßions & hard enough to retayne them. it must not tast to yᵘ as a negligence or carelesnes yᵗ I have not visited yᵘ Lad: in these dayes of yᵘ being here. call it rather a devout humylyty yᵗ I thus aske leaue & bee content to beleeue from him yᵗ can as impoßibly hy to yᵒ as hate yᵘ yᵗ by comandmªᵗ of our godmother throwne out of yᵉ towne so dayly and diuersly are soe tyme pered yᵗ are not oᵘʳ owne. at my retourne (wᶜʰ therfore I will hasten) I willbe bold to kiß yᵗ fayre vertuous hand wᶜʰ doth much in recrabing this letter & may do eaßly much more in spindring another to him whose best honour is that hee is yᵉ lieutenant of himself. finiting.

The Burley Manuscript, f. 295.

that in Ralegh's early "passionless love poems" to Queen Elizabeth "there is no stamp of a single, unique consciousness. . . . What remains is the fire which burns in the mind, the love which leads beyond the self, beyond time, beyond mortality . . . the highly generalized voice . . . merges so easily with hundreds of others just like it."[12]

In all the poems and letters that we know Donne wrote to Lucy, Countess of Bedford, both the verse letters and the published prose letters, the language fits the conventional mode.[13] Donne's epistles to Lucy are self-consciously crafted, full of elaborate, ingratiating compliments, professions of humility, and artful remarks about writing. In one prose letter Donne generalizes and distances his "love" for the countess by writing not about his own feelings but about "Letters"—in the plural—"by which we deliver over our affections, and assurances of friendship." Affection and friendship are topics for meditation, "the best faculties of our souls." There is no suggestion of intimacy. When Donne finally professes a "noble love unto you," that love is as elevated as he is subservient: "the best fruits that so poor a soil, as my poor soul is, can produce."[14] In this courtly letter of patronage, Donne adopts the form and style of what Angel Day calls a "speciall" letter; the relationship requires "both higher stile, and more orderlie deliverance, according to the waight of the argument . . . as bearing in them a resolute purpose and intendment seriouslie to discourse upon, to answere, mittigate or avoid any certain matter or causes, importing the present affaire whereupon the direction is framed."[15]

In a second prose letter to the countess,[16] Donne sounds only slightly more fa-

---

12. Quoted from Leonard Tennenhouse, "Sir Walter Ralegh and the Literature of Clientage," in *Patronage in the Renaissance*, ed. Guy Fitch Lytle and Stephen Orgel (Princeton: Princeton University Press, 1981), p. 238; Arthur F. Marotti, "John Donne and the Rewards of Patronage," also in *Patronage in the Renaissance*, p. 225; and Stephen J. Greenblatt, *Sir Walter Ralegh: The Renaissance Man and His Roles* (New Haven and London: Yale University Press, 1973), pp. 68, 74, 80. In "The Literature of Patronage, 1580–1630," *EIC* 2 (1952), p. 273, Patricia Thomson makes a point similar to Marotti's: "They establish the lady, the patroness, on a pedestal and allow the protégé, the poet, to grovel at her feet. The literary source of this familiar posture is found in Petrarch"; and Tennenhouse also observes "the formal Petrarchism of Ralegh's poem[s]" to Elizabeth that "exploit the same cultural myth of Elizabeth as Petrarchan mistress and goddess of chastity" (pp. 240, 244).

13. At various times "Twickman Garden," "The Funerall," and "A nocturnall upon S. Lucies Day, Being the Shortest day" have also been associated with the Countess of Bedford. In "John Donne and Patronage," p. 225, Marotti observes "some of the interesting disturbances in ['Twickman Garden' and 'The Funerall'] that threaten to subvert their conventions, if not the complimentary mode itself." C. M. Armitage, "Donne's Poems in Huntington Manuscript 198: New Light on 'The Funerall,'" *SP* 63 (1966), 697–707, makes a case for associating "The Funerall" with the Countess of Bedford, but it is by no means certain that any of these three poems expresses Donne's feelings about the countess. After examining the evidence, Helen Gardner concludes: "In view of all we know of Donne's relations with the Countess of Bedford and the tone of his letters to her in prose and verse, it seems incredible that either ['Twickman Garden' or 'A nocturnall'] should be thought to be concerned with Donne's actual feelings for his patroness" (*John Donne: The Elegies and the Songs and Sonnets* [Oxford: Clarendon Press, 1965], Appendix C: Lady Bedford and Mrs. Herbert, pp. 248–58).

14. *Letters to Severall Persons*, pp. 22–24.

15. Angel Day, *The English Secretary, or Methode of writing of Epistles and Letters*, 2 pts. (London: for C. Burbie, 1599), pt. 1, pp. 8–9.

16. *Letters to Severall Persons*, pp. 67–68.

miliar. Writing to ask Lucy for a copy of a poem she had written about him, Donne says: "I have yet adventured so near as to make a petition for verse, it is for those your Ladiship did me the honour to see in *Twicknam* garden, except you repent your making, and having mended your judgement by thinking worse, that is, better, because juster, of their subject"—presumably Donne himself. Donne's studied, cautious petition is both terribly hesitant and overly self-deprecating. Because Donne says the countess's poem "comes from your brain or breast," Arthur Marotti concludes, "Within the framework of socially decorous Petrarchism, such pieces may have been love lyrics."[17] Perhaps, but Donne's promise "that I will not shew them, and that I will not beleeve them" also suggests that the countess had written a poem of praise—like those Ben Jonson wrote to Donne—which Donne could, but will not, he assures the countess, exploit for his own professional advancement.[18] Although this letter is slightly more familiar than the preceding one, Donne is still highly conscious of the difference in social stature that separates him from the countess. Despite the reference to the countess's "breast," this is clearly a letter written by a humble poet to a patron of the arts, not by one lover to another.

Donne's verse letters to the countess are equally conventional and formal. The countess is "Gods masterpeece" and Donne prays God to "helpe mee" in praising her spiritual exaltation ("To the Countesse of Bedford: Reason is our Soules left hand," 33, 37). Donne describes not his own love but "the reasons why you'are lov'd by all" (13). He expresses his admiration in generalized abstractions, "Vertue, Art, Beauty, Fortune" ("To the Countesse of Bedford: You have refin'd mee," 2). In the verse letters to the countess, "beauty is but a code for this transcendent significance; his obeisance is the honor he pays . . . to the heavenly virtue transparent in the Countess' mortal womanhood."[19] Does Burley letter S16 fit the model of a poet writing to his patron, as Evelyn Simpson suggested? I think not, for reasons I will enumerate as we examine the letter in more detail.

The letter is addressed to "Madam" and signed "Anonimos." At first "Madam" may seem to imply a married woman, but in the Renaissance "Madam" was used in "subscribing a letter to a woman of any station" (*OED* 1). The second term of address, "your Ladyship," may also seem to suggest a client-patron relationship, but not necessarily. A lady was "a woman of superior position in society . . . originally the word connoted a degree equal to that expressed by *lord*, but it was early widened in application" (*OED* I.4). Since Ann's father, George More, was knighted in 1598,[20] Donne

17. Marotti, "John Donne and Patronage," p. 224.

18. Gardner, "Lady Bedford and Mrs. Herbert," p. 251, claims: "It would seem that these particular verses were verses of compliment to Donne, probably in reply to one of his Verse-Letters asking her favour."

19. Leonard Tourney, "Donne, the Countess of Bedford, and the Petrarchan Manner," in *New Essays on Donne*, ed. Gary A. Stringer (Salzburg: Institut für Englische Sprache und Literatur, 1977), p. 57. Shahla Anand, "Women and Donne," in *A Potpourri of Thoughts on English Literature* (New York: Vantage Press, 1975), p. 59, also says that Donne's verse letters to his patroness present "womanhood exalted—exalted to the point that the ideas become intellectual concepts."

20. According to the most recent and reliable biography of George More, by J. C. Henderson and M. A. Phillips, in *The House of Commons: 1558–1606*, ed. P. W. Hasler (London: Her Majesty's Stationery Office, 1981), 3:80–83.

might well have addressed Ann as your ladyship, particularly since a lady was also "a woman who is the object of a man's devotion; a mistress, lady-love" (*OED* I.2.c.). For Evelyn Simpson it is the signature, "Anonimos," that presents the real difficulty, since "Donne never disguised his Platonic admiration for Lady Bedford." For this reason, between the first and the second edition of *The Prose Works* Simpson became "extremely doubtful whether we should be justified in ascribing the letter to Donne."[21]

If, however, Donne was writing to Ann in order to arrange a clandestine rendezvous, he may well have signed himself "Anonimos," feeling at once playful about the adventure and anxious to prevent discovery. The placement of "Anonimos" in the middle of the last line confirms this sense of intimacy. As William Fulwood explains in the introduction to *The Enimie of Idlenesse*, letter-writing convention encouraged writers of familiar letters to show their familiarity by placing the subscription on the same level with the body of the letter. By contrast, writers addressing more formal letters to superiors were advised to signify distance and deference by leaving space between the body of the letter and the subscription,[22] a convention that Donne carefully followed in the published letters to the Countess of Bedford and the Countess of Huntington.

Burley letter S16 is not only unsigned but also undated. Yet if we can agree about the identity of "Madam" and "Anonimos," then we can fix the time quite closely. Donne writes "at this tyme of the yeare (when the sunn forsakes us) you come to us and suffer us not (out of your mercy) to tast the bitternes of a winter." It sounds like November, when the days have begun to shorten and the cold winter threatens but still holds off. After their marriage in December 1601, Donne wrote, "At her lyeng in town this last Parliament, I found meanes to see her twice or thrice."[23] It is tempting to speculate that this letter initiated the clandestine meetings that preceded Donne's marriage. During the summer of 1601, however, Ann was at Loseley and Donne was far from basking in the heat and rage of her presence. Consequently, the letter must have been written in the late fall of 1600. That was the year, following Lady Egerton's death, when the lovers spent at least part of the summer together at York House, where Ann remained "unchaperoned, the only lady (aged sixteen) of the household." "What conditions, spring and summer and early fall for the ripening of love!," Edward LeComte says.[24] Early that fall Ann left York House and went to live in the country with her father, Sir George More. Donne was still living at the Lord Keeper's. Since

21. Simpson, *Prose Works*, 2d ed., p. 322.

22. William Fulwood, *The enemie of idlenesse teaching a perfect platforme how to endite epistles and letters of all sorts* (London: for H. Middleton, 1578). In "Double Exposure: An Investigation of Audience Role in the Familiar Letter Collection," presented at the Modern Language Association annual meeting, 1978, Christina Marsden Gillis provided further evidence for the symbolic significance of the position of the subscription. When copying the letters into the Burley manuscript, the scribe seems to have respected the convention. In some letters he placed the subscription right after the text and in others he left a space between the text and the subscription. Of course, "Anonimos" may have been added by the copyist, but that seems unlikely since none of the letters on folios 294–300 contains a signature, and this is the only instance in which the scribe calls attention to the writer's anonymity.

23. *Loseley Manuscripts*, p. 328.

24. Edward LeComte, *Grace to a Witty Sinner: A Life of Donne* (New York: Walker, 1965), p. 77.

Sir George kept lodgings in the city, "Right over against the Lord Keeper's house above Charing Cross,"[25] it was quite convenient for the lovers to correspond, and even to meet when Ann accompanied her father to London.

The body of Donne's letter is divided into two sections. Donne begins, as convention dictated, with an *Exordium*, or introduction to the matter to be written of, "wherein either for our selves, or the cause we write of, or in respect of him, for or to whom we write, wee studie to win favor or allowance of the matter." Only after Donne has taken care to win Madam's favor with a charming *Exordium*, does he turn to the purpose of his letter, the *Narratio* or *Propositio*, "wherein is declared or proponed, in the one by plaine tearmes, in the other by inference, or comparison, the verie substance of the matter whatsoever to be handled."[26]

Donne's first letter to Lucy, Countess of Bedford contains an illustrative, conventional *Exordium*.

> Amongst many other dignities which this letter hath by being received and seen by you, it is not the least, that it was prophesied of before it was born: for your brother told you in his letter, that I had written: he did me much honour both in advancing my truth so farre as to call a promise an act already done; and to provide me a means of doing him a service in this act, which is but doing right to my self: for by this performance of mine own word, I have also justified that part of his Letter which concerned me; and it had been a double guiltinesse in me, to have made him guilty towards you.[27]

Donne begins by asserting his humility and the countess's stature: simply by "being received and seen by you" the letter acquires a host of "dignities." Slowly, cautiously, decorously, Donne demonstrates that the letter is "justified" (and the very word betrays Donne's self-consciousness and subservience) by her brother's mention of it.

By comparison the Burley *Exordium* sounds confident, direct, and informal. Rather than humbly begging leave to write, and carefully explaining why the letter is "justified" as he does in writing to the countess, Donne begins boldly: "I will have leave to speake like a lovor." Donne moves from one clause to the next, impatiently omitting the logical connective *though* before "I am not altogether one," assuming his correspondent already knows exactly what he means. As the following remarks reveal, the qualification that he is not "altogether" a lover refers to the fact that they have been separated since the summer. "I love more then any yett," Donne continues, becoming more direct, insisting that his love is unbounded, unprecedented, unequaled. Yet (for the word casually doubles as adverb and conjunction), "yett my love hath not the same marke and end with others." It does not have the same "end" because their separation and station make the ultimate end of marriage still uncertain. To some extent, Donne sounds proud to distinguish his love from others' love, proud that he is seeking a rich relationship rather than a large dowry or a passing fling. Still, there is an undertone

25. Mary Clive, *Jack & the Doctor* (London: Macmillan, 1966), p. 43.
26. Day, *The English Secretary*, pt. 1, p. 11.
27. *Letters to Severall Persons*, pp. 22–23.

of complaint, a hint of deprivation and self-pity, that shows how much he fears that some other lover may indeed win the "marke," the attention, and the "end," the proper betrothal, that is still denied him. "How charitably," he continues, "you deale with us of these parts?" As the statement veers so unexpectedly into a question, we suddenly realize that the only "marke and end" his love has hitherto achieved is just that: a surprising but pointed question mark. Even as Donne gamely tries to dispel his doubts with wit, he reveals the serious concern underlying his courtly compliment: how do you intend to deal with me?

But it is the following sentence that finally convinces me Donne is writing to his lover. When Donne alludes to "all that part of this sommer which I spent in your presence you doubled the heat and I lived under the rage of a hott sonn and your eyes," it becomes clear that Donne is describing a relationship not of patronage but of secret, unsanctioned passion that defies and redefines all conventional notions of honorable love. Whereas Donne's letters to the countess profess a "noble love," a conventional, generalized "affection and friendship," this letter asserts a mutual passion that sounds more sexual than spiritual. "You doubled the heat" suggests that the lady was as active and passionate as was Donne. Although it is, of course, conventional to compare the lady's eyes to the sun, Donne turns the trite metaphor into a remarkably frank expression of the "rage" and "heat" of great passion.[28] This is not the language of Petrarchan love poetry or patronage and clientage.

In these lines Donne used the half-playful, half-pleading language of ardent love, packed (like his poetry) with all the innuendo and boldness of private understanding, unabashed eroticism, and extreme intimacy. It is not surprising that Evelyn Simpson missed Donne's meaning, however, for the complexities of the lovers' relationship can be divined only by inference. The rich word play, the witty reversals, constant qualifications, and intimate innuendo are designed for someone who already understands the delicate ambiguity of the situation. As we shall see, this is exactly the kind of difficult, highly compressed love language, "In cypher writ, or new made Idiome" ("Valediction of the booke," 21), that Donne uses throughout the Songs and Sonets.

In Burley letter S16 Donne writes so artfully, playfully, and intimately that it sounds as if he is speaking directly to Ann. Although Donne prolongs the *Exordium* for more than half the letter, he uses the plain style, "utterlie devoid of anie shadow of hie and loftie speaches," that Angel Day recommends for familiar letters, including, of course, "epistles amatorie."[29] His sudden shifts of meaning, his fluid syntax, his loose logic,

---

28. Typical of conventional language of patronage are the following images of fire, all cited by Greenblatt, *Ralegh*, p. 97: "Praisd be Dianas faire and harmles light"; the "elementall fire / Whose food and flame consumes not"; the "vestall fier that burnes, but never wasteth"; the "durable fyre / In the mynde ever burnynge." In the verse letters to the Countess of Bedford, Donne uses the following even more exalted images of light: "Should I say I liv'd darker then were true, / Your radiation can all clouds subdue, / But one [the divine light of God], 'tis best light to contemplate you" ("To the Countesse of Bedford: Honour is so sublime perfection," 19–22); and "Vertues in corners, which now bravely doe / Shine in the worlds best part, or all it, you" ("To the Countesse of Bedford: T'have written then," 19–20).
29. Day, *The English Secretary*, pt. 1, p. 8. "Amatorie letters" are described in pt. 1, chap. 19, pp. 143–48.

imprecise conjunctions, and sparse punctuation all create the impression of spontaneous, private conversation that was carefully cultivated by writers of familiar letters.
"Indeed we should write as we speak," James Howell explains, "and that's a true familiar letter which expresseth one's mind, as if he were discoursing with the party
to whom he writes in succinct and short terms."[30] Donne's letters to the countess seem
a perfect example of what Robert Parker Sorlien calls "Donne's mature epistolary style
at its best—its slow rhythm, heavy punctuation, elaborately graceful courtesy, gravity
relieved by cheerfulness, and religious conclusions."[31] The Burley letter, on the other
hand, with its rapid rhythms, loose punctuation, casual inference, playfulness heightened by pleading, and amorous conclusions, suggests a more youthful and intimate
epistolary style.

After the compelling *Exordium*, Donne turns to the more immediate purpose of
the letter, the *Narratio* or *Propositio*. In this case, Donne has both a story to relate
"by plaine tearmes" and a proposition to suggest "by inference." First, he explains, he
failed to answer Ann's letter earlier, not out of "negligence or carelesnes," but because
he was out of town. Because the delay may have offended her, with "devout humylyty"
he "thus aske[s] leave" to visit her as soon as possible. This is the only point in the
letter when Donne sounds at all humble, and appropriately it is here, when Donne
is apologizing, that he addresses Ann as "your ladyship." Unfortunately, the reunion
must again be postponed, since he is "sodenly throwne out of the towne so dayly and
diversly are wee tempested that are not our owne." Although Donne is now talking
about professional responsibilities, his language, warmed by the memory of the summer's heat, all but explodes in a tempest of impatience and passion. The syntax is
unpunctuated, disconnected; the language seems complex, intimate, and spontaneous.
In planning their imminent reunion, Donne implies that his boldness, impatience, and
honesty are matched by Ann's daring, passion, and virtue: "at my retourne (which
therfore I will hasten) I wilbee bold to kiss that fayre vertuous hand which doth much
in receiving this letter and may do easyly much more in sending another." Evelyn
Simpson says, "The close of the letter may be compared with the last sentence of a
letter addressed to the Countess in the 1651 *Letters*: 'Here therefore I humbly kisse
your Ladiships fair learned hands, and wish you good wishes and speedy grants,'"[32]
but the difference in tone is notable. With the countess, Donne "humbly" acknowledges his subservience; in the Burley letter he "wilbee bold to kiss" Ann's hand. He

30. *Epistolae Ho-Elianae, or the Familiar Letters of James Howell*, 2 vols. (Boston and New York: Hough-
ton Mifflin, 1907), 1:3. David Manuszak described the colloquial style of familiar letters in "'A kind of
religion': James Howell on Friendship and the Art of the Familiar Letter in *Epistolae Ho-Elianae*," presented
at the Modern Language Association annual meeting, 1978. For a thorough survey of Renaissance guides
to letter writing, see Katherine Gee Hornbeak, "The Complete Letter Writer in English, 1568–1800," *Smith
College Studies in Modern Languages* 15 (1934).
31. For the distinction between "familiar" or "generall" letters and "speciall" letters, see Day, *English
Secretary*, pt. 1, pp. 8–9; Robert Parker Sorlien, "To Conject. or not to Conject.: Problems in Editing Donne's
Prose Letters," a report delivered at the Modern Language Association annual meeting, 1982, which echoes
Theodore Spencer's introduction to the published text of Donne's letter to Sir Nicholas Carey, 21 June 1625.
32. Simpson, *Prose Works*, 2d ed., p. 322.

apologizes for writing to the countess, but he tells Ann she "may do easyly much more in sending another to him," an assumption that would be presumptuous if the relationship were not extremely intimate.

To the countess, Donne professed a generalized, conventional "noble love." By contrast, he began Burley letter S16 by calling attention to the unusualness of his relationship with Ann. That is what he emphasizes in the final enigmatic description of himself as "him whose best honor is that hee is your leiuetenant of himself." Donne defines himself as Ann's vice-regent over himself, thus granting her ultimate power over him. Yet she relies on his strategic skill, and he creates the metaphor because he derives power and purpose from the role. As in his earlier remark, "you doubled the heat and I lived under the rage of a hott sonn and your eyes," Donne strives to find words that will convey the individual strength and mutual interdependence that make their relationship at once unique and precarious. Ann has accepted Donne as her devoted servant. What makes the relationship so special is that Donne's "best honor," his highest claim to personal title, his highest elevation of character, and his strictest allegiance to what is due or right (*OED*, 2) defies the conventional notions of honor. Their radical behavior forges its own rules—born of intimacy and courage. Despite the complexity of language and feeling, Donne is actually referring to something quite specific and recognizable—the private contract of love that he describes in the letter written to Ann's father after their elopement: "So long since as her being at York House this had foundacion, and so much then of promise and contract built upon yt as without violence to conscience might not be shaken."[33]

This first letter summarizes the state of affairs as Donne imagines it, based on the passionate, honest understanding of the summer they spent wrapped up in each other, blissfully scorning the world. Judging from this letter, Donne loves Ann for her fiery passion, respects her for her bold, independent standards of virtue, salutes her for daring to continue such a risky affair, and trusts her to appreciate his compressed, complex, witty, unconventional language.

Donne's language here is remarkably similar to that of "Loves growth," one of his most tenderly passionate, unidealized poems. Donne marvels, in the poem, that love does "of the Sunne his working vigour borrow" (10) and concludes "though each spring doe adde to love new heate, / . . . No winter shall abate the springs encrease" (25, 28). In the letter Donne recalls, "all that part of this sommer which I spent in your presence you doubled the heat and I lived under the rage of a hott sonn and your eyes. that hart which you melted then no winter shall freise." As this torrid love language implies, Donne claims the right to "speake like a lovor" because he and "Madam" spent the preceding summer as lovers—perhaps, as lovers in deed. If this is how Donne wrote to Ann More, she was clearly not a woman who appreciated only the "simpler and purer, the more ideal and tender of [his] love-poems." In fact, "Loves growth" explains the radical redefinition of love that the letter implies:

33. *Loseley Manuscripts*, p. 328.

Love's not so pure, and abstract, as they use
To say, which have no Mistresse but their Muse,
But as all else, being elemented too,
Love sometimes would contemplate, sometimes do. (11–14)

Donne uses the same pattern of imagery—"loves hot fires," "earths thrice-fairer Sunne," and "sterne winter"—in his verse letter "To Mr. C. B." Scholars agree that the verse letter was almost certainly written to Donne's friend Christopher Brooke. Since Donne asked Brooke to give the bride away at his clandestine wedding, surely Donne had also confided his love for Ann to his friend. Thus it seems natural to assume that "To Mr. C. B." describes Donne's love for Ann.

But, as Herbert Grierson notes, the verse letter evokes not the hot fires of mutual passion but the "scalding sighs" of unrequited love:

Strong is this love which ties our hearts in one,
And strong that love pursu'd with amorous paine;
But though besides thy selfe I leave behind
    Heavens liberall, and earths thrice-fairer Sunne,
    Going to where sterne winter aye doth wonne,
Yet, loves hot fires, which martyr my sad minde,
    Doe send forth scalding sighes, which have the Art
    To melt all Ice, but that which walls her heart. (7–14)

Because there was no evidence to suggest that Ann ever treated Donne icily, Grierson felt compelled to conclude, "possibly it was someone else."[34] It is at this juncture that the three Burley letters provide crucial information. Between the first and the second letters Donne learns—probably from Ann herself at their reunion—that her father has been told something incriminating. As the second and third letters reveal, that has an irreparable effect on their glorious intimacy. Her father's suspicions make it much harder—perhaps, for the time being, impossible—for the lovers to communicate freely and trust each other fully. Henceforth parental prohibition may well prevent them from ever having a proper marriage. But most devastating of all, her father's disapproval has begun to turn the heat and rage that once filled Ann's eyes into "Ice . . . which walls her heart" against Donne's love.

The verse letter "To Mr. C. B." brings together the complicated, shifting feelings that emerge in the course of the three Burley letters. It uses the ecstatic, passionate imagery of the first letter to describe the unfortunate events of the second letter and the "sad minde" and "amorous paine" of the third letter. Although the imagery is conventional, the remarkable correlation of attitudes, events, and words makes it seem

---

34. Grierson, ed., Poems, 2:168. John Shawcrosss suggests, "Perhaps this is an allusion to Donne's imprisonment in the Fleet in February 1602, where no sun would shine" (Complete Poetry, p. 203). But the parallels with the Burley letter suggest rather that the verse letter was written before the marriage, when Donne feared Ann would reject him.

more than likely that the verse letter "To Mr. C. B." and the three Burley letters all describe developments in Donne's courtship of Ann More.

Burley letter S15 is illuminated by the circumstantial evidence provided by Walton's account of the love affair: "Sir George had some intimation of it, and, knowing prevention to be a great part of wisdom, did therefore remove her with much haste, from [York House] to his own house at Lothesley."[35] Donne's second letter and Walton's account have not been previously connected because they overlap only indirectly. Donne frets over the details without recounting the story that Ann already knows, whereas Walton omits the details and bypasses the two issues that preoccupy Donne. How did the story get out? How will the incident affect Ann's feelings and behavior toward her lover? When we read Donne's second letter in the context of Walton's account and "To Mr. C. B.," we comprehend the ramifications more readily:

> Madam. I am intangled in a double affliction by being accused not only to haue heard (wch is a forfeyture of my service & place in y^r favor) but to haue spoken dishonorably of y^o. I find not my self to be so spungy either to take in or powre out so easyly. and I am sure y^o would not thinke me worthy to bee pardoned for any fault if I should confessingly aske a pardon for this. it would moue me less y^t ye envious world should speake this, because envy (wch cannot be driuen from accompanying vertue) is foule spoken; & therfore naturally slaunderous. but I must wonder wth greife y^t my lo: Latm^r whose discretion & allowaunce of my loue to him I should much prise one by no meanes (knowne to me) interested in y^r honor or compassionate in y^r dishonor otherwise then generall nobility borne in him instructeth him should load m^r Davies wth ye op^{r}ssion of having dishonored y^o & deriue it from him to me. I heere y^r father hath taken it for good fuell of anger against m^r davis & me pchaunce to. I do easylyer forgiue his anger then his credulity: for it is pitty he should haue beene any instrument in ye building of so fayre a pallace as y^o are and so furnishing it as his care hath done if hee would not be angry wth any defect. but (me thinks) it cannot be come y^t discretiō wch I think y^o inherit from him to vnbridle his suspiciō so much to ye p^{r}iudice of my vnderstanding & honesty. though my merites be not such as y^t they ever do works of superrogatiō, yet I durst vpon my conscience acquit him of ever conceaving vnworthyly of you. but ye reverence & respect I haue alwayes loued you comaunds me to employ all my force in keeping myself in y^r good thoughts & to leaue y^o well assured, not y^t I ever spake but y^t I never heard ill word from any man wch might be wrested to ye impeachment of y^r honor wch here I sweare to y^o by my loue & by y^t fayre learned hand wch I humbly kisse. & take leaue. / (f. 296)

Donne must have been extremely upset, for he does not take time to compose even the most perfunctory *Exordium*. Instead he begins abruptly with the *Narratio*, the matter at hand. The common, graphic metaphor of the spunge, following the elegant, conventional language of love, recalls those sudden shifts between high and low diction so familiar in poems like "The good-morrow." Ann must have been either very angry or very upset, for Donne treats her response most seriously: "I am sure you

35. Izaak Walton, *The Lives of Doctor John Donne, Sir Henry Wotton, Mr. Richard Hooker, Mr. George Herbert, and Doctor Robert Sanderson* (New York: Duffield, 1906), p. 6.

Madam. I am intangled in a double affliction by being
accused not only to have heard (wᶜʰ if a forfeyture of
my service & place in yᵉ favor) but to have spoken disho-
norably of yᵒ. if I find not my self to be so spongy either
to take in or powre out so easyly. and I am sure yᵒ would
not thinke me worthy to bee pardoned for any fault if
I should confessingly aske a pardon for this it would
move me less yᵗ yᵉ embwin world should speake this, because
envy (wᶜʰ cannot be denied from accompanying vertue) is
foule spoken; & therefore naturally slaunderous. but I much
wonder wᵗʰ griefe yᵗ my lo: latni whose discretion & advaunce
of my love to him I should much prayse one by no meanes kindver
to me I interested in yᵉ honor or compassionate in yᵉ dishonor
otherwise then generall nobility borne in Ami mistrusteth him
should load mr Davies wᵗʰ yᵉ oppresion of habwing dishonored yᵒ & derever
it from him to me. I heere yᵗ hᵉ father hath taken it for good faith
of angre against mr davies & me to. I do easilyer forgive his
angre then his credulity: for it is fitly hᵉ should have bene any
nistrument in yᵉ buildwing of so fayree a pallace as yᵒ are and so full
nothing it as his care hath done if hee would not be angry wᵗʰ
any defect. but (me thinks) it cannot become yᵉ discretion wᶜʰ I thinke
yᵒ inherit from him to unbridle his suspicē so much to yᵉ prejudice
of my understanding & honesty. though my merits be not
such as yᵗ they ever do worke of supererogatiō, yet I durst
upon my conscience acquit him of ever concealing vertue
thyts of you. but yᵉ reverence & respect I have alwayes bord
you comaunds me to employ all my force in keeping my self
in yᵉ good thoughts & to leave yᵉ rosh affixed, not yᵗ I ever
spake but yᵗ, I never heard ill bored from any may wᶜʰ
might be wrested to yᵉ mispeachment of yᵗ honor wᶜʰ heere
I sweare to yᵒ by my love & by yᵗ fayree learned hand wᶜʰ
I humbly kisse. & take leave ·/

would not thinke me worthy to bee pardoned for any fault if I should confessingly aske a pardon for this." Donne does not feel sufficiently confident of Ann's response to risk a playful phrase or a fanciful metaphor. Instead, he simply insists that he has honored their private contract, kept his word, and lived up to his "service and place in your favor."

Above all, Donne is anxious to soothe Ann. At the same time, he is angry, feeling betrayed by friends he trusted: "I must wonder with griefe that my lord Latimer whose discretion and allowaunce of my love to him I should much prise one by no meanes (knowne to me) interested in your honor or compassionate in your dishonor otherwise then generall nobility borne in him instructeth him should load Mr. Davies with the oppression of having dishonored you and derive it from him to me." Quite unlike the highly wrought, artfully ingratiating language with which Donne addresses his patrons and even less artful than the language of the first letter, this ungrammatical, uncontrolled outpouring of words shows that Donne is too distressed to worry about his style.

The events to which Donne alludes sound just like the kind of juicy gossip that is bred by secret affairs of the heart (and not by public affairs of patronage). If my reading is correct, the chain of information runs from Donne to Davies to Latimer to Sir George. Since Davies or Davis is such a common name, we can only speculate about the reference. Evelyn Simpson suggests John Davies of Hereford, and that seems plausible, since Donne knew him both at Oxford and at the Inns of Court.[36] Davies recorded sufficient positive remarks about Donne to justify Donne's confidence. Davies was also close to Christopher Brooke, who was so close to Donne that he later gave the bride away at Donne's illegal wedding. Davies could well have heard the story from his "deare and much respected friend, Arthur Maynwarring, Esquire, bearer of the purse before the Lord Chancellor."[37] As usher in Egerton's service, Maynwarring was in the perfect position to hear rumors floating about York House. If this is indeed how the story got out, we can well understand why Donne takes such pains to reassure Ann. She would think it all too likely that Donne told his close friend, Christopher Brooke, who told his friend Davies, who told Latimer, who took it upon himself to tell Ann's father.

Donne's reference to "my lo: Latm[r]" certainly refers, as Evelyn Simpson notes, to Edmund Nevill, who claimed the title Lord Latimer in 1590 upon the death of his father Richard Nevill, first cousin to John Nevill, Baron Latimer, who died in 1577. Edmund was never officially awarded the Latimer honors and properties, but he continued to call himself Lord Latimer until he later claimed the even more prestigious title *Earl of Westmorland*.[38] Edmund Nevill/Latimer was a Catholic, who became no-

36. Other possibilities are Sir John Davies, the poet; the Robert Davis who worked for Egerton; and the William Davies who was imprisoned in the Tower along with Latimer.
37. Davies addressed a poem "To my deare and much respected friend, Arthur Maynwarring, Esquire, bearer of the purse before the Lord Chancellor"; Bald, *A Life*, p. 97.
38. For example, the *Calendar of State Papers, Domestic, Elizabeth, 1585*, p. 269, records a letter written

torious when he disclosed William Parry's plot to kill the Queen. As Parry explains in his confession, "I offered to join with [Nevill] because I knew him to be a Catholic . . . [he] took his oath upon a Bible, to conceal and constantly to pursue the Enterprize for the advancement of Religion . . . the killing of the Queen was the matter." Nevill was apparently pardoned for disclosing the plot and saving the Queen's life, but Parry was found guilty of high treason on 25 February and executed on 2 March 1584.[39]

Donne was quite young at the time of Parry's plot, but Donne's and Nevill's mutual ties to Catholicism make it more than likely that they eventually came into contact with each other. Moreover, Nevill's history shows him to be just the sort of man to betray Donne and Ann to Sir George. After all, Nevill turned on Parry, who was not only a co-religionist but also a relative and friend, as Parry stresses several times in his confession: "my cousin Nevil (the Accuser) . . . came often to mine house, put his finger in my dish, his hand in my purse; and the night wherein he accused me, was wrapped in my gown."[40] Parry's sense of personal betrayal sounds remarkably similar to the grievance Donne expresses in Burley letter S15: "I must wonder with griefe that my lord Latimer whose discretion and allowaunce of my love to him I should much prise." I have not found any direct ties between Latimer and Sir George More, but that is not surprising since the Burley letter describes Latimer as "one by no meanes (knowne to me) interested in your honor or compassionate in your dishonor otherwise then generall nobility borne in him instructeth him."

Given the pertinence of all these details, I think we can say with growing confidence that this is indeed Donne's letter to Ann More. But perhaps the best evidence that Donne is writing to the woman he hopes to marry is that he worries throughout about her father's opinion. "I heere your father hath taken it for good fuell of anger against mr. davis and me perchaunce to. . . . it cannot become that discretion which I think you inherit from him to unbridle his suspicion so much to the preiudice of my understanding and honesty." If Donne has already compromised Ann's honor, not in words but in deed, as the first letter implies and this second letter neither confirms nor denies, then he has every reason to fear that Ann might say—or may have already said—something irreparable to her father. Donne seems uncertain how far the matter has gone, for in the Burley Manuscript (although not in the Clarendon Press transcript) *perchaunce* is written above the line. Of course, the scribe may have simply

by "Edmond Neville (signed Latimer), prisoner in the Tower, to the Earl of Leicester"; and the *Annals of the Reformation and Establishment of Religion, and other various Occurrences in the Church of England, during Queen Elizabeth's Happy Reign*, ed. John Strype, 4 vols. in 7 (Oxford: Clarendon Press, 1824), 4: 332–35, prints several letters from November 1595 signed "Edmond Latymer." On his tombstone Edmund Nevill is styled "Lord Latimer and Earl of Westmoreland"; see Daniel Rowland, *An Historical and Genealogical Account of the Noble Family of Neville* (London: by S. Bentley, 1830), p. 56.

39. *A Complete Collection of State Trials and Proceedings for High Treason and Other Crimes and Misdemeanors from the Earliest Period to the Year 1783*, compiled by T. B. Howell, 21 vols. (London: Longman, 1816), 1:1103.

40. *State Trials*, 1:1103.

added a word he erroneously omitted, but, given the situation, it seems more likely that Donne reread what he had written and decided to temper his language in order to strike a more hopeful tone. Donne was quite wary of Sir George's capacity for anger, as the Loseley letters also reveal.[41] Ann apparently inherited her father's hot temper, if we can judge from the cautious solicitation she occasions here and the rage and heat she radiated the previous summer. When Donne pointedly juxtaposes her father's ready anger and Ann's "inherited" discretion, his irony suggests the kind of private understanding that is born of true intimacy.

In Donne's mind their love remains as honest and precious as ever. Yet he knows that it has already begun to suffer the taint of the world's gossip and her father's anger. Worse, he fears that, at sixteen, Ann may be made to believe he exploited her innocence. To counter such accusations, Donne says, "the reverence and respect I have alwayes loved you commands me to employ all my force in keeping myself in your good thoughts and to leave you well assured not that I ever spake but that I never heard ill word from any." The missing words, the chaotic connections, and the long, impassioned, unpunctuated, unstructured sentence show that Donne is more distraught and worried than ever. Until now, he has acted boldly and adventurously. Now he sounds more like a victim, acted upon, maligned, "command[ed] to employ all my force in keeping myself in your good thoughts." The last phrase recalls the powerful language Carey finds throughout Donne, but in context it sounds more solicitous and beleaguered than aggressive or self-absorbed. Donne is worried that Ann might think him dishonorable, but he is equally worried about any "ill word . . . which might be wrested to the impeachment of your honor." This time instead of feeling "bold to kiss that fayre vertuous hand," he says, "I sweare to you by my love and by that fayre learned hand which I humbly kisse." It is this remark above all that seems to support Evelyn Simpson's suggestion that Donne is writing to Lucy, Countess of Bedford. However, this "fayre learned hand" also recalls the unique fact about Ann that Walton thought notable enough to record half a century later: she was "curiously and plentifully educated."[42] Ann's education not only earns Donne's love and admiration; it also sustains his hopes. Thus in this second letter he praises Sir George for "building of so fayre a pallace as you are and so furnishing it as his care hath done." Virtue is no longer sufficient. If she is to defy both the "envious," "naturally slaunderous" world and her hot-tempered, rigidly conventional father, Ann will need to muster all her independent intellectual strength.

Apparently, Ann failed to respond as Donne hoped. In the third letter, he is absolutely devastated, afraid of losing her altogether:

> I send to y^o now y^t I may know how I do bycause vppon y^r opinion of me all I depend: for though I be troubled wth the extremyty of such a sicknes as deserues att lest pitty if

---

41. For example, Donne wrote to Sir George More, "I humbly beg of you that she may not to her danger feele the terror of your sodaine anger. I know this letter shall find you full of passion" (*Loseley Manuscripts*, p. 329).

42. Walton, *Lives*, p. 6.

The Burley Manuscript, f. 299v.

not loue yet I were as good to send to a coniurer for a good fortune as to a phisition for health. indeed I am oprest w^(th) such a sadnes as I am glad of nothing but that I am oprest w^(th) it: if it had pleased y° to haue norisht & brought vpp so much loue in y^r brest as y° haue done greife pchaunce I should haue ~~had~~ as much loue in y^r service as I haue done greif: yet I should accompt even sorrow good payment if by myne y^(rs) were lessoned: now I vene & vrge my body w^(th) phisick when my desperat mind is sick as they batter citty walls when the citizens are stobborne: but by all this labor of my penn my mind is no more comforted then a condemned prisoner would bee to see his chamber swypt & made cleane: only y° know weth^r ever I shalbee better & only y° can tell me (for y° are my destyny) whether I were best to dy now, or endevor to liue & keep ye great honor of being

y^r servant   (f. 299v)

Now Donne is so distraught that he omits not only the exordium but also the salutation, unless, of course, Ann's name was discreetly omitted in the transcription.[43] Regardless, Donne gets to the point immediately, describing a sickness of the heart, not the body. Uncertain whether his love will be requited or rejected, begging for pity, insisting that only Ann can cure his mortal wound, Donne sounds like a typical Petrarchan lover. Or almost, for Petrarch found great solace and poetic inspiration in his idealized, always unfulfilled love for Laura. By contrast, Donne would rather die than live without the love he once had: "if it had pleased you to have norisht and brought upp so much love in your brest as you have done greife perchaunce I should have ~~had~~ as much love in your service as I have done greif." Ann could have chosen to sustain their mutual love. For choosing instead their mutual grief, Donne cannot forgive her. If the Burley Manuscript is an accurate transcription of the original letter, Donne went back to the sentence and crossed out the second auxiliary verb *had*. The Oxford edition omits the correction, but the distinction is important. Like the earlier addition of *perchaunce*, this correction shows Donne trying to make the situation seem less bleak and more hopeful. As it stands revised, the comment hovers between bemoaning an earlier, misguided decision ("if it had pleased you") and pleading for a less grievous and more loving future: "I should have as much love in your service as I have done greif." Donne simply refuses to believe that his "best honor," his "service and place in your favor," has all turned to grief. In the following clause he declares, "yet I should accompt even sorrow good payment if by myne y^(rs) were lessoned." Since "myne yours" makes no sense, Simpson apparently read the line to mean, if by it (that is, my grief), my years were lessoned; this makes Donne sound all too willing to die, as long as he dies quickly. However, *y^(rs)* certainly means *yours*, not *years*, because the letters on folios 294–300 repeatedly abbreviate *your* to *y^r*. Thus the line should be read, yet I would be willing to pay for my love with grief, if by mine (that is, my grief), yours (your grief) were lessoned. As the pun on *lessoned* (meaning both diminished and taught) suggests, the implicit logical conclusion of Donne's lesson is the lessening of their mutual grief.

43. None of the letters on folios 294–299v begins with a name. Folio 300 begins, "M. C." Three other quite intimate letters have no salutation. Only the two letters we have already examined begin "Madam." The rest begin "Sir."

Given the uproar and difficulties that their marriage in fact caused, Donne had good reason to fear Ann would continue to choose grief over love, and Ann had even better reason to consider giving up her love for Donne. By this time Sir George must have declared his firm opposition, for, as Walton says, "the friends of both parties used much diligence, and many arguments, to kill or cool their affections to each other."[44] With the world unanimously opposed, Donne now uses all his persuasive power to convince Ann that the decision rests solely with her: "uppon your opinion of me all I depend," he says, "my desperat mind is sick . . . only you know whether ever I shalbee better and only you can tell me (for you are my destyny) whether I were best to dy now, or endevor to live and keep the great honor of being your servant."

At this point, it is perhaps worth pausing to recall the historical fact that when a Renaissance couple like Donne and Ann More made a private contract of love without parental permission, they were not simply disregarding her father's wishes. They were challenging the patriarchal social structure on which all the country's laws were founded. We can see just how radical and threatening their action seemed by the elaborate moralizing it provoked from Walton, that bastion of tradition:

> love is a flattering mischief, that hath denied aged and wise men a foresight of those evils that too often prove to be the children of that blind father; a passion, that carries us to commit errors with as much ease as whirlwinds move feathers, and begets in us an unwearied industry to the attainment of what we desire. And such an industry did, notwithstanding much watchfulness against it, bring them secretly together,—I forbear to tell the manner how—and at last to a marriage too, without the allowance of those friends, whose approbation always was, and ever will be necessary, to make even a virtuous love become lawful.[45]

In the more joyful first letter Donne fought his own wariness and underlying fears by recalling his and Ann's mutual passion, courage, and trust. Now, with less confidence and more urgency, Donne tries a similar rhetorical strategy, urging Ann to act courageously and follow her own desires, since nothing less than Donne's life is at stake. Compared to the intimate placement of his earlier "Anonimos," the subscription of Burley letter S13 shows that Donne is much more conscious of the growing distance between himself and Ann. Although his closing is all one sentence, he now leaves a deferential space before signing himself, "your servant."

Evelyn Simpson says, "This letter appears to have been written in February 1601/2 when Donne was in disgrace after the disclosure of his marriage," because he writes other letters "in the same strain, complaining of the sickness . . . which was probably due to the anxiety and nervous strain which he underwent."[46] Given the circumstances at the time, however, it is hard to imagine that Donne could have written this poignant plea, "for you are my destyny," to anyone other than Ann. Yet after their marriage Donne would have had no reason to address such a petition to Ann; at that point,

---

44. Walton, *Lives*, p. 6.
45. Ibid.
46. Simpson, *Prose Works*, 1st ed., p. 301.

she no longer had the power to decide whether Donne could "keep the great honor of being your servant." If, however, during the previous year Ann thought of rejecting Donne for a husband her father chose and would support, then Donne would have had every reason to write her precisely this kind of letter.

Without more information, it is impossible to say just how long Donne's uncertainty lasted. We know the lovers were separated for most of the following year. When Donne later wrote to his father-in-law, he simply did not mention this period of hesitation and fear: "So long since as her being at York House this had foundacion, and so much then of promise and contract built upon yt as without violence to conscience might not be shaken."[47] The letters we have examined show just how much of Donne's "best honor" was wrapped up in these secret vows and the fear that they might be shaken. As the later letters to Sir George reveal, Donne was to experience a similar mental illness when he was jailed and terrified lest the marriage be discounted.[48] Thus Donne probably continued to worry, more or less desperately, from December 1600 until April 1602, when the courts finally removed all doubt that he had indeed won the hand of the woman he reverenced and respected and loved "more then any yett."

In these three Burley letters Donne is remarkably attentive to Ann's feelings and desperate at the thought of losing her love. He is not a domineering confident male egotist but an empathetic, solicitous, fearful lover. She is not a shadowy, powerless female, but an independent, witty, learned woman who doubles the heat and heightens the uncertainty of Donne's love. Unlike the letters written after Donne's marriage and published in *Letters to Severall Persons of Honour*, these three Burley letters consistently place love above personal ambition. In the first letter Donne speaks impatiently and resentfully of important assignments that take him away from Ann. In the second, he worries that her father will disapprove, not of Donne's inferior status or restricted finances, but of his "understanding and honesty." In the final letter, he says "Uppon your opinion of me all I depend." By then he is ready to give up everything either to marry Ann or to die of a broken heart. Rather than Carey's ambitious, self-seeking, aggressive careerist, it is this passionate, solicitous, devoted, and finally self-immolating lover—who derives his "best honor" from his "service and place in your favor" "(for you are my destyny)"—whom I find in the Songs and Sonets, where love "makes one little roome, an every where" ("The good-morrow," 11); where "All Kings, and all their favorites, / All glory of honors, beauties, wits . . . to their destruction draw" ("The Anniversarie," 1–6); where "All honor's mimique; All wealth alchimie" ("The Sunne Rising," 24); and where Donne willingly accepts a "ruin'd fortune" to be "*Canoniz'd* for Love" ("The Canonization," 3, 36).

Feeling, as Pope did, "how disagreeable it is to make use of hard words before a lady," biographers have often assumed that Ann could not possibly have understood Donne's more difficult poems.[49] Yet if these letters were indeed written by John Donne

---

47. *Loseley Manuscripts*, p. 328.
48. See ibid., pp. 328–44.
49. To cite just one example, Edward LeComte says, "She would not have understood his more intricate

to Ann More, they suggest that Donne's complex, unconventional love language was perfectly attuned to Ann's unusually well-educated, independent mind, as Donne perhaps acknowledges in "Valediction of the booke" when he advises his lady:

> Study our manuscripts, those Myriades
>> Of letters, which have past twixt thee and mee,
>> Thence write our Annals, and in them will bee
> To all whom loves subliming fire invades,
>> Rule and example found. (10–14)

This highly unconventional love story, commissioned by the poet and written by the lady, based on letters that have passed between them, expresses their unusually liberal view of love. Here, "in cypher writ, or new made Idiome" (21), other sublimely impassioned lovers "may finde all they seeke, / Whether abstract spirituall love they like" (29–30) or "chuse / Something which they may see and use" (33–34).

We have traditionally assumed that only the "simpler and purer, the more ideal and tender of Donne's love poems" are the expression of his love for Ann More. When we examine Donne's poems more closely, however, we discover that even Donne's most tender and ideal poems are not simple and pure. The idealized, Neoplatonic view of Donne's courtship and marriage captures only one aspect of the love poems I think he wrote to Ann More. What it cannot account for or explain is just how radical a redefinition of love and honor Donne strives to achieve. If, as the three Burley letters suggest, John Donne's love affair with Ann entailed a wider range of feelings and experiences than we have assumed, it probably also inspired a larger, more various group of poems than we have considered.

As far as I know, poems like "The Anniversarie," "Womans constancy" and "Breake of day" are never associated with Ann. Many critics have found "The Anniversarie" particularly disturbing, since it describes a tender, exalted, unmarried love affair. As John Carey explains, "'The Anniversarie' indicates that the woman addressed was not Donne's wife ('Two graves must hide thine and my coarse'), so who, worried critics have asked, was she?" Carey solves the dilemma by ridiculing critics who think "poems must have some factual basis."[50] Yet, like his worried predecessors, Carey tacitly makes the same factual assumption that worried his predecessors, and it prevents him from seeing the simplest explanation: that John Donne wrote "The Anniversarie" for Ann More when her name was still More.

Other critics have assumed the sexually liberated women who appear in "Womans constancy" and "Breake of day" must be prostitutes. Yet these female speakers proclaim their self-respect and honor with great confidence and wit. In "Breake of day," for example, the unmarried woman insists that her willingness to engage in a clandestine sexual relationship shows just how devoted and honorable is her love:

---

or his cynical poems. She was not a reader" (*Grace to a Witty Sinner*, p. 94). The Pope citation is from the dedicatory epistle to Mrs. Arabella Fermor, preceding "The Rape of the Lock."

50. John Carey, *Life, Mind and Art*, p. 92.

Light hath no tongue, but is all eye;
If it could speake as well as spie,
This were the worst, that it could say,
That being well, I faine would stay,
And that I lov'd my heart and honor so,
That I would not from him, that had them, goe. (7–12)

In "Womans constancy" the female speaker is wittily and warily jockeying for reassurance—and, if that fails, for an honorable retreat—because her love is still tenuous and uncertain, having stood the test of only "one whole day" (1). In this reading of the poem, the phrase *lovers contracts* (9) refers not to payment for services rendered but to a private agreement that only mutual devotion and personal honor can sustain— exactly the kind of agreement Donne later claimed for himself and Ann: "So long since as her being at York House this had foundacion, and so much then of *promise and contract* built upon yt as without violence to conscience might not be shaken" (emphasis supplied).[51]

Just as Donne's first, most joyful letter to Ann is complicated by wariness and uncertainty, his most exalted and exuberant poems are constrained by secrecy and disturbed by "true and false feares" ("The Anniversarie," 27). In "The Sunne Rising," "The good-morrow," and "The Canonization," Donne proclaims the uniqueness of the lovers who are confined to "one little roome," but he also shows the limitations and worries of lovers who cannot appear together in drawing rooms. Because their all-encompassing, unprecedented love is clandestine, it is always subject to the death blow of discovery and condemnation. In "A Valediction of my name, in the window," Donne's passionate, tender devotion suddenly gives way to blunt and startling jealousy. Of course, the poem could be addressed to the speaker's wife as many readers have assumed. I think it is more dramatically convincing, however, if the unsanctioned, insecure nature of the affair makes the speaker suddenly fear that in his absence his lover will marry "one, whose wit or land, / New battry to thy heart may frame" (45–46), just as John Donne may have feared that Ann More would abandon him for a suitor who had more solid ground to stand on.

The first Burley letter can help us to understand the unique isolation, the unconventional sexuality, and the fearful discord that often appear amid Donne's declarations of honorable love. The last two Burley letters can help us to see the tender, vulnerable love that underlies some of Donne's more patently angry and cynical poems. For most of this century critics have interpreted the brutal cynicism of these poems as an impersonal, aesthetic response to existing poetic conventions, rather than as an expression of the poet's, or even the speaker's, impassioned love and anger. Yet in a variety of tones and guises, ranging from tenderness to anger, betrayal to retribution, many of these poems make the same point as the third Burley letter: "only you can tell me . . . whether I were best to dy now, or endevor to live and keep the great honor

---

51. *Loseley Manuscripts*, p. 328.

of being your servant." In "The Message," in a tone resembling the mingled bitterness and hurt tenderness of the third letter, Donne calls, unconvincingly, for an end to an affair that he fears Ann has already ended. In "The Funerall" and "The Dampe" Donne carries out his threat to "dy now": he presents himself as the victim and skeleton of disappointed love. When Ann threatens to reject him for a more socially acceptable suitor, Donne attacks the conventions of poetry and society with a mordant wit and a vengeance so unsettling that most readers have preferred not to take him seriously.

Perhaps, more than any other premodern poet, Donne is renowned for the difficulty of his poems. Ben Jonson feared they would perish for want of being understood. They have not perished, but I do not think they have been fully understood either. In and of itself, the new biographical information provided by the Burley letters does not change any of Donne's poems, but it does suggest new ways to comprehend and assess the disturbing mixture of tones and attitudes that makes Donne's love poems so unconventional and baffling. Once we adjust our point of view, "Womans constancy" and "Breake of day" suggest not a prostitution of honor but the radical redefinition of honor that made Donne's love for Ann More so precarious and precious. Even if the course of true love never does run smooth, the parallels between the Burley letters and the Songs and Sonets suggest that Donne's was an unusually intense and complicated affair. Because Donne had not only an amorous heart but also literary genius, Songs and Sonets became an extraordinary collection of love poems. And because his "best honor" required absolute secrecy and his imagination thrived on verbal complexity, the precise circumstances of the affair are brilliantly hidden by the difficulty of Donne's language. Donne made his poems enigmatic and elusive, full of private ironies and meaningful ambiguities, for much the same reason he made his letters to Ann More so cryptic and anonymous that their authorship and contents have remained doubtful and undeciphered all these years. Because of the danger and delicacy of his love affair, Donne was anxious to keep his true meaning private and undiscovered. As he says in "The undertaking," "I have done one braver thing / Then all the *Worthies* did, / And yet a braver thence doth spring, / Which is, to keepe that hid" (1–4).[52]

Appendix

Since the three letters examined in my essay are neither signed nor preserved in Donne's handwriting, the question of their authenticity remains unresolved. The sole

52. For invaluable help with this essay, I would like to thank in particular Dennis Flynn, who provided me with crucial information about Nevill/Latimer; the staff of the preservation department of the Leicestershire Record Office, who patiently examined the Burley Manuscript with me; Robert Volz, of the Chapin Rare Book Library, who advised me about my description of the Burley Manuscript; Lee Dalzell, Sarah McFarland, and Barbara Prentice of the Williams College Library, who helped me to track down information on Latimer; John Shawcross, Claude Summers, and Robert Bell, who gave me very helpful suggestions on earlier versions of this argument; and Benigno Sanchez and Ernest Sullivan, who provided me with information about conventions of letter writing in the Renaissance.

surviving text of the letters is the Burley Manuscript. Because this manuscript has been seen by only a handful of Donne scholars, it is worthwhile to trace its history and to describe its makeup.

Logan Pearsall Smith first discovered the connection between Donne and the Burley Manuscript when he was preparing *The Life and Letters of Sir Henry Wotton* (1907). He described the manuscript as a "commonplace book" belonging to Donne's close friend Henry Wotton or to someone associated with Wotton (2:489–90). Smith thought a few of the letters contained in the manuscript were by Wotton to Donne, many by Donne to Wotton. Alerted to the collection's existence by Smith, Herbert Grierson concluded that the Burley was a "manuscript of great importance for the editor of Donne's letters. . . . Amid its varied contents are some letters, unsigned but indubitably by Donne; ten of his *Paradoxes* with a covering letter; and a few poems of Donne's with other poems" (*The Poems of John Donne*, 2:cx).

In 1924 Evelyn Simpson printed the letters from the Burley manuscript in *A Study of the Prose Works of John Donne*, though not from the manuscript itself, believing that to have been "destroyed in the disastrous fire at Burley-on-the-Hill, so that the transcript made by order of the Clarendon Press is now our sole authority for the letters" (1st ed., p. 282). Simpson attributed many of the letters to Donne, two with absolute certainty: a prose postscript added to one of Donne's verse letters to Wotton and the cover letter preceding the paradoxes. All speculations about the rest rely on internal evidence and stylistic inference. There was an extensive but inconclusive debate in the 1952 *Times Literary Supplement* (22 August, p. 556; 12 September, p. 597; 19 September, p. 613; 26 September, p. 629; 3 October, p. 645; 24 October, p. 700; 14 November, p. 743; 19 December, p. 837) about whether or not the earliest letter could have been written by Donne during the 1597 Islands expedition. References to Essex's Irish expedition of 1599 and his house arrest at the Lord Keeper's leave little doubt that some of the letters are from Donne's correspondence with Henry Wotton, one of Essex's secretaries.

After Simpson's edition, scholars naturally assumed the Burley manuscript had indeed been destroyed. Then, quite unexpectedly, in 1960, I. A. Shapiro discovered it at the National Register of Archives. Shapiro, who was preparing an edition of Donne's letters, had possession of the manuscript for several years. In a telephone conversation, he was kind enough to give me his opinion of the three letters discussed in this essay. Although he thinks the first letter was definitely written to a lover and not a patron, he sees no connection between these three letters and Donne's life or poetry. Moreover, he explains, the Burley manuscript is a miscellaneous collection of heterogeneous materials. Since these three letters are not in the same part of the manuscript as the letters clearly written by Donne, Shapiro sees no reason to associate them with Donne.

Somehow the manuscript was again misplaced, and for several years scholars again assumed it was irretrievably lost. In 1976 it was rediscovered in a safe-deposit box in the University Library at Birmingham, where it remained, under Shapiro's protection. Peter Beal examined the manuscript in Birmingham after having completed the

Donne entries but while preparing the Wotton entries for *The Index to English Literary Manuscripts* (London: Mansell, 1980). Beal observes, "The Burley manuscript proves upon examination to be a large folio of numerous independent documents bound together" (vol. 1, pt. 2, p. 262). I am indebted to his account for the more recent events of the manuscript's curious history.

When I was in England in January 1983, I discovered that the Burley manuscript is now finally available to scholars at the Leicestershire Record Office, where it is classified as part of the Finch Collection, shelfmark D. G. 7, Lit. 2′. Thus I had the good fortune to examine the only extant text of these letters while working on this essay. With the exception of three interesting details that I discuss in the text and a few minor spelling variations, the transcript of the three letters in question made for the Clarendon Press and printed by Simpson is accurate, down to the abbreviations and commas.

The miscellaneous character of the Burley manuscript is a major concern in determining the authenticity of the letters, making an examination of the original bound volume absolutely crucial. Although Shapiro saw no connection between the parts of the manuscript containing the disputed letters and the parts containing the canonical letters, my examination of Burley revealed a close link. Physically, the bound volume divides into four main sections, which I will call parts 1–4. Part 1, folios 1–121, consists of gatherings made up of a heavy, uniform, untrimmed paper with many pages left blank; it looks like a substantial, independent folio volume containing copies of various documents. Part 2, folios 122–234, is a composite miscellany of self-contained, oddly sized, individual pieces, clearly collected over a period of time and subsequently bound into the larger Burley Manuscript.

Part 3, folios 235–316, contains the Donne letters and poems. Like part 1, it appears to be a separate, integral volume that was later bound together with the other pieces of the Burley Manuscript. The gatherings vary in length throughout and seem to have been prepared by the scribes as needed. Before part 3 was added to the rest, its pages were trimmed to a uniform size, visibly smaller than the untrimmed pages of part 1. The paper, of a uniform texture and weight, is lighter than that used in part 1. The first page contains five epigrams of the sort that would normally appear at the beginning of a manuscript of private poems and letters. The first epigram seems particularly pertinent to the clandestine love story told by the three letters examined in my essay:

> Who so hath leave within this booke to prye
> Must have a Canthars toung and Eagles eye
> An eye most sharp all secrets depth to pearce
> A toung most mute no secrets to rehearce.

Part 4, folios 317–73, resembles part 1 physically. The heavy, untrimmed paper is the same size, weight, and quality. The same watermark appears in both. Parts 1 and 4 look as if they originally belonged together. At first glance, it seems surprising that parts 2 and 3 were interposed; however, the order makes sense when the contents are examined more closely. Part 2 adds to the official letters and documents, associated with Henry Wotton and his Venetian embassy, that predominate in part 1. Part 3, like part 4, is composed primarily of poems and private letters.

The Burley Manuscript as a whole is a miscellaneous collection of numerous, independent documents. The sewn, plain vellum binding suggests that the volume may well have been bound as is in the seventeenth century. Nonetheless, the miscellaneous nature of the larger Burley Manuscript has little bearing on the Donne poems and letters, because they appear in part 3, which was originally a separate, autonomous manuscript volume. The three letters discussed in my essay appear on folios 295, 296, and 299v (numbered by Simpson as letters 16, 15, and 13, respectively). Thus they are not very far removed from the two letters on folios 286 and 308v–309 that are indisputably Donne's. The first is not really a letter but a brief prose postscript, appended to Donne's verse letter "To Sr H:W: going into Venice." Understandably, the postscript appears not with the other Donne letters but amid a group of poems by Donne and others. Following the poems, on folios 294–300, appears a substantial group of letters, including the three in question, that look as if they were all copied into the manuscript at the same time from a single packet. Evelyn Simpson attributes most of them to Donne, with a few to Wotton or friends of Wotton. They follow piece by piece, in the same meticulous script, with no gaps. In every respect, they look as if they belong together. The scribe seems to have planned the layout carefully. Whenever possible, he finished the page with a completed letter, adjusting the side margins from ¾ to 2 inches, allowing the bottom margins to vary from ½ to 2½ inches. When a long letter ends in the middle of a page, he fills in with a short letter. He may have copied many of the letters in their original order (Simpson confuses matters by printing them out of the manuscript's order), but on occasion he seems to have sacrificed chronology for neatness. For example, what is probably the earliest letter about the 1597 Islands expedition appears not first, but third, where it is used to fill the space remaining on folio 294v. If the letters were copied not from a prior manuscript collection but from individual sheets, this matching of letters to pages would have been the most efficient and reliable way for the scribe to calculate and control the number of pages required.

Given the appearance of the manuscript, it is puzzling (and of course disappointing) that the genuine Donne letter and paradoxes on folios 308v–315 do not follow directly after the disputed letters on folios 294–300. Visually distinct from the intervening pages, the two groups seem to be connected by the same handwriting, ink, and layout. Indeed, I think they belonged to a single packet that the scribe intended to copy together into one gathering.

What seems to have happened is this. After carefully calculating that he needed about thirty-two pages for all the letters and paradoxes, the scribe (whom Simpson calls Dl) prepared a gathering of eight sheets folded in half. He copied the main group of letters onto folios 294–300, and, having finished about half of his task, he took a break. By mistake, another scribe picked up and used the half-empty gathering. We know this scribe was working in the opposite direction (from the back to the front), because the writing on half of folio 303v and folios 304–306v is upside down, and because "Et," which begins folio 304, appears as the catchword in the bottom margin of folio 304v. The less orderly appearance of these pages suggests that the second scribe was working more casually and quickly than Dl. I suspect he simply failed to notice that the signature was already half used. The gathering had probably been turned over so that the blank pages were on top.

When the original scribe returned to finish his task, only folios 300v–303 remained blank—clearly not enough space for the remaining Donne letter and the accompanying collection of paradoxes. He could not resume where he left off on folio 300v, because the paradoxes would then have been interrupted in the middle. Consequently, he left folios 300v–303 blank and prepared a short, new gathering just long enough for the remaining letter and paradoxes (including an extra sheet as a margin of error). At some later date, a third scribe (whom Pearsall Smith identified as William Parkhurst, Wotton's secretary) used the intervening blank pages for a separate group of letters, which Simpson thinks may have been written by Donne to Wotton a few years later.

This hypothesis seems the best way to explain the puzzling appearance of this section of the manuscript: the careful layout of folios 294–300, the visual similarities with folios 308v–315, the more chaotic layout of the intervening pages, and the writing that suddenly appears upside down. But the best evidence for the theory is the fact that the remaining letter and paradoxes occupy fourteen pages in the new gathering. We know the scribe was carefully fitting the letters into the space allotted on folios 294–300. Before his plan was disrupted, he had fifteen pages left in the original gathering (ff.300v–307), just enough room (with one page to spare) for the remaining letter and paradoxes.

If this hypothesis is correct, it means that the scribe carefully planned for the entire group of letters and paradoxes to appear together in one self-contained gathering. This closer connection between the authentic Donne letter and the disputed letters gives us good manuscript authority to associate the three letters in question with John Donne. Although we still do not have incontrovertible evidence, I think that connections between the three letters and Donne's life and poems make a convincing case for Donne's authorship.

When I returned from England, I learned that Robert Parker Sorlien, who is currently preparing an edition of Donne's prose letters, had also examined the manuscript within the last year. In a paper delivered at the 1982 meeting of the Modern Language Association, Sorlien argued that in addition to the two letters judged authentic by Simpson, her No. 32 is also "surely by Donne." Since then Sorlien has concluded that an additional twenty-two of the Burley letters, including the three discussed in this essay, are "possibly by Donne."

4. POETRY, PERSONAL AND IMPERSONAL
The Case of Donne

JOHN T. SHAWCROSS

Many authors—particularly poets—are beset with criticism stemming from either of two approaches: the biographical or the philosophical. "Beset" because other approaches may be not only possible but also more meaningful and because at times these approaches misrepresent the literary work. The commentary on some of Donne's poems provides excellent examples of indefensible biographical or philosophical interpretations. This is not to say that some of Donne's poems do not have biographical origins or overtones, or are not the result of philosophic questioning and concepts. But too frequently a poem like "The Relique" has been subjected to erroneous explication because of a single misappropriated reference (here to Mary Magdalene) or a poem like "Womans constancy" has furnished evidence that Donne, seriously considering the problems of the sexes, resignedly accepted incompatability.[1]

To the contrary, literature should first be viewed as literature—not as biographical statement, even when biography has direct influence; not as philosophy, even when the work propounds strong ideologies. For if there is nothing of worth but biographical interest or philosophic concept, the piece of literature has moved out of the imaginative—or evocative, or "creative"—into the informational—or referential, or expository. A poem—a good poem, that is—is seldom, if ever, just reeled off without planning or without revision. Preliminaries require more than simply an experience to recount, an idea to express, an emotion to communicate. The building materials of a good poem subtend form, structure, development; they consist of metrics, sound, imagery, symbol, metaphor, strategy, and tension. That is, to employ well-known language, the vehicle with its many mechanical parts is ascertained to achieve a desired tenor. Such mechanical parts should be so meshed that their interworkings are not apparent. If the poet has not fully predetermined all such elements, revision evolves them, and in any case attempts to make them as consistent, complete, and logical as is necessary for the experience or idea or emotion. At times, of course, a beginning recommends itself without such preliminaries, but what happens as the poem progresses and as it is revised makes the difference between a poem like Vaughan's "The Timber" and his "They are all gone into the world of light!"[2]

---

1. Even R. C. Bald in *John Donne: A Life* (Oxford University Press, 1970), pp. 182–83, seems to accept H. J. C. Grierson's assignment of the first in *The Poems of John Donne*, 2 vols. (Oxford: Clarendon Press, 1912), 2: xxv, 49–50. And Arnold Stein, reading the second as spoken by a male voice, for instance, writes, "there are latencies in the situation that are not developed but that may be part of a private and personal poem which only pretends or threatens to be an epigram" (*John Donne's Lyrics: The Eloquence of Action* [Minneapolis: University of Minnesota Press, 1962], p. 104). Compare the biographical reading of the first poem by John Carey, in *John Donne: Life, Mind and Art* (New York: Oxford University Press, 1981), pp. 44–45. He discusses the second on pp. 194–95. I use the term *philosophical* to imply the conceptual, thought divorced from emotion or effect even from the contextual.

2. I have previously discussed a literary work as the result of its pre-text (structure, themes, genre, and

What is here suggested raises a question of poetic intention, but in a sense of the word that is different from the excesses of nineteenth- and early twentieth-century critics against whom W. K. Wimsatt was reacting in exposing the intentional fallacy. To speculate on the external circumstances that have created poetic expression or to allege a psychological or emotional bias on limited evidence, engendered primarily by the critic's attitude toward a work, is patently invalid. Frequently the search for either external or internal evidence became an end in itself, the literary work disappearing from consideration. We cannot resurrect the exact circumstances under which a work was written. But undoubtedly a writer does have "intention" in the sense that there is a reason for his writing. This is obvious in expository or argumentative prose; it should not be less obvious in imaginative literature. To speculate on little evidence or little analysis, or to disregard the work itself, is unacceptable; but to employ evidence (including psychological analysis) to determine an author's point of view and impetus for writing is fitting and proper. In trying to correct an ill of criticism the taboo of intentional fallacy has diverted criticism from a proper path. Oddly, the aim of such correction was to allow the literary work to stand on its own merit; yet it seems that it has blocked out those elements that underpin merit by denying—for many slavish avoiders of the fallacy—the author's reason for writing and consequently his "building materials." The reader in the poem is important, and he should be attuned to what in the poem creates his response. But we should not forget that it was the author who put those materials together, who in that sense is also in his poem, and whose "intention" is inferable thereby.

The demonstrable misreading of Donne has sprung from many roots. One is a picture of Jack Donne, the fickle and cynical roué, seeking "soul" and finding only "body," and of John Donne, the loving and faithful husband, and eminent divine. Another is a belief that Donne is "sincere," by which one apparently means "is writing about an actual emotional experience," a belief that partially arises from the critics' lack of knowledge of other poets as different as George Gascoigne and Sir John Davies who rejected "pretty" verse, or who, like Fulke Greville and Sir Edward Herbert, experimented with metaphor. Donne should not be read as isolated poet but within his contemporary poetizing context. Finally, misreading springs from a cursory reading and inattention to tone and poetic stance. Specific examples of these contentions will clarify the issues. First, let us look at "The Autumnall," which has not generally been viewed under the intention that I would urge for Donne. Thus we may evaluate the poem better by recognizing its significant compositional elements. Next, "The Relique" will illustrate false biographical interpretation; and "Womans constancy," false philosophical statement. From these we can proceed to examine some works that seem to have varying degrees of biographical statement in them, and then to a discussion of works that we may call "personal."

---

so on) and its execution (the writing process itself, the imagery, the style, and so on). See *With Mortal Voice: The Creation of "Paradise Lost"* (Lexington: University Press of Kentucky, 1982). A literary work's metaphoric meaning, I believe, proclaims a conscious control by its author.

"The Autumnall" has been included among the love elegies, although it is clearly in a stanzaic pattern. Perhaps that mislocation has aided in its inadequate reading over the years. Izaak Walton, in his *Life of George Herbert* (1670), p. 15, and such a late manuscript as the O'Flahertie MS (ENG MS 966.5, Harvard University) assign the subject of the poem as Magdalene Herbert, a friend of Donne's and mother of his friends Sir Edward Herbert, Lord Cherbury, and George Herbert. The indecorousness of many lines, directly as well as metaphorically, has not always been admitted by students of Donne. Lines like 25–28 emphasize older qualities (the autumn):

> This is loves timber, youth his under-wood;
> There he, as wine in *June*, enrages blood,
> Which then comes seasonabliest, when our tast
> And appetite to other things, is past.

On the other hand, lines 37–42 stress extremely old qualities (the winter):

> But name not *Winter-faces*, whose skin's slacke;
> Lanke, as an unthrifts purse; but a soules sacke;
> Whose *Eyes* seeke light within, for all here's shade;
> Whose *mouthes* are holes, rather worne out, then made;
> Whose every tooth to'a severall place is gone,
> To vexe their soules at *Resurrection.* . . .

Inappropriate for Mrs. Herbert are *cradles* (the womb as birth place) and *tombs* (the womb as place simply to die, a pun for sexual intercourse) in line 46.[3] Once we rid ourselves of the biographical context we see Donne the poet examining another aspect of love such as the Songs and Sonnets focus on: here the topic is love of an older woman, in contrast, one imagines, to other poets' glowing apostrophes to their young mistresses. It is not dissimilar in intent to Shakespeare's mannerist sonnet, "My mistress' eyes are nothing like the Sun" (no. 130). The point is that despite the philosophic seriousness that often may be induced from Donne's poems there is also a strong element of poetic rivalry among a coterie of young students or post-students that shapes them.[4]

Lines 13–16 are typically inappropriate for Donne to have written about Magdalene Herbert:

3. In her appended account of Donne and Mrs. Herbert, Helen Gardner concludes, "We should give some credence to Walton and that we may accept that in his praise of an 'autumnal beauty' Donne had Mrs. Herbert in mind" (*John Donne: The Elegies and the Songs and Sonnets* [Oxford: Clarendon Press, 1965], p. 252). She places the poem at the end of the elegies, although the Contents separates it from them as a poem without generic classification. My reading of this poem attempts to make it available for a deconstructed approach without accusation that significant contextualization has been ignored.

4. Compare M. Thomas Hester's words concerning Everard Guilpin's satires: "He wants *in*, not *out* of the confines of the generic conventions—and not because satisfaction of the norms and forms of the genre insures any social reformation in his readers but because his exhibition of those standards and examples includes him in the literary game gentlemen wits play." See "'All are players': Guilpin and 'Prester *Iohn*' Donne," *South Atlantic Review* 49 (1984), 14.

> Call not these wrinkles, *graves*; If *graves* they were,
>   They were *Loves graves*; for else he is no where.
> Yet lies not Love *dead* here, but here doth sit
>   Vow'd to this trench, like an *Anachorit.*

It is unlikely that he would have stressed whatever wrinkles she may have shown. It is unlikely that they would be viewed as so deep that they become trenches. It is unlikely that the pun on the wrinkle or trench or grave as the place in an older woman in which Love sits would have been made, for the obvious contrast is with the usual place in a woman in which Love sits. There Love does "die"; here he is not dead. There one does not "withdraw" (the etymological meaning from which *anchorite* derives) to become a religious recluse; here, Love does devote himself to that which he considers divine. The contrast in vows is likewise inappropriate, for the poem is not simply a statement of reverence for an older woman, mother of his friends, but revels in the constant play between the nonsexual love for an older woman and the usual sexual love for other women. Note, for example, the final two lines of the poem: "Not panting after growing beauties, so, / I shall ebbe out with them, who homeward goe." "Panting"? "Growing"? "Ebbe out"? Besides interpretation of the poem, the biographical facts also gainsay Magdalene Herbert as subject of this poem. Mrs. Herbert was only seven years older than Donne. When the speaker rejects relating the woman to "living *Deaths-heads*" because they are "*Antique*," "not *Ancient*," he implies that she is *Ancient*, though not *Antique*. The words may derive from similar roots, and their meanings are similar. The punning play of one against the other suggests that the woman is an old person (ancient) though not a prized remnant of the past (antique) as would be a *death's-head*. Neither word is appropriate for Magdalene Herbert, and certainly not when it comes from one only seven years her junior. The poem was written before the end of 1614, for it appears in the Group I MSS, whose progenitor, it would seem, was produced by the beginning of 1615. Donne would have been around forty-two and Mrs. Herbert around forty-nine. She would have been of an age not yet with definite certainty beyond childbearing, and not quite the implied fifty of the poem. And if it were composed with Mrs. Herbert in mind, one would think, it should have been written prior to her marriage to Sir John Danvers in 1608, when Donne would have been around thirty-five and she around forty-two—hardly an "Ancient" and barren age.

Two important points that remove this poem from the biographical context so uncritically repeated are (1) the date of composition, which may lie with most of the Songs and Sonets before 1601, and (2) the poet's intention in the poem, that is, to present another kind of love from those usually depicted by Elizabethan poets, apparently in a kind of poetizing competition common to the 1590s when Donne was still pursuing formal education or was off on expedition or was first engaging in definite employment. It should be noted that in all five manuscripts of Group I the poem appears in the same medial postion among various Songs and Sonets: "The Indifferent," "Loves Usury," "The Canonization," "The triple Foole," "Loves infinitenesse," "Song:

Sweetest love, I do not goe," "The Legacie," "A Feaver," "Aire and Angels," "Breake of day," "The Prohibition," "The Anniversarie," "A Valediction of my name, in the window," "The Autumnall," "Twicknam garden," "Epitaph on Himselfe," "Valediction of the booke," "Communitie," "Loves growth," "Loves exchange," "Confined Love," and "The Dreame."5 Dating is, of course, uncertain, but most of these are usually placed before 1601, and we should therefore question some poems' suggested dating based on biographical readings. I refer to "Song," "A Feaver," "A Valediction of my name," "Twicknam garden," "Epitaph on Himselfe," and "Valediction of the booke." "Twicknam garden" will be discussed later. "Epitaph on Himselfe" appears in two versions (consisting of lines 1–16 and 7–24, respectively), and the added title "To the Countess of Bedford" occurs only with Group III MSS (the earliest date of which is in the late 1620s); the Phillips MS, giving lines 7–24 only, calls it "Another on the Same" with reference to Mrs. Boulstred. The other poems have been related to Ann More. But aside from probable date of composition, the ludic urge that has been expressed as the performing self in recent critical studies of literature, and particularly in studies of sixteenth-century England, cannot be overlooked. The false specter of Romantic effusion has blighted poetic criticism for a long time—as if the poet cannot write without parallel experience, as if all that is said is fully and firmly believed as he or she writes. A deeper study of the poetizing of Donne's period—look at the sonnet sequences alone—unavoidably points to writing as process rather than as expression of heartfelt emotion or of burning thought; writing that should be judged alongside other writing in kind.

"The Relique" has likewise been connected with Magdalene Herbert, and again removal from that context allows an earlier and more defensible date of composition for it and provides us with another example of witty love poetry for the sake of witty love poetry.6 Primarily it is the reference to Mary Magdalene in line 17 that has suggested Mrs. Herbert's connection with the poem, and also the fact that the woman and the poet have a "Platonic" rather than a sexual relationship. But the implication of a possible sexual relationship and the emphasis that the reference gives to Mary Magdalene's sinfulness seem most inept for Mrs. Herbert. (The citation of Mary Magdalene in the sonnet entitled "To the Lady Magdalen Herbert, of St. Mary Magdalene" stresses Mary Magdalene's reasons for sainthood and passes over explicit reference to her demoniac identification.) In "The Relique" Donne plays upon sexual puns of contrast, where the lovers do not know sex in life but do symbolically in death. It is a miracle that they have not touched the seals that nature sets free (that is, have not engaged in sexual intercourse) but that "late law" has imposed (that is, man's inhibitions against sex between two unbetrothed or unmarried people, the law being religious law). But after death, symbolically, things will be different. When his grave

---

5. These are numbered 37–57 in my edition, plus no. 147, "Epitaph on Himselfe." Cambridge University MS Additional 5778(c) and its cognate, the Leconfield MS, omit "The Prohibition" and "Epitaph on Himselfe."

6. Gardner dissociates this poem from Mrs. Herbert; see *Elegies and Songs and Sonnets*, pp. 257–58.

is redug for the burial of another body, the gravediggers will find the memento of "A bracelet of bright haire about the bone," a commonplace symbol of avowal of love. (The symbol appears often in literature, for example, in Shakespeare's *Midsummer Night's Dream* 1.1.30–33.[7]) But Donne makes the symbol an obscene pun by preceding it with the idea that women are promiscuous and take more than one lover and by following it with the idea that the gravediggers will think that a *loving* couple is reposing there. The bone becomes a phallus as well as an arm, and bright hair becomes not only a tress cut when the hair of the head was bright but also pubic hair little dimmed with age. Needless to say, such images are inappropriate to a poem concerning Mrs. Herbert; and needless to say, Donne's poetizing coterie of friends would have snickered over the subtlety of the joke and its obscenity.

"The Relique" is concerned as well, though, with the "mis-devotion" of people who revere bits of bone and hair and funerary items in their idolatry and their devotion to things rather than to God. Donne, the sexist, as the modern age would call him, says that "All women shall adore us, and some men" when such a relic as the bracelet of bright hair about the bone is found. These being relics of their sainthood in the religion of love (Cupid being God), the woman will become a Mary Magdalene (one who has often had "more then one a Bed" but who has been reformed and sainted), and the speaker will become "A something else thereby." There would seem to be some play of a Christ image here, since Mary Magdalene discovered and announced the resurrection of Jesus, but Donne may have thought rather of David. In "An hymne to the Saints, and to Marquesse Hamylton," he wrote, "let it bee / Thy wish to wish all there, to wish them cleane; / Wish him a David, her a Magdalen" (40–42). Hamilton had died on 2 March 1625, probably by poison administered by enemies. Donne counsels him to wish all repentant sinners now in heaven to wish all those left behind him to be clean (to be washed in the blood of the Lamb), so that each male repentant sinner in heaven becomes a David, who had repented his sins and begged the Lord not to punish his people because of him (2 Samuel 24:17) and who had even forgiven Shimei who had cursed him (1 Kings 2:8–9); and each female repentant sinner in heaven becomes a Mary Magdalene, whose reformation made her worthy of announcing the resurrection. In "The Relique" the reference to Mary Magdalene suggests that for the people the bracelet of hair will have the magical power of bringing reformation from sinfulness for women and thus possible sainthood; this is the kind of miracle the people seek, but the greatest miracle is the woman of the poem who, contrary to the usual ideas about woman's sexual appetite and inconstancy, was nonsexually inclined in her relationship with the speaker. And the possible reference to Christ suggests that male abstinence such as has been his miracle in life (in this particular relationship, that is) will bring salvation (like those who "were not defiled with women" in Revelation 14:4); the possible reference to David (one decidedly not

7. Compare Phillips D. Carleton, "John Donne's 'Bracelet of Bright Hair About the Bone,'" *MLN* 56 (1941), 366–68.

virginal) suggests that the people will learn repentance through the miraculous powers of the relic. Removal from a biographical context allows "The Relique" to be grouped with such similar poems as "The Will," "The Funerall" (which also remarks "That subtile wreath of haire, which crowns my arme"), and "The Dampe," the poems with which it is generally associated in the manuscripts.

A poem like "Womans constancy" may seriously consider the age-old idea that it is woman who is fickle and promiscuous and that she deserves some consideration as well as man, but it is largely concerned with wit: wit in metaphoric language, wit in stanzaic and rhyme pattern, wit in humorousness and paradox, wit in reversal of what one might expect. For the poem is spoken by a woman, as the epithet "Vaine lunatique" and the probable sex of the person who leaves—the "Vaine lunatique"—make clear. Rather than producing a love poem such as Michael Drayton might write (even such a later sonnet as "Since there's no help"), Donne takes a similar situation or theme and plays it in variation. The praise of his achievement should lie not in the philosophy expounded (for in poems like this there is no originality of thought), but in his artistic working of that situation or theme to make it more meaningful or memorable or various of interpretation, and thus original of execution.

First we must attend to the speaker of the lyric. Often the speaker is treated as being a man, and man is traditionally a constant lover; such an attitude classifies woman as fickle and promiscuous. As male, the speaker argues that he will not attempt to alter his mistress's potential infidelity since soon he, too, may wish whatever relationship has come to exist between them to be dissolved.[8] It becomes a kind of philosophic statement that without mutual fidelity there can be no fidelity at all; it becomes part of Donne's attempt to find an eternal "soul" in woman, somewhat like the poet of "Loves Alchymie." Since there is no way that woman can be true or unchanging (being inconstant as the moon), he professes a "sour-grapes" attitude. But note that "thou" has been visiting "I's" rooms and will be leaving the next day. Perhaps women did visit "bachelor quarters" in those days, but were they women with whom one was concerned about maintaining a relationship? Rather, in our male-oriented world, is it not usually man who visits woman and who leaves for business or whatever else carries him away from her embraces? The "I" of the poem certainly gives no hint of having to leave for business or the like. (Comparison with "Breake of day," which most agree is spoken by a woman, reinforces the point.) Instead, I would urge, the "thou" is a man and the "I," a woman. The "vaine lunatique" of line 14 cannot be woman influenced (physically and emotionally) by the moon, but a man who is made lunatic by the moon, which is a female symbol (classically, Diana). The "vaine lunatique" is "thou," the lover of the woman, one made lunatic by the moon, and here one who

---

8. Seeing the speaker as a man causes Wilbur Sanders to call the woman a whore (*John Donne's Poetry* [London: Cambridge University Press, 1971], p. 46). The usual interpretation may be observed in Donald Guss's discussion in *John Donne, Petrarchist* (Detroit: Wayne State University Press, 1966), pp. 113–14; here he even sees Donne as the "I" of the poem: "The arguments [of the person leaving] are not meant to persuade the reader—Donne assures the lady that he can refute them."

is both inadequate (*vanus*, idle, empty, inconsequential) and conceited. Once we get the speaker straight we come to see another level of irony in the poem. Although woman was noted for her inconstancy, the woman speaker of the poem is really arguing for constancy in this affair; but suspecting that such constancy on her part would be ill-rewarded, she counters that she, too, might become inconstant. The reversal of the expected idea is witty and indicates why woman has become so inconstant as to be proverbial: she is forced to give man some of his own medicine or be man's fool.

The poem, we thus see, comments on the way in which man achieves sexual alliance—by vowing eternal love (after all man *is* the constant one)—only to break that alliance once he has been sexually satisfied by making a new vow (of love for another, or marriage, or the like) that he *says* was made before his avowal of eternal love for the present woman. Or he might break the alliance by saying that they are not now the kind of people they were then (divorce courts hear this plea repeatedly), and continued alliance would be strained and meaningless. Or perhaps any vow made by awe of love and fear of Love's reprisal can be denied; or perhaps, by the analogy of die and sexual intercourse, contracts are voided by death. Or perhaps not to be woman's fool the man has made up his mind prior to their coition to be fickle and to tell her the lies she wants to hear. Thus only by breaking their alliance does he show constancy to himself and truth to his personal oath. Well, says the woman, I could confute you but I won't because tomorrow I may be very glad to be rid of you as lover. The delineation of the male-female battle is different from what we observe when we read the speaker as male. It suggests psychological understanding not otherwise possible. Yet it is the witty use of dramatic situation, of metaphor, and of tone that most strikes one about the poem. We are not really concerned about the cynic lover (male or female), but we are taken by the way in which Donne is able to achieve a dramatic scene, a single vision of what we can believe was a real experience, and an actual speech and emotional pattern. Part of the means to this achievement lies in the shortened lines (two of 8 syllables, one each of 6 and 4) and a varied rhyme scheme from what is expected; part, in the fact that it is one stanza with each line tied to the others by rhyme or parallelism.

Other Songs and Sonets that have often been invalidly tied to biography or philosophy, I would argue, include "The good-morrow," "The Sunne Rising," "The Canonization," "Twicknam garden," "Valediction of the booke," "The Extasie," "The undertaking," and "The Primrose."

Of course, at times, biographical—as well as philosophical—contexts do surround some of the poems. The verse epistle "Reason is our Soules left hand, Faith her right," while epideictically praising the Countess of Bedford, hints that the countess's patronage may have faltered through her reason instead of being unhesitatingly unabated as a result of her faith in Donne. And the famous "A Valediction forbidding mourning" does, from all accounts, proceed from Donne's travel to the Continent with Sir Robert Drury; yet its statement of faith in love is more than just biographical. Contrasting with the sublunary lovers (perhaps like those of "The good-morrow," certainly those of "Loves Alchymie") who find love only in sense and bodily parts are (if biographical) John and Ann, who have achieved the transmutation of their individualities into gold through their faith in each other. I neither urge biographical interpretation nor dismiss it. The poem may have had general biographical origins as a result of Donne's various travels, even before he met Ann, but such origins are not integral to a reading of the poem. The biographical may add another dimension, but the main point is psychological and has philosophic import: only affective separation is separation.

"The triple Foole" seems to draw one of its allusions from biographical fact. Lines 12–16 allude to poems that have been set to music; such musical settings make the speaker feel the pain of his love again:

> But when I have done so,
> Some man, his art and voice to show,
>   Doth Set and sing my paine,
> And, by delighting many, frees againe
> Griefe, which verse did restraine.

He is a fool for loving, since it is thwarted; a fool for writing of it in "whining Poetry"; and now a fool again for having his poem set to music. Of course, the reference does not demand that only Donne and his poetry set to music are meant, for others had the same experience. But such poems as "The Expiration," "Breake of day," "The Baite," "Song: Sweetest love," "The Message," and "The Primrose" had early been set in musical versions ("The Expiration" and "Song" appear in two different settings). We are thus led to conclude that biographical detail may lie behind the poem or its images, although in this poem such background does not alter our reading of it.

Another case in point is surely "A Valediction of my name, in the window." We do not know what circumstance evoked the poem; it has been suggested that Donne refers to trips into London during 1605–1609 when the family lived at Mitcham, or to Twickenham, the residence of Lucy, Countess of Bedford, during 1608–1610, or to the Continent with Sir Walter Chute in 1605–1606 or with Sir Robert Drury in 1611–1612. But it does celebrate some leavetaking, and the speaker argues that symbolically he is with his loved one by the etching of his name in a window for her to look upon: "Here you see mee, and I am you [through reflection]." The name is given mystical powers: it is a "charme," and in gematria—in which numerical values are given to letters—the usual signature, "Jo: Donne," equals seven and thirty-six, two very powerful numbers; seven implies infinity. The name is as long-lasting as the diamond that cut it into the glass, and thus symbolically he is always with her though physically separated. Other biographical details are given: he is emaciated from illness ("My ruinous Anatomie") and his name is "ragged bony," for indeed his normal signature does have the contour of a T-bone, and he seems to allude to his usual practice of underscoring the signature. The play of death imagery and of eternalities suggests that the circumstances of the poem may have been a time when "Neere death" afflicted him. If indeed the poem is based on reality, composition may have occurred around

1607–1608 when he was seriously ill, perhaps with a recurrent typhoidal fever. Soon after this siege with near-death, he wrote his satire on suicide called *Biathanatos*. What we see in this "Valediction," therefore, are biographical elements, and we are led to read biographical matter out of the poem; for example, that the loved one is thus Donne's wife, Ann. But this is a dangerous critical procedure, and many commentators, apparently because of the loved one's potential new love affair, avoid the issue of biographical import.[9]

Among the poems that may be considered for personal views—that is, poems that are built on some biographical experience or that offer some kind of direct emotional or psychological experience—are the verse letter to Sir Henry Wotton beginning "Here's no more newes" and the holy sonnet "What if this present were the worlds last night?" The verse letter is dated 20 July 1598, when Wotton was in the service of the Earl of Essex and thus not always in London, as Donne usually was as secretary to Sir Thomas Egerton. At the time of writing, however, Donne was probably with Egerton in Greenwich where Queen Elizabeth had gone with her entourage.[10] In line 2 ("I may as well / Tell you *Calis*, or St *Michaels* tale for newes") Donne refers to two events in which he himself took part, the Cadiz expedition and the Islands expedition; and it is evident that at this time he has connections with the royal court. Out of this same set of circumstances came the satires, the affinities with the last two (nos. 4 and 5) being strongest. "Here's no more newes" is part of an exchange of verse letters between Donne and Wotton including "Sir, more then kisses" and Wotton's "'Tis not a coate of gray, or Shepheards life."[11] Bald's view of the poem as, "in effect, a consolatory epistle, designed to raise Wotton's mind above the pleasures of the court in which he cannot share" (*A Life*, p. 103), totally misses the ironic humor. The problem is, Bald fails to recognize the poem as a fine example of the ludic level of so much coterie verse of the time. While a verse letter generally involves some degree of biographical context (the only exception being the totally fictitious situation, as in Rochester's "A Letter from Artemisia in the Town to Chloe in the Country"), it is a lyric and thereby demands that we read its biographical elements contextually. The personal, I argue, should be remarked, but the impersonal—that is, the craft of the poem as poem—must also be examined. Too often critics can find nothing but the biographical to discuss; cases in point are provided by Milton's Latin elegies. Donne's verse epistle to Wotton is calculated to demonstrate his rhetorical adeptness, his ability

9. Curiously, Bald does not even mention this poem; and Carey, while he seems to say that Donne is the speaker of the poem, concerns himself with the way the ending "suddenly shrugs off the poem we have been reading, disowning it as mere pretence" (*Life, Mind and Art*, p. 195). While postmodernist critics would ignore even the possibility of such extratextual matters as I have mentioned here, the possibility must be dealt with (and I hope dismissed as often inconsequential even when a good case can be made for it) because that is the way Donne has been read over and over again. Turning one's back does not make anything go away.

10. See Bald, *A Life*, pp. 102–3.

11. On these verse letters as a three-part sequence, see Ted-Larry Pebworth and Claude J. Summers, "'Thus Friends Absent Speake': The Exchange of Verse Letters between John Donne and Henry Wotton," *MP* 81 (1984), 361–77.

to communicate by allusion and implication, the humor in turning ideas or attitudes of the recipient back upon themselves—in a word, his wit.

The communication in "Here's no more newes" is that the court is as it has usually been—vicious, corrupt, suspicious, lacking in honesty and integrity. Those who show any opposing virtues do so but for a short time before they, too, are corrupted. The place is beset with rumors; its inhabitants acknowledge no wrongs; its greatest achievements "Are but dull Moralls of a game at Chests" (24). Donne is thinking of such adages as "pawns are expendable" and "never leave the queen unguarded." His disgust with the world of the court suggests why he eventually turned to religion as his life's work, although for the intervening seventeen years he vacillated among the fringes of the worlds of the court, diplomacy, religion, and literary patronage. Donne would still seem to be in the process of initiation into the world of sham and evil, and at the age of twenty-six seems strangely retarded to have any more ideals to lose. Was Jack Donne only now recognizing the kinship of his wild oats sowing and public life? Has he finally seen who are the wretched and who the wicked (see "Satyre V") in terms of the haves and the have-nots? Is the answer to "Be . . . thine owne home, and in thy selfe dwell" ("Sir, more then kisses," 47)? or to "Let falshood like a discord anger" man to action ("Who makes the Past, a patterne for next yeare," 41)?

What is curiously interesting and what thus emboldens our understanding of the coterie nature of the poem is that when Donne wrote this verse epistle to Wotton there indeed was a great deal going on in and around the court. "Here's no more newes, then vertue" is surely an untruth that Wotton would have immediately perceived as the ironic understatement that it is. That irony makes even more incisive Donne's last line, "*At Court*; though *From Court*, were the better stile." Wotton was an adherent of the Earl of Essex, who had half-drawn his sword in the presence of the Queen, had been banished from court, and was off sulking on his country estate. The "dull Moralls" noted just before take on very specific, ironic meaning when we remember this phase of the Essex affair. Donne, indeed, had news to tell, as well, of Burghley's being near death and the confusions of the Irish situation. The poem is not an autobiographical verse epistle; it only employs biographical contexts. It is rather an excursion into the classical anticourt theme memorably set forth in Spenser's contemporary "Mother Hubberd's Tale" (1591).

To turn to a poem that seems to offer direct emotional and psychological experience, we can look at one of the holy sonnets. The date of the group of sonnets of which "What if this present were the worlds last night?" is a part may be around 1609 (although an earlier date will not alter our reading of it), after Donne's serious illness, during his patronage by the Countess of Bedford, and before his association with Sir Robert Drury. This specific sonnet seems to reflect the kind of contemplation of death, associated with the siege of illness, that we have already noticed. The poem meditates that Judgment Day may come unannounced. (The millennium was expected by the devout sometime during the seventeenth century; later, it was more precisely expected in 1657.) But the circumstances of the poem do not really matter; what does is the psychological thrust of the poem as the speaker thinks about his worthiness and the means by which worthiness may be evidenced or measured. For the I of this poem the concept of the crucified Christ—man's redeemer, a martyred saint, one whose great love for man brought him torture and death—reassures him that the Judgment of the Son on him will not doom him to hell but will forgive him his sins. Since beauty is a sign only of pity, and the cross to be engraved in his heart where his soul dwells is beautiful, he is convinced of the Son's pity on him. What should we stress here? The speaker's repentance for his sinfulness? His rationalization that God will show mercy on him? A justification of the past or a prospectus of his future? His reference to idolatry of his profane mistresses implies that he has replaced this with love of a divine mistress, religion. The sonnet would seem, by itself, to assume purgation and to have moved to illumination. The poet is not yet on a unitive path, for he has not asserted positive action that he will undertake. But he has prepared for such action by renunciation of the past. While the sonnet is undoubtedly applicable to any Christian, it seems to represent a personal meditation and resolution, which, when reviewed in chronological pattern with other data, will develop a perspective view of Donne at a period of crisis.

Finally, for consideration of poetry, personal and impersonal, in Donne, we might contrast two further poems. "Twicknam garden" persistently is viewed as a poem written for the Countess of Bedford, whose home was in Twickenham. The poem offers a stock Petrarchan theme of male love/female rejection, accompanied by the usual sighs and tears, but with overtones of the lost Eden due to the fall of Eve by the seduction of the serpent. Here, in contrast to the usual Petrarchan poem, the lover is thwarted by the fidelity of the woman. As Gardner says, "it seems incredible that [the] poem should be thought to be concerned with Donne's actual feelings for his patroness" (*Elegies and Songs and Sonnets*, p. 250). Yet she persists in making that association because of the title given in Group II and III MSS. The Bridgewater MS gives only "In a Garden," and, most significantly, the Group I MSS omit any title at all. It should be clear that in the mid-1620s the title "Twicknam garden" was attached to the poem, which was apparently not titled by Donne; this attachment of a title is part of the regularization and sophistication of the text that is repeatedly observable in Group II MSS. On the basis of the false title, commentators have extrapolated biographical and psychological meaning from the poem and have often slighted the variation on the theme that Donne is playing with for his coterie poetizers.[12]

On the other hand, "The Dissolution" seems clearly to relate to the death of Ann (15 August 1617), and we have thus a poem that delineates emotional and psychological reaction to this loss. The poem does not appear in Group I MSS (deriving from a compilation made around 1614/15), nor even in Group V MSS (largely dated in

---

12. While still relating the poem to the title ("he felt it necessary to pretend to be a suitor utterly and hopelessly dedicated to the Countess of Bedford"), Earl Miner in *The Metaphysical Mode from Donne to Cowley* (Princeton: Princeton University Press, 1969), pp. 55–57, does examine the strategies of the poem; what he misses, I think, is the playfulness.

the late 1610s or early 1620s, including the Bridgewater MS, but often reflecting early texts); it is found only in the Group II MSS, from which the Group III MSS derived it. The poem should be read as poem, divorced from any external element, but the externality of the real-life world out of which it comes gives an added dimension for an understanding of Donne the person. It is therefore reprehensible that neither Bald nor Carey mentions this poem.

The personal view of "The Dissolution" places the poem after 15 August 1617, when Ann Donne died, the seventh day after the birth of her twelfth child (stillborn), and thus relates it to "A nocturnall upon S. Lucies Day," if we accept the latter poem as referring to Ann's death, as it is often viewed. "The Dissolution" presents a Donne who is on the verge of becoming the "Nothing" of "A nocturnall" through the dissolution of self as a result of overabundant, overburdening elements—his "fire of Passion, sighes of ayre, / Water of teares, and earthly sad despaire," the four elements of life. His elements so increased by loss of her will "soonest breake," and his fire (passion) growing with its fuel will, by its excessive heat, cause his "soule more earnestly [to be] releas'd" rather than allow him to "live long wretched so." We see a Donne envisioning his own dissolution (as in an alchemical experiment) because of his loss, a psychologically depressed lover who has lost "loves securitie" and who sees only bleakness for himself. Walton tells us that he "betook himself to a most retired and solitary life" immediately thereafter and rededicated himself to God, preaching at St. Clement Danes (where Ann and her child had been buried) as his first public act thereafter.[13] Bald remarks the alterations in Donne's life from this point onward (*A Life*, pp. 328–32); the surviving evidence indicates his return to public life was not until 2 November 1617, when he preached at Whitehall. We have, thus, in "The Dissolution" and "A nocturnall" material for a fuller psychological view of Donne than his biographers (or biographically oriented critics) have pursued.

But what of the impersonal view of "The Dissolution"? Waht is to be stressed, I would suggest, is the craft of the poem. The twenty-four-line poem appears at first to break into three-line groupings, but then clearly abandons any certain ordering: 6, 8, 10 / 6 (7), 8, 10 / 10 / 6 (7), 8, 10 / 6, 10, 10, 8, 10 / 6, 8, 10 / 10, 6, 4, 10, 10, 14. The "first Elements" of the prosodic line have themselves dissolved by growth. Yet that dissolution is less dissolved than at first appears, for the lines of 6 and 8 syllables combine into 14, the length of the last line. And this has been adumbrated by the previous 4 and 10 (or should we remark only 6 and 4?). The varying prosodic line reflects, indeed, the substance of the poem. The rhyme scheme begins as if unrhymed, progressing to a couplet form: *a b c d b a c d e e f f e g g h h i i j k k j j.* That is, it moves from disorder to order in reverse of the concept of dissolution, but it is subtle because line stoppage and enjambment counter a feeling that we have moved to couplet form. The craft of the poem duplicates, first, the thought of the poem,

<hr />

13. Izaak Walton, *The Life of Dr. John Donne* (London: for R. Marriot, 1658), pp. 52–55. Perhaps Walton is accurate, but there is no proof of this delivery of this sermon.

then its implication: the disorder of self that her death has brought as he tends toward nothing and the order that will emerge as his own former self transcends into a new being, one in which the first, air, water, and earth have been reassembled. The implication (to be developed in "A nocturnall"), created by the craft, will emerge for us only as we contemplate the alchemical result of dissolution: a resultant maleness uninvolved in male/female union. All that is needed is redirection.

As we read Donne's poetry, we should remember the way in which he has interwoven biographical details into the poems, the way in which they may inform us of biographical—or more usually ideational or psychological—matters, and the way in which they may represent an imaginative and artistic artifact without significantly direct biographical overtones. An author does write out of himself—his experiences and his thoughts and his total being; but a major factor in the evaluation of a piece of literature is the execution of the work itself and the result of that execution (the literary artifact), not what we have learned about the author. The dependency of evaluation on reader response—what the reader has been made aware of, in what way the reader is made to reconsider himself or the world about him, what has influenced the reader's action or thought—is likewise significant. Analyses of Donne's poems should stress these evaluative factors. A poem like "A Valediction of weeping," or the holy sonnet "Since she whome I lovd," or the verse epistle to T. W., "At once, from hence, my lines and I depart," divorced from biographical contexts, will rise in evaluation and poetic significance for the reader. Not only will the form (and structure) of the work be allowed its due but the thought will emerge as factor in an enlarging world of thought. The reductionism of pinpointed event will be reversed, and an important poem like "The Anniversarie" will be freed from such implications as lie in Gardner's comment, "It breathes the same scorn for the Court from which Donne was an exile" (*Elegies and Songs and Sonnets*, p. 199). And a maligned poem like "A Jeat Ring sent" will be revalued for its riddling play and cleverness of language; and these are but part of the definition of the author's intention for his poem.

IN **CYPHER WRIT,**
OR **NEW MADE IDIOME**

5. DONNE AND PROPERTIUS
Love and Death in London and Rome

STELLA P. REVARD

Of the Latin love elegists of the first century B.C., Ovid rather than Propertius is usually considered the major model for Donne, providing him with the design for at least two of his elegies, those beginning "Fond woman" and "Come, Madam, Come," and influencing the voice of the lover in both the elegies and the Songs and Sonets. Ovid in the *Amores* and the *Ars Amatoria* advertised himself so widely as the leading *preceptor amoris* of the ancient world that we have taken for granted that poets of the sixteenth and seventeenth centuries, and especially Donne, took him at his word and mimicked his attitudes on women and love throughout their poetry, particularly when they affected the airs of the witty man-about-town, content to take pleasure widely and view women and women's constancy with a cynical eye. Yet, if we look more closely at the Ovidian lover, we find little more than superficial resemblance between him and the persona or personae of Donne's poems. Ovid's lover is, above all, straightforward in his approach to sex and women; he seeks success and pleasure, for himself and for his mistress. He worries little about his own or his mistress's fidelity and he hopes, if she is unfaithful, that she will be discreet. Once he accepts her infidelity, he even relishes a rival (it adds zest to the affair). He stands up and gives advice on any and all aspects of love; he is capable of laughing at his own and others' follies; he considers love, in sum, part of the delightful game of life.[1]

If this is a fair assessment of the Ovidian lover, and I believe it is, little more than surface resemblance links him to the Donnean lover, and that only in the lyrics and elegies in which Donne assumes a witty nonchalance that often masks bitterness. Even such poems as these ("Womans constancy" and "The Indifferent," for example) may owe less to Ovid than to the elegy tradition that includes Propertius and Tibullus. The two most famous Ovidian imitations, moreover, "Fond woman" and "Come, Madam, Come," follow Ovid (*Amores* 1.4 and 1.5) more in general subject matter than in dramatic development, rhetorical strategy, or character delineation. In 1.4 Ovid advises his mistress how to go to a banquet with her husband and still manage, eluding his watchfulness, to give secret signs to her lover. He re-creates the proposed situation: the mistress's arrival at the banquet, her conduct throughout, and the departure. He then offers counsel for that night and the morning after. Donne's "Fond woman," while duplicating the husband-lover-mistress triangle of the Ovidian elegy, only echoes Ovid

---

1. I wish to express my thanks to Carl Conrad, Department of Classics, Washington University, St. Louis, to whom I am indebted for much that I know about the Roman elegists.

Ovid's *Ars Amatoria* is exemplary for its positive view of love: it leads the lover through all the stages of the affair and culminates with mutual gratification for lover and mistress. For examples of Ovid's casual approach to infidelity, see *Amores*, 2.19, 3.4, and 3.14. Du Quesnay contrasts Ovid's frank enjoyment of sex with Propertius's and Tibullus's anguish. See I. M. Le M. Du Quesnay, "The *Amores*," in *Ovid*, ed. J. W. Binns (London: Routledge and Kegan Paul, 1973), p. 7.

69

directly in those few lines in which the lover observes that he and his mistress can no longer trick the husband in his own presence ("Nor at his boord together being satt, / With words, nor touch, scarce lookes adulterate," 19–20). Rhetorically more convoluted, Donne's elegy begins by exploring the mistress's contradictory reactions to her husband's jealousy: she fears his disapproval, yet desires her liberty. Donne's lover does not express directly, as does Ovid's, his resentment of the husband who legally possesses the mistress's favors, but he indirectly caricatures the husband first as a dying man, swollen with poison, then as a glutton, "pamper'd with great fare," and finally as a tyrant prince. The poem becomes less a dramatization of the lovers' dilemma than an exploration of their feelings about their situation; they run the gamut in emotion from fear to joyous exultation at prospective liberty. Similarly, Donne's "Come, Madam, Come" is indebted to Ovid (*Amores* 1.5) for its subject, Corinna's secret midday visit to her lover's chamber, where she disrobes and the two make love. Donne's elegy, however, dramatizes only the disrobing and describes it from the lover's point of view as he urges his mistress to remove one garment after another. Normally connected with the Ovidian elegy on Corinna, Donne's elegy may, as we shall see, owe more to Propertius and his elegy on lovemaking with Cynthia.

Donne's attitudes in both these elegies are different from Ovid's, and though Donne, no less than Ovid, is concerned with exploring feelings in love as well as situations, he is definitely more contradictory in his feelings and more elusive than Ovid both in these elegies and throughout his work. The Donnean lover is noted for the constant shifting of stance and attitude, now affirming, now denying his love, forever anxious, doubtful, questioning, unable to take his own or his mistress's motives at face value, obsessed with real or imagined falseness. Does he have all his mistress's love? Is her love worth having? Is his? Is the experience everything it might be? Isn't it threatened by the limits that human mortality always imposes? Doesn't death await the lovers to annihilate them and their love, unless death prove the ultimate and greatest union? John Carey has commented that Donne's "restless sexuality" is basically different from the "urbane indecency" that is at the heart of most of Ovid's elegies. Donne, he argues, is continually obsessed with the "shadow of separation and loss," "whether he flaunts it with cynical nonchalance, or writhes in exasperation, or celebrates the blissful release from his phantom which he finds in a girl's arms."[2] There is a world of difference between him and Ovid, who, though he may explore difficulties in love, assumes that sexual gratification is an obvious and wholly satisfactory goal for the lover.

Therefore, though Ovid may have been an important model for Donne in defining situations for the love elegy, he little influenced Donne's conception of the lover himself. We might be led to think at this point that Donne is wholly original in his portrayal of the restless, self-examining lover if there did not exist in the school of love elegists before Ovid an elegist who has given us the very prototype of the self-examining lover: neurotic; intelligent; witty but eccentric; learned but difficult in his learning;

2. John Carey, *John Donne: Life, Mind and Art* (London: Faber and Faber, 1981), pp. 41, 37–38.

cold and sensual at the same time; forever defining and redefining his feelings and those of his mistress. I mean, of course, Propertius, Ovid's own master, known in the Renaissance but less popular than Ovid, and a more complex, if less witty and smooth, practitioner of the love elegy.[3] For Propertius, love is not an occupation, as with Ovid, but an obsession, for he has no other goal in life than to comprehend totally and possess completely his mistress in an all-consuming relationship. This relationship, however, is persistently threatened by his own and his mistress's falseness and by the necessary limitations of life and perforce of death.

Critics have not left Donne's debt to Propertius unnoted. Classicists have remarked how alike the two are in wit, objectivity, and dramatic power, as well as in difficulty and obscurity.[4] Editors of Donne have cataloged borrowings from Propertius, fewer in number than those from Ovid, but nonetheless significant, such as the arguments in "Loves Warre" or the *adunata* in "Song: Goe, and catche a falling starre."[5] Yet few have urged closer connection than a temperamental likeness and the occasional borrowing on Donne's part of a conceit or phrase from the earlier poet. There is, I believe, a closer link. It seems likely that Propertius provided Donne with the model for the self-examining restless lover that we observe in so many of Donne's elegies and Songs and Sonets. In Propertius, Donne could find an introspective lover who was different from the Petrarchan model that had dominated love poetry in the sixteenth century, one absorbed in the love affair but not necessarily subservient to it, a lover not less frank than the Ovidian lover about his own sexuality but insistent on finding more in sex than simple gratification. Donne became interested in the love elegy because it offered a different experience of men's and women's relationships than did the Petrarchan sonnet tradition. He found in Ovid form and subject matter, but turning to Propertius he discovered a greater range and depth of personality and the possibility to exploit not one but many stances in love.

First of all, there is the almost deliberate contrariness of the lover that we find in Propertius's elegies and in Donne's elegies and lyrics. The persona is continually shifting in his attitudes toward his mistress, sometimes in the same, sometimes in consecutive poems. Chameleonlike, he is now bitter and accusing, now tender and sincere. He proclaims at one moment that all women are worthless and inconstant, then at the next that they are incomparable paragons of virtue to whom he can entrust his whole heart and soul. For example, in a great many poems Propertius tells us that Cynthia, his subject throughout the first two books of elegies, is a cold hard wanton, whose behavior is notorious throughout Rome. His reactions to her unfaithfulness range from bitter denunciation to suicidal despair to detached amusement. In two par-

---

3. For a contrast of Ovid and Propertius, see Du Quesnay, "The *Amores*," pp. 6–8.

4. See "Propertius" in *The Oxford Classical Dictionary*, 2d ed. (Oxford: Clarendon Press, 1970); also J. P. Sullivan, *Propertius: A Critical Introduction* (Cambridge: Cambridge University Press, 1976), p. 52; and Margaret Hubbard, *Propertius* (London: Duckworth, 1974), p. 64.

5. See the notes in *The Poems of John Donne*, ed. Herbert J. C. Grierson, 2 vols. (Oxford: Oxford University Press, 1912); and *The Elegies and the Songs and Sonnets*, ed. Helen Gardner (Oxford: Clarendon Press, 1965). See especially Gardner, pp. xxii–xxvii, 128, 152.

ticularly strong companion poems he tells of the despair to which her cruelty has led him.[6] These poems use the descriptions of outer scenes of rage and desolation to depict the state of the poet's inner mind. In the first he embarks on a voyage to a distant place and suffers on shipboard a raging storm, whose angry buffeting winds are symbolic of the unruly passions to which Cynthia has subjected him. In the second, having arrived at the unfriendly land, the poet portrays his utter misery by describing the desolate landscape.

> Haec certe deserta loca et taciturna querenti,
>   et uacuum Zephyri possidet aura nemus.
> hic licet occultos proferre impune dolores,
>   si modo sola queant saxa tenere fidem. (1.18, 1–4)

> Here indeed is a lonely and silent place for my lament,
> where only the breezes of Zephyr possess the vacant grove;
> here freely is there sanction to pour out my secret sorrows,
> if solitary rocks at least know how to keep faith.[7]

It is a familiar enough poetic device to use the backdrop of a real or imagined landscape to portray a desolation of heart, and Donne also effectively uses background or landscape to compare or contrast with his mood of despairing love in such poems as "Twicknam garden" and "A nocturnall upon S. Lucies day." In the first, he contrasts the mood of the lover, "Blasted with sighs, and surrounded with teares" to the spring scene before him and wishes that "winter did / Benight the glory of this place, / And that a grave frost did forbid / These trees to laugh" (1, 10–13). The wished-for winter portrays the lover's desolation; in the "nocturnall" the darkness of the day's and year's midnight actually serves to convey the deadness, emptiness, and privation that the lover is feeling.

Donne and Propertius, however, are equally effective in painting the lover's anger as his despair. Both poets threaten to expose the lady for her perfidy and to pay her back in kind. For example, Propertius tells Cynthia in 2.5 that he will have his revenge, not by striking her or tearing her hair but by publishing in his poetry that, though her beauty is great, her vows are empty. Or, says he in another poem (2.11), he will simply cease to write of her so that she will go to her grave unknown. Donne, similarly, takes a moral tone in such lyrics as "The Legacie" or "The Message," where he wills the lady's own false heart back to her or attacks her for having made "jestings / Of protestings" and having crossed "both / Word and oath" ("The Message," 12–15). After such righteous indignation at falseness, the reader would hardly expect

6. For commentary on these elegies, see Friedrich Solmsen, "Three Elegies of Propertius' First Book," *Kleine Schriften* 2 (Hildischeim: Georg Olm Verlagsbuchhandlung, 1968), pp. 289–92; and Hubbard, *Propertius*, pp. 34–35.
7. Propertius's elegies are quoted from Propertius, *Elegies I–IV*, ed. L. Richardson, Jr. (Norman: University of Oklahoma Press, 1977). All translations, unless otherwise noted, are my own.

a poet to turn about and express an attitude of calm and amused detachment at woman's infidelity, but this is precisely what both Donne and Propertius do. In two poems Propertius ironically comments on Cynthia's infidelity. In the first (2.9), he contrasts his mistress who could not remain faithful one night with the long-enduring Penelope and Briseis and remarks that women are by nature changeable as the south wind. In 2.32 he pretends to excuse Cynthia's falseness by saying that she is only doing what women throughout the ages have always done, and he then describes such famous ladies as Pasiphae, who was seduced by a bull, and Danae, who could not even preserve her chastity in a brazen tower. Certainly, says Propertius with a smile, Cynthia has chosen to emulate the most illustrious women of Greece and Rome, and, this being the case, she is entirely free from his censure. We can almost hear the later mocking echo of Donne, who, in a similar mood, suggests that one is as likely to catch a falling star or impregnate a mandrake root as find a woman "true, and faire."

But neither Donne nor Propertius lets the matter rest with ironic detachment; both admit to infidelities of their own and suggest that free-ranging desire is natural to both sexes. As Donne remarks in "The Indifferent," if women were true, it would be to those who are false to them. This famous propaganda piece of Donne's, "I can love both faire and browne," seems directly related to an equally famous apology for philandering in Propertius (2.22). Propertius confesses that a great many girls delight him equally, causing a great many difficulties to come his way. Wherever he goes, he sees lovely girls with white arms, with white breasts all unveiled, and with hair curling seductively on their brows. With a heart tender to each, he cannot bear to deny any, and, should one refuse him, another will be willing. Donne's and Propertius's poems seem to be confessions of avowed philanderers, but both are more subtle than they appear at the outset. Donne's easy libertine air in the first stanza of "The Indifferent" is complicated by the contradiction of the final line, "I can love any, so she be not true" (9). Does the final line unmask the man who boasts of his inconstancy because he fears that, as he can be constant to no one, no one can be constant to him? If this is so, then the poem is more than a celebration of profligacy, and Donne is closer still to Propertius in his attitudes than critics have proposed.

In 2.22B, 23, and 24 Propertius reveals that his free-ranging libertinism is not due merely to a heart too susceptible to female beauty. He complains about the coyness of women who lead men on rather than saying yes or no directly as a prostitute would, mistresses who prefer keeping men at their beck and call to honestly satisfying them or refusing their favors (2.22B, 23). In 2.24 he lays his inconstancy to Cynthia's charge, claiming that were she not inconstant, he would not be either. Donne could easily have learned from the Roman master of elegy his habit of inquiring into paradoxes and motives after an initial disarming celebration of inconstancy. His technique in "Womans constancy," as in "The Indifferent," is similar to what we have observed in Propertius. He begins by anticipating how the lady will excuse her breaking of vows and concludes by intimating that he perhaps is as wanton as she. Yet, as in Propertius, we cannot take either the opening lines or the turnabout at the conclusion at face value. We have the feeling that the lover is defending himself with his confession of inconstancy against his fear of the lady's inconstancy:

> . . . I could
> Dispute, and conquer, if I would,
>   Which I abstaine to doe,
> For by to morrow, I may thinke so too. (14–17)

This extraordinary introspection into the contrariness of male feeling and behavior carries over to a degree into insight into female feelings. Two poems by Propertius and one by Donne explore the love affair from the point of view of the mistress of the wandering lover. In Propertius's elegies 1.3 and 2.29 Cynthia lies at home, faithful as Penelope, while her lover wanders the streets at night, drunken. In 2.29 a group of little boys, winged cupids with their torches and arrows, accost the lover and lead him home through the streets, cautioning him to keep better his pledges of love and learn to stay home with his mistress. In 1.3 the lover returns to Cynthia's house after a bout on the town; he fears to wake his mistress, but the busy old moon ("luna moraturis sedula luminibus" [32], the busy moon with lingering light), like the sun in another poem by Donne, peers through the window to rouse her. Cynthia pours out her reproaches, to which her lover listens without a word. Only once does Donne let the lady speak her case without interruption. Cynthia could well have been a model for the woman in "Breake of day," who, though in different circumstances, voices a complaint against her lover's behavior. In leaving her, she says, he reveals his casual attitude toward the affair, for he urges the demands of business over those of love: "He which hath businesse, and makes love, doth doe / Such wrong, as when a maryed man doth wooe" (17–18). Donne and Propertius, however pressing they make the demands of the lover in the majority of their poems, are well aware that a love affair has two sides.

To characterize the love poetry of Donne and Propertius as miscellanies of attitudes or as simple explorations of aspects of love affairs would be a mistake, however. For, though the lover adopts different and even contradictory stances, there is throughout the elegies and lyrics of both poets a peculiar possessiveness, an obsessive fervor, that marks even the dismissals of love and the denials of the mistress. Love for each is the touchstone for defining everything else, the goal toward which each strains, the transfiguring experience, the absolute in life, and the means for reaching beyond even the grave. In no classical elegist but Propertius could Donne have found so persistent a preoccupation with the mistress as the sum total of earthly experience. Propertius cries out that his mistress is everything to him: Cynthia was the beginning and shall be the end ("Cynthia prima fuit, Cynthia finis erit," 1.12, 20). She has utterly transformed his personality; he no longer is what he has been. He has no other muse but Cynthia, no other subject but love, no other joy but to write of his mistress (2.1; 2.13). She alone is to him home, parents, and all sense of joy: "Tu mihi sola domus, tu, Cynthia, sola parentes / omnia tu nostrae tempora laetitiae" (1.11, 23–24). It is difficult not to connect Donne in the romantic sublime with Propertius, or to cite the many instances in the Songs and Sonets when Donne finds identity and totality in his mistress. In "The Sunne Rising" he proclaims, "She is all States, and all Princes, I, / Nothing else is" (21–22); in a similar mood in "Loves infinitenesse" he plays upon the words *one* and *all* to express the completeness of the lovers' relationship: "so wee shall / Be one, and one anothers All" (32–33). The famous image of the twin compasses at the conclusion of "A Valediction forbidding mourning" expresses a sentiment like Propertius's, for Donne, too, finds beginning and end in his love: "Thy firmnes makes my circle just, / And makes me end, where I begunne" (35–36).

The sense of oneness is expressed in two ways, by union in love and by union in death. Side by side, Donne and Propertius celebrate the ecstatic togetherness in the bed and in the grave, sensually experiencing the conquests of both domains. Another such night as this, says Propertius, and I would be immortal: "immortalis ero, si altera talis erit" (2.14, 10). Likening his experience to the conquest of a great kingdom, he says that he felt like the Atrides when Laomedon and its great wealth fell to them. Though by no means an unusual metaphor in love poetry—we find lovers compared to conquerors in Ovid (for example, *Amores* 2.12) and many other poets— it is worth noting that Donne also thinks of sexual conquest in terms of winning a wealthy empire. Both "The Sunne Rising" and "Come, Madam, Come" compare the mistress to lands conquered: "the India's of spice and Myne" ("The Sunne Rising," 17) and "Oh my America! my new-found-lande, / My kingdome, safeliest when with one man man'd, / My Myne of precious stones, my Emperie" ("Come, Madam, Come," 27–29). Yet the exploitation of this metaphor of "masculine" conquest does not preclude in either Propertius or Donne the use of the gentler and softer metaphors to express the joy of "feminine" yielding. Oddly enough, these metaphors are not applied exclusively to the mistress, but to lover and mistress together or to the lover himself. Propertius, for example, compares his joy at winning Cynthia not only to the joy of the Atrides but also to that of Electra at her brother's return or of Ariadne on seeing Theseus safely through the Daedalian maze (2.14). So complete is the union, says Propertius, describing the same night of love in the elegy following, that their embrace was like the yoking of doves:

exemplo iunctae tibi sint in amore columbae,
masculus et totum femina coniugium. (2.15, 27–28)

Let doves joined in love be example to you,
Male and female in total union.

The point is that union annihilates the differences between war and peace, male and female, for love makes the two, now become one, indistinguishable in feeling and being. It is a state of being that Donne explores throughout his love poetry, speaking in "The Extasie" of the single soul created by the two lovers' souls joining or in "The Canonization" of the two lovers as "the Eagle and the dove" or as the "Phoenix": "we two being one, are it. / So, to one neutrall thing both sexes fit" (24–25).

Even so frankly sensual a poem as "Come, Madam, Come" has in its conceit of unclothing the notion of lovers revealing themselves fully to one another in order to achieve intellectual as well as physical union. The model for Donne's poem, moreover, is the second of the pair of elegies in which Propertius celebrates Cynthia's yielding.[8] Propertius tells how he strove with Cynthia to reveal her nakedness before they put out the lamp. Urging her to cast off the last garment, he praises those who revealed themselves fully to their lovers, Helen to Paris as she rose naked from Menelaus's bed, and Endymion, who first appeared naked to Diana before he lay naked with the goddess. He even threatens to tear the clothes from his mistress if she will not reveal herself in full nakedness. It is not Propertius, however, but Donne who declares: "Full nakedness, all joyes are due to thee" ("Come, Madam, Come," 33). Although Ovid's elegy (1.5) deals with a comparable subject, unlike Donne's "Come, Madam, Come" and Propertius's elegy 2.15 it approaches the topic with physical and not metaphysical terms. Donne persistently alludes to the undressing of the body as the unclothing of the soul: "As soules unbodied, bodies uncloth'd must bee" (34). What is finally to take place is a mystic union, as though somehow the consummation on earth were to lead to other consummations. In this Propertius provides the cue, for he depicts his happiness in terms of the blessedness of immortality or of the gods. There is no limit to what he feels, nor can one be set: "errat, qui finem uesani quaerit amoris" (2.15, 29): he errs who seeks to set an end to raging love. Its limits are life and death alone, and, to conclude this poem celebrating the consummation of physical love, Propertius says: hers I shall be alive, and hers dead ("huius ero uiuus, mortuus huius ero," 2.15, 36). Donne's witty summary in "The Canonization" would not better express the ultimate union beyond death that consummation in life looks forward to: "Wee can dye by it, if not live by love" (28). For both, death is the unavoidable measure for love.

Throughout love poetry death is often the symbol of the ultimate union of lovers. What makes Donne unique among Renaissance poets in his treatment of love-death and what links him with the Latin elegist Propertius is not so much the use of this common metaphor but the vivid and sensual realization of it. With ever so much care and detail Donne tells us about the physical experience of being dead, of being carried to the grave, of becoming bones and dust and mingling with the bones and dust of his beloved. The pleasure that he takes in imagining and re-creating death seems almost as great as that he takes in sex. Moreover, in this preoccupation with death, with graves, with funerals, he follows exactly in the line of Propertius. How many of Propertius's poems deal not only with his death but also with his and Cynthia's funerals. When he is annoyed at Cynthia's scorn and threatens to write of her no more, it is the neglected tomb of his mistress that he evokes. Let the grave consume her beauty and her fame, he writes. Let her sink to ashes unknown so that the traveler going by will contemn her grave and neither recall nor say that these were the ashes of a

---

8. Gardner cites Propertius 2.15 as the source for Donne's praise of nakedness in "Come, Madam, Come."

learned lady: "et tua transibit contemnens ossa uiator, / nec dicet: 'Cinis hic docta pu-ella fuit'" (2.11, 5–6). He is likewise obsessive about his own death and fears that Cyn-thia may show no grief at his funeral and after neglect his grave. If she cannot be faith-ful to him in life, at least, he hopes, she may attend him in death. When in 1.17 he fears that he may die at sea, it is not his death that he dreads but the missing funeral obsequies. Had he stayed in Rome, he would have enjoyed at his death the proper rites for a lover. Cynthia would have stood beside his pyre, tenderly laid his body on rose petals, cried aloud his name. This sensually sweet funeral would have ful-filled in death what he lacked in life: the devotion of a mistress. Bitterer than death itself, cries he two poems later (1.19), is the fear that Cynthia will deny him even in death, causing death to become the means of their final separation rather than of their union.[9]

> Non ego nunc tristes uereor, mea Cynthia, Manes,
>   nec moror extremo debita fata rogo;
> sed ne forte tuo careat mihi funus amore,
>   hic timor est ipsis durior exsequiis. (1.19, 1–4)

> No longer now do I dread the sad shades, my Cynthia,
>   nor delay the doom due to the final pyre;
> but that my funeral rites should want your love;
>   this fear is bitterer than the funeral obsequies.

For Donne, as for Propertius, the attitude toward the grave often defines that to-ward the love affair. How many love poems of Donne open with references to the lover's death: "When I dyed last" ("The Legacie," 1); "When I am dead" ("The Dampe," 1); "Before I sigh my last gaspe" ("The Will," 1). Some of these, such as the opening line of "The Apparition"—"When by thy scorne, O murdresse, I am dead" (1)—are surely witty allusions to the lover's so-called death as a result of the mistress's disdain, but others cannot be so easily passed over. There are the anguished thoughts of the mistress's loss in death: "Oh doe not die, for I shall hate / All women so, when thou art gone" ("A Feaver," 1–2); or the first line of "The Dissolution"—"Shee'is dead" (1). Death, which in these poems threatens to dissolve the bond between the lovers, proves, however, the more lasting union. There is no fonder thought in Donne than the idea of the lovers joined in the grave itself. As Propertius imagines with pleasure the devo-tion of the final obsequies, Donne pictures the joy of the grave as marriage bed. In "The Anniversarie" it is only the prospect of separate graves that causes him distress: "Two graves must hide thine and my coarse, / If one might, death were no divorce" (11–12). In "The Relique," the memento of love, the "bracelet of bright haire about the bone," provides the means by which the lovers maintain their union in the grave. Fear of death in Donne, as in Propertius, is by extension the fear of the impermanence

---

9. Hubbard comments that in Roman funerary cults the bones do love and have power as bones: "*manes*, like the bones and ashes of the dead, inhabit the funerary urns; indeed they *are* the bones and ashes, con-ceived as still *empsycha*, possessed of sensation and feeling" (*Propertius*, pp. 35–36).

of love. If the lovers can join one another in death, dying by love as they cannot live by it, then they can defeat impermanence. The progress of "The Canonization" charts just such a course, and it is perhaps no accident that the most memorable image in the poem is that of the well wrought urn.

I would like to think that Donne took this striking image of the funeral urn directly from Propertius. As Donne argues that the "well wrought urne becomes / The greatest ashes, as halfe-acre tombes" (33–34), Propertius praises the modesty of the poet's funeral over the elaborate display of state funerals. He only desires, he tells Cynthia, a little urn. Let his faithful mistress and his three books of elegies be his sole attendants at the funeral. Further, let his tomb be shaded with laurel and inscribed with two lines to commemorate his faithful service to love. Like the canonized lovers of Donne's poem, Propertius imagines that he will become after death the "saint" of love, his tomb renowned to faithful lovers and served by a mistress herself deified by love. Interestingly enough, this elegy on "love's last rites" (2.13) immediately precedes the two elegies that celebrate its initial consummation (2.14 and 2.15), where Cynthia first yields to Propertius. Its delight in the unearthly joys of the "saints" of love contrasts with the joy of physical consummation. For both Propertius and Donne, the grave is a most fine and private place for the last embraces of the lovers.

To conclude with the eschatological sublime of Propertius's funeral elegy and Donne's "The Canonization" would be to misrepresent the range of experience that these poets explore. Both are capable of undercutting their own exultation and examining the comic dimensions of love beyond the grave. Consider, for example, a situation exploited by both poets in which one of the two lovers returns as ghost to haunt his or her unfaithful partner. This is exactly what occurs in one of Propertius's last elegies on Cynthia (4.7), a poem that may well be the inspiration for Donne's "The Apparition." In Propertius's elegy, Cynthia returns, a pale ghost, and bends over the bed of her sleeping lover; in Donne's poem, the lover threatens to come as a ghost to his false mistress and find her in worse arms than his. Both poems are exercises in the comic macabre, and both turn absolutely upside down the romantic notions of union after death that their authors celebrate elsewhere. Part of the technique the poets use is to make realistic a basically unrealistic situation. Propertius describes Cynthia's ghost with graphic detail: she looks to him just as she did when borne to her grave, the fire having eaten away the clothing at her side and the beryl ring on her finger. Donne portrays realistically the mistress's reaction to the ghost rather than the ghost itself. She, "poore Aspen wretch," is "bath'd in a cold quicksilver sweat," lying beside her present lover, whom she dare not "pinch to wake," lest he think she calls for more. The focus for both poets is on the discomfiture of the lover or mistress at being caught by the previous partner he or she thought dead and buried. Both portray comically, though in different ways, the lover or mistress shrinking from the reproaches of the visitant ghost.

It is supremely ironic that Propertius in this first of the final pair of poems on Cynthia permits the mistress, whose infidelity he had complained of in poem after poem, to speak the final word on her own faith. Now it is she who accuses him: of neglecting her funeral rites and the erection of a proper monument, of having forgotten her utterly, and of letting the "prostitute" with whom he now lives scorn her memory and reign in her place. Further, she asserts, it was not she who was unfaithful, though all his poetry reported her so, but he, who now has won renown through his songs to her. Yet, she says, despite all, she will have him still, and she proclaims, almost threateningly, that she will consummate that last lovers' reunion beyond the grave that his own poems celebrated.

> nunc te possideant aliae: mox sola tenebo:
>   mecum eris, et mixtis ossibus ossa teram. (4.7, 93–94)

> Now let others possess you; soon I alone shall hold you;
>   with me you will be, and bone mixed with bone, I shall wear you down.

The lover in Donne's poem has come on a mission not unlike Cynthia's: to say in death that last word that he did not speak in life to his scornful mistress. But what exactly that word will be Donne does not tell us. Though he portrays vividly the future ghost's visit and the mistress's reaction, he lets her and us imagine the reproach.

> What I will say, I will not tell thee now,
> Lest that preserve thee;'and since my love is spent,
> I'had rather thou shouldst painfully repent,
> Then by my threatnings rest still innocent. (14–17)

The effect of the lover's silence and of Cynthia's speech is the same; the "ghost" reverses the roles the lovers played in life and gains an ascendancy over the partner that, dying, he or she was denied. The threats of the vengeful ghost and the shrinking of the absurdly trapped lover provoke our laughter, holding up to ridicule not only the lovers but also love itself.

Coming full circle from sublimity to bathos, this final set of poems demonstrates, I believe, the astonishing versatility of Propertius and Donne in changing their stances on love. Yet they are not mere chameleon-poets, adopting now this pose, now that, and believing in none. Whether celebrating love's sublimity or holding love up to scorn, they explore every facet of the experience with a peculiar obsessiveness. For them love and death were the absolutes, and the ultimate experience was to look on both together. For this reason, it seems more than likely that Donne, having first discovered the love poem with Ovid, went on to master its range with Propertius as his ultimate model.

As a final biographical note in this study of two poets in two distant lands, let me repeat the conflicting accounts that ancient tradition has left us on what happened to Propertius after his comparatively brief career as elegist and man-about-town. One tells us that he died of love, the other that he married, retired from poetry, and raised a family.[10] What happened to Jack Donne we all know.

---

10. Sullivan, *Propertius: A Critical Introduction*, pp. 1–3.

6. DONNE'S EPIGRAMS
A Little World Made Cunningly

M. THOMAS HESTER

"If he would," suggested William Drummond of Hawthornden, Donne "might easily be the best epigrammatist we have found in *English.*" Ben Jonson agreed:

Who shall doubt, *Donne*, where I a *Poet* bee,
When I dare send my *Epigrammes* to thee?
That so alone canst judge, so'alone dost make.[1]

Modern judgment seems not to concur, however — if the amount of critical attention given this group of poems is any indication. Perhaps the epigrams have been neglected simply because ours is not "an age of the epigram"[2] — although the ubiquity of sententious bumper stickers and emblazoned T-shirts on our campuses would seem to indicate otherwise. Nevertheless, the judgment of Drummond and Jonson is well founded, for Donne's epigrams offer an instructive example of his poetic achievement *in parvo.* Although admittedly not as complex as many of the lyrics, the epigrams manifest that "sophistrie too subtile" of Donne's best poems, exhibited here in the daring exploration of the limitations of deriving definitive conclusions from speech acts and of the traps that reside in tropes driven toward epigrammatic closure.

One must be careful, of course, not to blur the rhetorical differences between epigram and lyric. As Norman Farmer points out, "One simply cannot read an epigram as he reads a lyric," for "it follows different rules and fulfills a totally different pleasure principle" — or, in Donne's case, at least plays with and manipulates different generic expectations. Taxonomically, the two forms respond to different rhetorical pretexts. The lyric is self-enclosed and private, an overheard address to a fictive reader within the borders of the poem's metaphoric world; the epigram is topical and public, addressed to us directly by the poet (not a persona) about its referend. Both forms also relate to the world differently, the lyric accommodating that world to the emotional requirements of its own amorous perspective, the epigram accommodating itself to

---

1. William Drummond, in *Critical Essays of the Seventeenth Century*, ed. J. E. Spingarn (Oxford: Clarendon Press, 1908–1909), p. 216; Jonson, *Ben Jonson*, ed. C. H. Herford and Percy and Evelyn Simpson, 11 vols. (Oxford: Clarendon Press, 1925–1952), 8: 25.

2. Mario Praz, *The Flaming Heart: Essays on Crashaw, Machiavelli, and Other Studies in the Relations between Italian and English Literature from Chaucer to T. S. Eliot* (Garden City, N.Y.: Doubleday, 1958), points out that "the epigrammatic tendency is discernible in all the literary works" of Donne's age (p. 207). As to the treatment of Donne's epigrams, H. H. Hudson does not mention them in his study of genre in the Renaissance, T. K. Whipple grants them less than a page in his study of the English heirs of Martial, and J. B. Leishman devotes only a paragraph to them in his study of the Donne canon. The only lengthy consideration of the epigrams is Frank S. Caricato, "John Donne and the Epigram Tradition," Ph.D. diss., Fordham University, 1973. All citations of Donne's epigrams are from W. Milgate's edition: *John Donne: The Satires, Epigrams and Verse Letters* (Oxford: Clarendon Press, 1967). All other quotations from Donne follow the John T. Shawcross edition.

the world beyond its borders.[3] But Donne's poems in these two forms are not parallel lines that never meet. They find their conjunction in similar challenges to the borders of genre and metaphor as modes of signification, in the testing of the polysemous character of language and genre as metaphoric frames for Donne's poetic definitions. To appreciate the wit of his more famous lyrics, we turn profitably to his formal epigrams.

Among Donne's epigrams, poems such as "A Selfe Accuser," "Klockius," and "The Antiquarie" reveal his mastery of the satirical or "Roman" mode of the genre as exemplified in the works of Martial and Catullus, just as "A Burnt Ship," "Hero and Leander," and "Pyramus and Thisbe" disclose his skill with the lapidary epigram *à la Grecque*. Both groups exhibit the dialectical skill demanded of the form—the building up of "hyperdetermination" and verbal tension so as to set up a sharp reversal or "sting" in the Roman mode, or the satisfaction of the building tension by a sententious or proverbial truism in the Greek form.[4] But perhaps the best introduction to the complex (and complicating) generic manipulation and surprise that reached its fullest achievement in Donne's lyrics is provided by his lapidary epigram "Sir John Wingfield":

Beyond th'old Pillers many'have travailed
Towards the Suns cradle, and his throne, and bed.
A fitter Piller our Earle did bestow
In that late Iland; for he well did know
Farther then Wingefield no man dares to go.

Suitable as an inscription on the valiant colonel's tomb, resonating with the verbal tension and encapsulated proverbial wisdom demanded of the genre, this poem displays Donne's expertise in the Planudean form of the sepulchral epigram, fulfilling admirably the epigram's function as an abbreviated transfer of cultural codes and values.[5] As a proverbial epigram it memorializes the intrepid hero of the 1596 Cadiz expedition who was slain near the Pillars of Hercules, those promontories that mythologically marked the boundaries of the known world (and that Emperor Charles V and

3. Norman K. Farmer, Jr., "A Theory of Genre for Seventeenth-Century Poetry," *Genre* 3 (1970), 295.

4. Such a distinction between "Greek" and "Roman" modes is not evinced by the contents of *The Greek Anthology*, of course, for it contains witty and satirical as well as sententious epigrams; and Martial as well was proficient in both modes of the epigram. However, in the Renaissance the distinction was made, based on the fact that the majority of the Greek epigrams were proverbial or sententious and the majority of those by Martial were satirical. Helpful studies of the dynamics, conventions, and interpretation of the epigram are Barbara Herrnstein Smith, *Poetic Closure: A Study of How Poems End* (Chicago: University of Chicago Press, 1968); and Rosalie L. Colie, *Shakespeare's Living Art* (Princeton: Princeton University Press, 1974) and *The Resources of Kind: Genre-Theory in the Renaissance* (Princeton: Princeton University Press, 1974).

5. Over four thousand epigrams are collected in *The Greek Anthology*, first collected by Constantinus Cephales in the tenth century and then lost. The Planudean Anthology of 1301, by Maximus Planudes, offered the only poems of the collection available for the Renaissance until Salmasius discovered the Cephales collection in the Heidelberg Palatine Library in 1607. The Palatine additions were not fully available until the nineteenth century (adding over a thousand poems to the collection known to the Renaissance). On genres as codes see Colie, *Resources of Kind*, chap. 2. I have examined the Wingfield poem more fully in "*Genera mixta* in Donne's 'Sir John Wingfield,'" *ELN* 16 (1979), 202–6.

Philip II designated as the *terminus a quo* of the supposedly endless Spanish Empire). Donne presents Wingfield as an embodiment of the Hercules emblem: his heroic labors and sacrifice provide a model and a boundary beyond which human heroism dare not on its own aspire.

This same kind of commemorative typology figures in two of Donne's epigrammatic riddles. In "Hero and Leander," just as the English colonel's monumental "travail" across the span of the known world (from "cradle" to "throne" to "bed") proves Wingfield's mythic stature, so the universality of the lovers' amatory conduct is figured forth in the Empedoclean circularity of their immersion in the four elements:

> Both rob'd of aire, we both lye in one ground,
> Both whom one fire had burnt, one water drownd.

The "just circle" of their love has transformed the fragmented, elemental flux into a *concordia*. There is a note of irony here, however, in the image of the two lovers as an emblem of the elemental unity of love. For they have achieved an elemental "perfection" only through their deaths, so the "circle" of their love is "just" only through their destruction. Rather than an image of eternality only, then, we are left with a sad completeness, for the poem suggests only a "literary" immortality. The "circle" of the lovers' actions "lies," as the pun suggests—they are victims ("rob'd") as much as conquerors; their completeness is achieved only through their final immersion in death. The situation is similar in "Pyramus and Thisbe":

> Two, by themselves, each other, love and feare
> Slaine, cruell friends, by parting have joyn'd here.

The oxymoronic exigencies of the lovers' situation—"by themselves"/"by each other," "by fear"/"by love," "friends"/"cruel," "parting"/"joyn'd"—are presented as having been overcome, or "unmetaphorized,"[6] by the essential love of this "two-in-one." In the Wingfield encomium, the "late Iland," rendered dead by the death of the colonel and the victory of the English, becomes literally the scene of a sententious proverb that recalls the enduring (and prevailing) nature of his example and provides a reminder of the eternal standards and spiritual cause that Wingfield, Essex, and the English represent.

"Sir John Wingfield," then, displays Donne's ability in the Planudean mode of the epigram. Nevertheless, to see the Wingfield poem as an example of this mode only is to miss most of its fun and complexity, for it, too, manifests the same generic mixing and witty inversions evident in the explicit assaults of "A Licentious Person" and "Antiquarie." "A Licentious Person" presents an ironic literalization of the Psalmist's admission that his sins are "more than the hairs of mine head" (Psalms 40:12) through an amusing amplification of the joke about the syphilitic's "French crown":[7]

---

6. Colie, *Shakespeare's Living Art*, discusses various forms of mythic and metaphoric play with genres in the Renaissance.

7. Pointed out by Caricato, "John Donne and the Epigram Tradition," pp. 155–56.

> Thy sinnes and haires may no man equall call,
> For, as thy sinnes increase, thy haires doe fall.

These satirical thrusts are extended by the pun on "haires"/*heires* (which is prepared for by the synecdochic "thy sinnes increase"). This pun not only intimates the extent of the satiric victim's contagion but also transforms the witty Roman epigram into a verification of both the Psalm adage and the biblical proverb about the visitation of the sins of the father on the son. "Antiquarie" also transforms biblical figure into topical insult:

> If in his Studie Hammon hath such care
> To'hang all old strange things, let his wife beware.

The victim here appears to be the same Haman derided at the conclusion of "Satyre V," who lost all "when he sold his Antiquities" (87), and who is identified there with the traitorous priest of Esther 5–7 who sold his treasures in order to pay off assassins but ended by being hanged on the gallows that his wife advised him to erect for the faithful Mordecai. By selling his "Antiquities," God's people and the wisdom of their religion (*OED* 2: 5, 6), Haman lost his life. In "Antiquarie," it is Hammon's *wife*, not his life, that is threatened. In this poem the caustic variation on the traditional image of woman as vessel (*ware*)[8] and the bitter level of topical satire combine with the fallacious ambiguity to create the sort of surprise-through-equivocation central to "A Selfe Accuser" and "A Lame Beggar" also.[9]

As H. J. C. Grierson suggests, "Antiquarie" may present an oblique attack on a specific person and, as he suggests, John Hammond, the civilist, interrogator of Campion, cohort of the notorious Topcliffe (who was infamous for the torture of Catholic recusants in his home), and reputed originator of "The Bloody Question," seems the most likely candidate. "Hammon" (or some spelling like it) appears in the Group III and Group IV manuscripts (and in others such as Hawthornden), whereas the printed texts and the Group II manuscripts have "he hath so much care." The poem, then, seems to have survived in two different versions of equal textual authority. I would speculate that "he" is the later version, written after John Hammond's son had become the physician of James I and Prince Henry, whom he attended in his last illness (an association that would suggest why Donne might have rewritten the poem, removing the satirical thrust at the civilist); or that Donne changed "Hammon" to "he" in a later version in order to replace the dated, topical reference when he was preparing the proposed edition of his poems in the last years before his ordination.[10] In support

8. For a study of this motif, see Aubrey L. Williams, "The Fall of China and *The Rape of the Lock*," *PQ* 41 (1962), 412–25.

9. Caricato provides a helpful distinction between the fallacy of equivocation and the fallacy of amphiboly, "John Donne and the Epigram Tradition," p. 175, n. 54.

10. The latter suggestion I owe to Clayton Lein, who, along with John Shawcross, has been most generous in sharing his expertise in the Donne manuscripts with me. Only Grierson suggests an allusion to John Hammond here, although several editors note that there is probably a contemporary reference here

of the topical attack on Hammond we might recall that *strange, old,* and *thing* are nearly unanimous epithets for Catholics among Establishment controversialists; in "Satyre IV," for instance, Donne ironically applies these terms to the court provocateurs in order to indict the hypocrisy of the Establishment's administration of the "huge statute lawes." And even if such a topical level is not readily obvious in the poem, "Antiquarie" retains its sting and its satirical typology in its unfolding syntactical disclosure that Hammon's "care" for his wife should make her "wary."

Returning to the Wingfield encomium, if we remember that the imperial motto that Philip of Spain inherited from his father was *plus oultra* ("Farther than") — a motto that was transcribed across the Herculean Pillars and above an ever-rising sun in Spanish heraldic emblems — then Donne's epigrammatic "pillering" of the Spanish is apparent. The emblematic sun of Philip, which was supposed never to set on the Empire, the pillars that marked not the boundary but the start of the nation's empire, and the motto that expressed their expansionist achievements are all here rendered applicable to the daring colonel who pillaged their ports — "Farther then [*plus oultra*] Wingefield no man dares to go." The Spanish having been stripped of their goods and their pride by the daring raid on Cadiz, Donne the assaulting epigrammatist now defiantly waves their own banners in their faces. Ironically entitled "On Cavallero Wingfeild" and "Il Cavalliere Gio: Wingef." in the only two manuscripts in which it survives (O'Flahertie and Westmoreland), the lapidary epigram has become not only a riddle and a joke but also a witty assault fully in the spirit of Martial's comic deflations of his Roman enemies. The encomium ends with "a sting in its tail."

In addition to the clever retort to the implicit boast of the Empire's impressa, Donne exposes at the same time the dangers of epigrammatic enclosures; by turning Philip's epigrammatic heraldic emblem against him, he shows the impossibility of (pre)determining the significations of public speech acts. Literally and generically anglicized by Donne (*plus oultra* = Farther then), the elements of the Spaniard's emblem are compressed into the final line's epitaph for Wingfield and re-create the emblem/epigram, leading into vistas of signification beyond the boundaries of Philip's "hyperdetermined" intentions. Here, as in the other epigrams (and in the radical re-formations/deconstructions of Petrarchan motifs in his lyrics), Donne shows that no metaphor can be subjected to the imperialism of any single hermeneutic. The empire of metaphor is finally heuristic; its boundaries are not pillars of interpretive restrictions but imaginative traces of human "travail." Even in his most "Greek" epigram, then, Donne's tendency is to open

---

and in "Satyre V." Only Shawcross points out the biblical reference (*The Complete Poetry of John Donne*, p. 398), on which I elaborate in *Kinde Pitty and Brave Scorn: John Donne's Satyres* (Durham, N.C.: Duke University Press, 1982), pp. 115–16, where I also examine the controversialists' epithets. Shawcross has suggested a connection also between the wife in the epigram and Haman's wife. In the biblical account Zeresh advises her husband to erect the gallows, but her advice backfires: not only is Haman destroyed, after having bribed the king to get position, but she is also exiled and her ten sons are killed during the Jewish Purim. Both husbands, then, are rich, "strange," and murderous; both wives are rich, "strange," and victims of their husbands' "hanging" proclivities.

up the genre in which he works, here by mixing modes of epigram in order both to fulfill and to surprise generic expectations.

In addition to the Wingfield poem, two, perhaps three, of Donne's epigrams focus on events surrounding the Cadiz expedition: "Cales and Guyana"; "A Burnt Ship," which most likely describes the Spaniard's deliberate destruction of their major ship, the *San Felipe*; and "Fall of a Wall," which probably recalls the death of Captain Sydenham, who, along with thirty or forty of his corps, was killed at the seige of Corunna in 1589 during the English expeditionary response to the Armada.[11] All four poems are lapidary epigrams that commemorate the fate of their subjects; but all four are also balanced by a level of irony, ranging from the explicit tragic antitheses of "A Burnt Ship" to the veiled insults of the Wingfield riddle. Each of these epigrams, while it describes the unfortunate death of its subject, embeds a wry or critical comment on the impermanence and instability of human endeavors. In "Fall of a Wall," for example, the epideictic prospect is drastically problematized:

> Under an undermin'd, and shot-bruis'd wall,
> A too-bold Captaine perish'd by the fall,
> Whose brave misfortune, happiest men envi'd,
> That had a towne for tombe, his corps to hide.

Different in tone and imagery from the unqualified praise of Wingfield, this poem wryly undercuts the subject's heroism by the application of the terms "too-bold" and "brave" to his actions, by the description of his death as "perished by the fall," and by the troubling conclusion that the collapse of the wall gave his "corpse" (or "bones") a place to "hide." These unflattering modifiers suggest that, in addition to exemplifying the fickle "misfortune" of man, the death of the captain provides a witty reminder that "pride goeth before a fall."

As intimated by the pathetic fallacy of the opening line, which anthropomorphically identifies the fate of the wall/town with that of the captain, "Fall of a Wall" exploits that most familiar of Renaissance motifs—the macrocosm-microcosm correspondence of body/town–soul/commander, which Donne uses most memorably in "The Extasie": "a great Prince in prison lies" (68). But, once again, Donne's treatment creates surprising complications. Like mortal man, the metonymic wall of the town is "undermin'd" and "bruis'd" (Gen. 3:15); and the proud captain is trapped by the mortality of the wall, just as the spirit is entombed within the body. Both suggestions are unified by the riddling oxymoron of the third line, which renders or literalizes the paradox of man's condition: capable of courage ("brave") but doomed to sin ("misfortune"), man is capable of happiness but inclined to envy. Only the "happiest" men—those capable

---

11. Donne could have attended the Corunna expedition or read about it in the account of Sir George Buc, as R. C. Bald suggests in "Three Metaphysical Epigrams," *PQ* 16 (1937), 402–5. John Shawcross points out, however, that it is more likely that Donne based his poem on the 1589 account by Hakluyt; Donne's language is closer to that version, which, in accordance with several of the manuscripts, suggests "bones" rather than "corps" in the last line ("The Source of an Epigram by John Donne," *ELN* 21 [1983], 23–24).

of a spiritual perspective—can appreciate the captain's true liberation from the "bruis'd" flesh; but, unhappily, they more often envy him for the wrong reasons, for the grandeur of his "tombe," thus extending their own entombment by the limited, the "undermin'd," the fallen.[12] Once again, then, the panegyric of the lapidary epigram is problematized (or undermined) by a surprising play of metaphor that questions the wisdom of the "brave example" the epigram ostensibly praises.

Furthermore, given Donne's love of word-play with proper names, it is possible that "Fall of a Wall" is a subtle variation on the practice of embedding the subject's name in the epigram, presenting a metaphoric cipher of the captain's name—Sydenham. This is intimated by the ironically appropriate conclusion that the "too-bolde" captain had a town for a tomb, "his corps to hide." Killed by the fall of a wall while sieging Corunna, the proud adventurer enacted the mortal riddle of his natural name, for *side* (or *syde*) is obsolete English for "proud or boastful" ("too-bolde") and *ham* is Old English for "town." The manner of his death unfolds the aptness of his name; he becomes a literalized emblem of the biblical warning that the wages of sin/pride are the town of death. Both the "happiest" and most envious of men should recall that Sydenham's death, after all, resulted from the Fall. Donne did delight in playing with proper names, as his famous puns on "more" and "donne" in his poetry and prose illustrate, and as shown by his play in the epigrams on "Wingfield" and "Hammon." In the same vein, the tenor of "Phryne" is clarified by the association of the "painted" lady of the epigram with the Greek courtesan of the fourth century B.C. and by the mocking suggestion that, unlike the beautiful courtesan—who was said to have been the model for the Aphrodite of Apelles and for that of Praxiteles, and who was acquitted of impiety when Hyperides the Orator exposed her breast to the jury—the beauty of the Elizabethan Phryne is mere "paint":

> Thy flattering picture, *Phryne*, is like thee,
> Onely in this, that you both painted be.

Both "painted ladies" commissioned "flattering" works of art to themselves (there was a gilded statue of Phryne at Delphi that Pausanius says she dedicated to herself), but the modern "picture" only confirms how unfounded is the vanity of the modern Phryne.[13]

12. The same combination of terms and criticism of the *too-bolde* victim appears in stanza 40 of "Metempsychosis," in Donne's description of the mouse's destruction of himself and the elephant whose proboscis he entered; after crawling to the brain of the mammoth, the mouse

. . . gnawed the life cords there; like the whole *town*
Clean *undermin'd*, the slain beast tumbled down,
With him the murderer dies, whom *envy* sent
To kill, not 'scape; for only he that meant
To die, did ever kill a man of better room,
And thus he made his foe, his prey, and *tomb*;
    Who dares not to turn back, may any whether come. (394–400)

13. For a study of the ancient and medieval origins of such Renaissance verbal realism, see Ernst Cur-

The typically Donnean radical reversal of the first line of "Phryne" by the sarcastic second line is exhibited in a much more daring and provocative form in "Cales and Guyana." (Being "surprised by syntax," after all, is an experience central to most of Donne's poems.) This poem also illustrates the poet's witty reductions and expansions of the epigram; and just as the parody and puns of "Sir John Wingfield" transform a proverbial form into a topical insult, so "Cales and Guyana" intimates Donne's dissatisfaction with the *vraisemblance* of the closed form, his apparent discomfort with the terminal closure that characterizes the epigram:

> If you from spoyle of th'old worlds farthest end
> To the new world your kindled valors bend,
> What brave Examples then do prove it trew
> That one things end doth still beginne a new.

Editors disagree about the identity of the addressee here. Some suggest Ralegh, others Essex, and others both leaders of the Cadiz raid. But it seems most likely that the poem is an imaginary address to Ralegh, for the wordplay and dexterous similitudes create a note of uncertainty, perhaps even a note of criticism, intended to question the wisdom of Ralegh's position (and thus to endorse that of Donne's would-be champion, Essex). Certainly "the new world" would suggest Ralegh, whose *Discoverie* (1595) had announced his own advice about the directions of further assaults against the Spanish treasures—an opinion that was extended in his *Opinion of the Alarum about the Spanish Attack* (1596), which openly asserted his disagreement with Essex about the most profitable use of English forces. If the "you" addressed here is Ralegh, then, given his avid competition with Essex, it is possible that the poem is more sarcastic than has been supposed, that it is an ironic response to Ralegh's wish that "her Majesty will undertake it [Guiana], for whatsoever prince shall possess it, that prince shall be lord of more gold, and of a more beautiful empire, of more cities and people, than either the king of Spain or the great Turk." To many readers of Ralegh's tracts, in fact, the "brave" adventurer's account was "simply a fantastic potpourri of well-known fabrications. . . . Ralegh was up to his old tricks of deceiving people, [and Elizabeth's] silence and her persistent refusal to restore him to favor may be eloquent testimony of her own lack of trust in his veracity. Even more damning was her utter disinterest in doing anything about Guiana . . . and the Queen's opinion was all that mattered."[14]

Furthermore, if Donne's attempt to attach himself to the rising star of Essex, Ralegh's rival for the approval of the Queen, and the nearly official disagreement with Ralegh's scheme are not sufficient to explain the subtle satire of the poem, there is

---

tius, "Etymology as a Category of Thought," in *European Literature and the Latin Middle Ages*, trans. Willard R. Trask (New York: Harper & Row, 1953), pp. 495–500.

14. The description of Guiana is taken from Ralegh's "Voyage for the Discovery of Guiana," in *The Works of Sir Walter Ralegh, Kt.* (Oxford: Oxford University Press, 1829), pp. 389, 397. The appraisal of public and official response to his tract is taken from Willard M. Wallace, *Sir Walter Ralegh* (Princeton: Princeton University Press, 1959), pp. 120–21, which offers also a thorough account of the Cadiz and Islands expeditions (pp. 123–55).

also the disappointment about the results of the Cadiz expedition that many blamed on Ralegh. That raid concluded as it had begun, with considerable controversy about the aims and operations of the force among its leaders, Essex, Ralegh, and Lord Howard. After the conquest and looting of Cadiz, a pillage that Essex kept from being more violent and rapacious than it was, Essex named himself governor of Cadiz and urged that the force remain and waylay the rich Spanish fleet from America. Fearing mass desertions and overreaching the limits of their charge from the Queen, Ralegh urged a swift return to Plymouth, with only a few brief excursions against northern Spanish ports. Essex finally relented, and the English fleet returned—missing the Spanish Plate Fleet laden with 20 million ducats of treasure by less than twenty-four hours as it arrived at Lisbon by the Tagus River. Donne did return to sea, of course, in the 1597 Islands expedition under the generalship of Essex and in patriotic response to Philip II's assemblage of a second Armada—in defense of "England to whom we'owe, what we be, and have," he wrote Christopher Brooke ("The Storme," 9)—and may even have served in one of the ships under Ralegh's command at the capture of Fayal. But even in his accounts of that expedition he is critical of its management and directions—"Guyanaes harvest is nip'd in the spring . . . ; slownes is our punishment and sinne; / Perchance, these Spanish businesse being done, . . . / Our discontinued hopes we shall retrive"—and reflects on the doubtful "Vertue" of that undertaking—"Is not Almightie Vertue'an India? / If men be worlds, there is in every one / Some thing to answere in some proportion / All the worlds riches" ("To Mr. R. W.," 18, 22–23, 26–30). And before accepting the apparent encomiastic tenor of "Cales and Guyana" (and the possibility that Donne was among those English adventurers whose hopes for more raids against the rich Spanish strongholds were "kindled" by Ralegh's rationale), we should recall Donne's description in "Satyre III" of those adventurers who "lay / Thee in ships woodden Sepulchers, a prey / To leaders rage, to stormes, to shot, to dearth" as "desperate coward[s]" fighting "forbidden warres . . . for gaine" (17–19, 29, 32, 26).

"Cales and Guyana" intimates some of the same "wise doubt" about the "brave Examples" of the valorous (or suicidal) Elizabethan adventures. First, there is that troublesome word "brave," with its implications of "presumptuous and foolish"; then the syntagmatic dénouement of "end" and "a new" (or "anew") does not clarify the denotations of this sign; and the oxymoronic "still beginne" aborts any singular interpretation of the "new" adventure. Ostensibly, the imperative of the epigram urges the adventurers to validate analogically (and fallaciously) Aristotle's theorem about the generation of matter: the victory at Cadiz should generate quite naturally a "new" spoiling of Guiana.[15] But the final pun suggests more than this, extending the pejorative connotation of "kindled" as "the offspring of animals" and the possibility that a "new" ad-

---

15. Caricato, "John Donne and the Epigram Tradition," p. 150. In *Of Generation and Corruption*, Aristotle says that "every generation is a corruption of another and every corruption is a generation of another . . . ; generation is the corruption of non-being, and corruption is the generation of non-being" (book 1, chap. 3, p. 319 of the 1831 Bekker edition, cited in *Aristotle Dictionary* [New York: Philosophical Library, 1962], p. 274).

venture is of the same "kind" as the "old" in the worst senses. The axiom that "one things end doth still beginne a new" intimates that the corruption ("spoyle") is all that is beginning anew: an empassioned ("kindled") "thing" is being generated by Ralegh's "new" revival of "old" promises about the treasures awaiting those "brave" enough to follow him. (Such a view of the appeal would accord with Donne's description of the Islands expedition in the verse letters as a dark hell of divine "*Fiat*" ["The Storme," 72] at which "Heaven laughs" ["The Calme," 6] because of man's misdirected motives.) The "new," as connoted by the sylleptic modification of both "old" and "new" by "spoyle," is now to be corrupted by further expeditions after treasure.

In other words, on one level of evocation, the final pun surprises as an epigram should; it is just the right word, playing on the antithetical resonances of "spoyle" and "new" in order to insinuate that the "spoyle" of the "new" world should now be initiated: the "new" proves "trew" by being the "old." But, at the same time, the ambiguous conclusion contradicts such a reading. Are not the "new" flames of English bravery only more of the same? What "kind" of "thing" is being "kindled" (or "kenneled") in the world? And, if the pejorative connotations of "kindled" and "bends" are followed, by what kind of animal passion are the young English adventurers being "imprisoned"? "Bend," after all, derives from the Old English *bindan* ("to tie or fasten") and during the Renaissance denoted a civic or religious commitment and a form of imprisonment, carrying the scriptural meaning of "to forbid" (Matt. 16:19), as well as being a nautical colloquialism for "a ship." Into what kind of "bondage" does Ralegh's "brave Example" promise, then? And, for that matter, what does his "brave Example" (at Cadiz? in his fantastic travelogue?) "prove"? We do not know—and that is the problem raised by Donne in the poem and by the poem; it does not yield that ultimate termination expected of the genre. In effect, the result is a problematic rather than a closed form, mirroring the multiple and contradictory possibilities of human determination that it unfolds. Like the aspirations of the adventurers, the direction of the epigram "bends" toward unexpected results, toward "new ends" that are "trewer" to human "example." Thus, the poem may indicate Donne's own conflicting opinions about the wisdom of the English expeditionary adventures or his attempts to side with Essex in the continuous struggle for royal favor; but at the same time it illustrates his desire to open up genres to more irony than sententiousness (or to sententious irony), to surprise and even frustrate generic expectations.

If a genre is an invitation to match form to matter, or a set of metaphoric problems to be solved,[16] then Donne in this and other epigrams seems to be exploring or testing the poetics of the epigram itself. We get the pun we expect (usually),[17] the hyperdeter-

16. Claudio Guillén, *Literature as System* (Princeton: Princeton University Press, 1971).

17. Although it is impossible to prove, the same kind of generic surprise may occur in the conclusions of many other of the epigrams, where we do not get the precise rhyme word we expect. In "Pyramus and Thisbe," for example, we are left with "here" to rhyme with "feare," when we rightfully expect *bier*. In "Ralphius" we get "bed" with "bred" instead of *dead*; and in "Niobe," "become" and "tombe" instead of the dominant word awaiting us, *womb*. More often, though, the rhymes create contradictions, providing oxymorons that encapsulate the situation of character being described: Hero and Leander form an elemental *round* by the

mined closure required of the epigram whether it is assaulting, dedicatory, sepulchral, ecphrastic, or amatory. But we also get "more than conventionally ought to fit into such a small space, expanding the one sign" (whether the pun or the form as a paradigm) into all "kinds" of relevant, interrelated, and contradictory meanings.[18] A genre is a metaphor and, as such, in Foucault's words, "no more than a play of resemblances, . . . a network of marks in which each of them may play, and does in fact play, in relation to all the others, that of secret or of indicator."[19] And what we get in Donne's epigrams is a dramatic illustration or the affective experience of the limitations (or "supplementarity") of this form — and perhaps, by implication, the innate limitations of any sign or series of signs to enclose the vagaries and interrelated possibilities of human action and expression.

In his epigrams (as in his lyrics) the movement is toward the compression of the speaker's utterance into as small a space as possible, almost to reduce the poem to a phrase or even a word. This, of course, is a given of the genre (and, if Riffaterre is correct, a central feature of all poetry). In most cases, the Donne epigram (or lyric) does just the opposite of "elaborating" on a motif or metaphor. This practice is equally evident in some of the epigrammatic lyrics, in "The Flea," for instance, where the bold sophister's entire argument is compressed into that single word conspicuous by its absence, *die*; and in the generic amphiboly of "The Apparition," where the final word "innocent" is framed by two opposed and opposing sets of generic frames (the idealistic, Petrarchist "solicitation" and the realistic, Ovidian "my love is spent"). In these senses, Donne seems always to be testing the power or potentiality of words to signify, for the compression of signs into a single phrase or word both satisfies and at the same time destroys the dialectical movement toward clarity and closure. The final turn, twist, or adage, with its expected terminal closure, only opens up the impossibility of signs to resolve the human dilemma presented or signaled in the poem: these "sullen Writ[s] . . . just so much court thee, as thou doest" them ("Metempsychosis," 511–12).

One of the major impulses of Donne's works, Dennis Quinn suggests, is reaction to the "wane of wonder." The Donne poem aims, he urges, to "re-awaken . . . us to the mysteries of life and death, goodness and evil," and it is not skepticism or curiosity that results from these poems but rather a "sense of wonder" that helps us see "the mysterious character of the natural."[20] One slight amplification of this observation is

---

rhyming of "ground" and "drown'd"; the victims of "A Burnt Ship" come their "way" to meet "decay," and those not found are "drown'd"; the heir of "Disinherited" gets "good title still" by his father's "last Will." One might conclude that Donne works variations in the epigrams on his favorite figure, the paradox, but the poems are more complex than this, for Donne not only blends various short forms in the poems but also mixes stances, strategies, and conventions of genres in order to open them up rather than to enclose them. For Donne, genres are always unfolding, not infolding—or are infolding in order to unfold.

18. This is indebted to Rosalie Colie's description of how "puns act out overtly what all words must do": *"My Ecchoing Song": Andrew Marvell's Poetry of Criticism* (Princeton: Princeton University Press, 1970), p. 152.

19. Michel Foucault, *The Order of Things* (New York: Pantheon, 1971), pp. 41, 34.

20. Dennis Quinn, "Donne and the Wane of Wonder," *ELH* 36 (1969), 626–47.

helpful, though. Donne is primarily concerned with the wondrous character of experience. But, as the epigrams exemplify, his poems explore the inability as well as the ability of words to re-create those wonders: "All language, I should passe," he writes in "The Relique," "Should I tell what a miracle shee was" (32, 33). His most popular epigram, "A Lame Beggar," suggests the same admission:

> I am unable, yonder begger cries,
> To stand, or move; if he say true, hee *lies.*

The final equivoque, *"lies,"* turns the formal properties of the utterance into a paradox, showing or at least questioning the reliability of words themselves while wittily signaling their ability to suggest the wondrous mysteries of human motivation. We often experience the same "mingled pleasures"[21] in the epigrammatical couplets (or couplet epigrams) that conclude the addresses of Donne's witty sensualists. In poems ranging in tone from the defiantly problematical "Aire and Angels" with its surprising axiomatic resolution, to the hyperbolically assertive "The Canonization" with its hectoring epigrammatical claim for another form of amorous superiority, from the string of epigrams that constitutes "Communitie," to the apparently self-defeating epigram that concludes "The Message," so also in his formal epigrams Donne's poems move toward a concluding compression of genres or words that creates an explosion of relevant and interrelated significances. If, as Augustine claims, the usefulness of all things inheres in their signifying function, then Donne's manipulation of epigrammatic strategies and conventions serves to bring into question and open up the adequacy and the creativity of human forms and signs. This is not a function unique to Donne's poems, of course, as the examples of Herbert and Marvell especially show, but what is unique about his poems is that they explore precisely this function of signs.

Before it begins to appear that I, like Donne, am avoiding closure, I wish to suggest in conclusion that the type of play with syntagmatic and paradigmatic expectations in Donne's epigrams typifies the kind of dialectical surprise and purposeful sophistry that creates the wit of his lyrics. Without closing, allow me to conclude by suggesting, in brief, that we should look closely at how Donne's manipulation of epigrammatic conventions in the lyrics creates a generic open-endedness in those poems also. Such an investigation would reaffirm, I believe, that if there is a poetics of space in Donne's lyrics, that space is not bedrooms and parlors, doorways and entrances, but the spaces between word and thing. The complicated and complicating surprises of Donne's poems, to use his own term, "lie" in that interstice or (poly)seme between sign and signification. And one of the best introductions to Donne's play with the problematics of signification is provided by the cunningly made little world of his epigrams.

---

21. Quinn cites Richard of St. Victor's *Benjamin Major*—"wonder consists of sudden light mixed with darkness, the light of vision mingled with remnants of incredulity and with the darkness of uncertainty"— and Donne's description of wonder in one of his sermons as an experience "in the midst, between knowledge and faith" (ibid., pp. 628, 627).

7. DONNE'S CHRISTIAN DIATRIBES
Persius and the Rhetorical Persona of "Satyre III" and "Satyre V"

JAMES S. BAUMLIN

Despite the popularity and critical attention "Satyre III" has enjoyed, our present understanding of its relationship to the classical models, and its use of genre, remains partial at best. Clearly the poem avoids the raging, Juvenalian style that Alvin B. Kernan places at the heart of the Elizabethan imitation of classical satire.[1] It avoids with equal vigor the jesting, self-deprecatory manner of Horace. Its rejection of these models, however, has led some of the poem's best critics to question its conformity to the classical genre. N. J. C. Andreason, for example, calls "Satyre III" "a soliloquy conducted in meditative isolation," and a number of critics, most notably M. Thomas Hester, have suggested the direct influence of meditative techniques on the poem's structure and argument. Thomas Sloan, on the other hand, argues for the public and persuasive nature of the poem, or for the poet as "rhetor."[2] And "Satyre V," if less popular than the third satire, has proved no less problematic in its use of genre and convention.[3] Donne's method, as I view it in both these poems, is one stressing persuasion over vituperation and meditative self-reflection, one in which the poet indeed speaks as homilist or rhetor; but, Donne is no less a formal satirist for being deliberative or rhetorical, and indeed Donne imitates a specific kind of rhetoric, both in "Satyre III" and in "Satyre V." Abandoning Juvenal's *saeva indignatio* and Horace's *sermo* style, Donne turns in these poems to the protreptic zeal and the diatribe style of a third and, for the Renaissance, equally important Roman model, Persius.

As with his imitation of Ovid in the elegies, Petrarch in the love lyrics, Spenser in the epithalamia—or any other of his models in style or structure—Donne's re-creation of a Persian voice avoids close verbal imitation. Donne's contempt for slavish imitators ("wit-pyrates," as he calls them in the poem "Upon Mr. Thomas Coryats Crudities") is patent, expressed most fully in "Satyre II" and in his prose "Character of a Dunce." An alternative to this slavish imitation, however, is counseled by such writers as Vives,

---

1. Alvin B. Kernan, *The Cankered Muse: Satire of the English Renaissance* (New Haven: Yale University Press, 1959), pp. 81–140.

2. Thomas Sloan, "The Persona as Rhetor: An Interpretation of Donne's *Satyre III*," *Quarterly Journal of Speech* 51 (1965), 14–27; N. J. C. Andreason, "Theme and Structure in Donne's *Satyres*," *SEL* 3 (1963), 69. Arguing for the poem's "union of private and public discourse, its concomitant meditative and satirical stance," M. Thomas Hester compares the structure of "Satyre III" to the stages of meditative devotion, as outlined in the *scala meditatoria* of Johan Gansfort and translated by Joseph Hall in his *Arte of Divine Meditation* (*Kinde Pitty and Brave Scorne: John Donne's Satyres* [Durham, N.C.: Duke University Press, 1982], p. 71).

3. John R. Lauritsen finds in "Satyre V" an "anti-satiric sentiment" ("Donne's *Satyres*: The Drama of Self-Discovery," *SEL* 16 [1976], 129), while Emory Elliott suggests, "The speaker has abandoned the role of the satirist" ("The Narrative and Allusive Unity of Donne's *Satyres*," *JEGP* 75 [1976], 115). In contrast to both these views, Hester argues that "Satyre V" "is cast simultaneously as meditation and as oration" (*Kinde Pitty*, p. 103).

Bembo, and Petrarch: while the poet should avoid another's words, he may make use of another's invention and rhetorical devices; so Petrarch suggests to Boccaccio—and so Bembo suggests, in greater detail, to Pico della Mirandola, pointing out how the imitation of models ranges through "their *sententiae* or their similes, comparisons, and other figures and colors of rhetoric" as well as through their "arrangement and logical sequence."[4] Donne, evidently, agreed. He returns to many of his Stoic model's themes, giving them a Christian significance; but his imitations of Persius rest also on these broader elements of rhetoric, on similarities in persona and relationship to audience, on similar devices of argument and rhetorical development. The elocution of "Satyre III" and "Satyre V," then, is a major focus of this essay. Before turning to these poems, though, we should consider, if briefly, the Renaissance attitude toward Persius and his satiric art: the reputation enjoyed by this Roman can explain, in large measure, why Donne chose to explore so serious an issue as Christian faith ("Satyre III") and address such powerful individuals as the Queen and Egerton ("Satyre V") in a Persian voice.

To his Renaissance critics Persius was both a serious moralist and a proto-Christian in his teachings, qualities that made him the satiric model most capable of conveying spiritual subjects to a Christian audience. Pietro Crinito, Bartolommeo della Fonte, Johann Baptista, and other critics and editors of Persius allude to this Roman's *sanctitas scribendi*[5]—as Joachim Vadian states, "This I dare say about Persius: among teachers of morals he is unsurpassed in gravity and elegance, and he, most of all, is in accord both with the truth and with our religion."[6] In contrast to Horace's moral eclecticism and Juvenal's generally unphilosophical approach to moral issues, Persius's Stoicism grants to his satires a firm and consistent ethical foundation. In the *Prolegomena* appended to his famous edition of Persius, Casaubon notes, "Unswerving in his devotion to virtue, a steadfast and constant enemy of vice, always consistent, [Persius] enriched poetry by means of graver arts. Finally, he never forgot his Stoic profession."[7] And in a general defense of this moral philosophy Juste Lipse describes Stoicism as that

---

4. "De Imitatione ad Picum," in *Giovanni Pico della Mirandola, Opera Omnia* (Hildesheim: Georg Olms, 1969), 2:201: "Quis non aut sententias, aut similitudines, comparationesque, aut alias scribendi figuras atque lumina . . . aut ordinem aliquem ac seriem . . . aut aliarum omnino rerum exemplum aliquod ab iis capiat, quos multum perlegerit." Petrarch, *Le Familiari*, ed. Vittorio Rossi (Florence: G. C. Sansoni, 1941), 4:206: "Utendum igitur ingenio alieno, utendumque coloribus, abstinendum verbis."

5. Pietro Crinito, "De Satyrographis": "a divo Hieronymo disertissimus nuncupatur: nec immerito: nam et sanctitate scribendi, et sententiarum gravitate, et verborum pondere, et satyrica urbanitate nulli postponendus esse videtur"; quoted in Joannes Murmellius, *A. Persii Flacci Satyrae sex* (Cologne, 1568), sig. H7r. See also Baptista, *Flacci Persii Poetae Satyrarum Opus* (Venice, 1495), p. 311; and Fonte, *Auli Flacci Persii Poetae Satirarum Opus* (Venice, 1482), sig. a1.

6. "Id ausim de Persio dicere: salubrium eum praeceptorum gravitate et concinnitate a nullo superari, et cum veritati tum religioni nostrae cum primis esse consonum" (*De Poetica et Carminis Ratione* [1518], ed. Peter Schäffer [Munich: Wilhelm Fink Verlag, 1973], 1:263, my translation).

7. Translated by Peter Medine, "Isaac Casaubon's *Prolegomena* to the *Satires* of Persius: An Introduction, Text, and Translation," *ELR* 6 (1976), 290. Earlier in the *Prolegomena* Casaubon claims that Horace "was too inconsistent, nor did he act as a sure teacher of virtue. . . . Often [Horace] may speak as a Stoic, often as an Epicurean or an Aristippean. . . . Just as frequently he derided and bitterly ridiculed the Stoics, in

"way of Wisdom . . . which certainly is such, as (in conjunction with the holy Scriptures) will lead us to tranquility, and peace."[8] I do not suggest that Donne speaks as a Stoic in "Satyre III"—or, for that matter, "Satyre V"—but the moral seriousness of his Stoic model does provide an appropriate vehicle for Christian subject matter. It is for this reason, above all, that Donne chose a Persian voice and manner for "Satyre III."

Persius's forceful and exhortative manner of writing on behalf of Stoic precepts has led one modern critic, Ulrich Knoche, to describe the Roman's third satire as a *protreptikòs pròs philosophian*, a "persuasion to philosophy."[9] And Donne, following Persius, takes persuasion as his goal when he exhorts his audience to seek true religion. Persius's *Satire III* offered Donne the broad thematic, stylistic, and structural model for his own poem on religious choice: if Persius's third satire is a *protreptikòs pròs philosophian*, Donne's is a *protreptikòs pròs pistín*—a persuasion to religion. Persius's *Satire III* is a lively and forceful diatribe against moral sloth—specifically against a young friend's (perhaps a student's) lack of discipline and commitment to Stoic values. The young man's lethargy and his "whining evasions," indeed his choice of a vicious life even after he has been taught the true and the good, are all particular examples of the poem's general proposition: apathy is a part of and perpetuates moral weakness. The virtue Persius urges on this young man—and on his larger reading audience—can be attained only by assiduous study and total devotion to a moral ideal; and he represents the moral struggle concomitant with this study, as the "steep path" forming part of Pythagoras's famed letter: "But you have learnt how to distinguish the crooked from the straight; you have studied the doctrines of the learned Porch . . . and the letter which spreads out into Pythagorean branches has pointed out to you the steep path which rises on the right. And are you snoring still? Yawning off the debauch of yesterday . . . ? Have you any goal in life? Is there any target at which you aim?"[10] For Isidore of Seville, as well as for St. Jerome, the Pythagorean symbol becomes a thor-

---

the possession of whom alone in that age was the teaching of wisdom." And he adds, "We know nothing of the morality of Juvenal. In his satires he touched on 'philosophical matters' in such a way that appears certain that he labored for a longer time with the rhetor than the philosopher" (p. 289).

8. Juste Lipse, *Two Books of Constancie*, trans. Sir John Stradling, ed. with intro. by Rudolph Kirk (New Brunswick, N.J.: Rutgers University Press, 1939), p. 203.

9. Ulrich Knoche, *Roman Satire*, trans. Edwin S. Ramage (Bloomington: Indiana University Press, 1975), p. 131. Giovanni Britannico, a Renaissance editor of Persius, likewise speaks of this Roman's protreptic zeal: "ex praecepto Senecae monet, consolatur, et protrepticus est" (*Flacci Persii Poetae Satyrarum Opus*, p. 317; cited in Medine, "Isaac Casaubon's *Prolegomena*," p. 274).

10. *Juvenal and Persius*, trans. G. G. Ramsay, The Loeb Classical Library (Cambridge, Mass.: Harvard University Press, 1940), *Satire III*, 52–67:

Haut tibi inexpertum curvos deprendere mores,
quaeque docet sapiens bracatis inlata Medis
porticus . . .
. . . .

et tibi, quae Samios diduxit littera ramos,
surgentam dextro monstravit limite callem;
stertis adhuc? . . .
. . . .

est aliquid quo tendis, et in quod derigis arcum?

oughly Christian conception: it is "an emblem of human life," as Isidore glosses it, "whose right path, though steep, yet tends toward a blessed life, while the left path, though easier, leads to ruin and death."[11] As Persius continues the diatribe his words no longer have just his youthful and morally slothful friend as their object but explicitly include his larger reading audience as well: "Come and learn, O miserable souls, and be instructed in the causes of things: learn what we are, and for what sort of lives we were born . . . what part God has ordered you to play, and at what point of the human commonwealth you have been stationed."[12] This call to self-knowledge, we may note, is one that appealed greatly to St. Augustine, who quotes the passage in *De Civitate Dei*, 2.6. By making so frequent use of Persius, the Church Fathers once again baptized this poet—and particularly this poem—for the Renaissance critics and imitators of his satiric art.

It is a commonplace that the stylistic techniques Persius uses in such pungent moral exhortations derive largely from the Cynic and Stoic diatribe, the polemical method of the popular moralists of Greek antiquity.[13] Persius found in the diatribe a complex rhetorical form that combined both elements of harangue and sharpness of rebuke with serious efforts at moral teaching; and among its typical stylistic and structural devices—devices Persius himself used, especially in his third satire—are paradox, hyperbole, catachresis and other forms of "violent" metaphor; *prosopopoeia* and an impassioned, second-person address; rhetorical questions and such schemes as *subjectio* and *ante occupatio*; and, above all, monologistic dialogue, with its abrupt transitions in both speaker and argument. All these elements are an essential and easily recognizable part of Persius's satiric method. These same diatribe elements inform Donne's "Satyre III."

Donne's own poem is a plea for each individual to commit himself to discovering religious truth. Like Persius's moral polemicist, Donne's satirist exhorts his audience to leave its apathy, here toward religious doctrine, and question the automatic, because convenient, adherence to *any* dogma not sanctioned by the individual conscience. Thus

---

11. *Isidori Hispalensis Episcopi Etymologiarum sive Originum Libri XX*, ed. W. M. Lindsay (Oxford: Clarendon Press, 1966), 1.3.7: "Y litteram Samius ad exemplum vitae humanae primus formavit . . . cuius dextra pars ardua est, sed ad beatam vitam tendens; sinistra facilior, sed ad labem interitumque deducens. De qua sic Persius ait [*Sat.* 3, 56]." Translation mine. Ramsay notes that the letter was originally written with a straight stem, Ꙍ, thus yielding the steep right and sloping left paths (Loeb, p. 349).

12. III, 66–72, Ramsay translation:

discite et, o miseri, causas cognoscite rerum:
quid sumus et quidnam victuri gignimur . . .
. . . .
quis modus argento, quid fas optare . . .
. . . quem te deus esse
iussit et humana qua parte locatus es in re. . . .

13. The seminal text on Persius's use of the diatribe style is François Villeneuve, *Essai sur Perse* (Paris: n.p., 1918), pp. 119–40. See also Edwin S. Ramage, *Roman Satirists and Their Satire: The Fine Art of Criticism in Ancient Rome* (Park Ridge, N.J.: Noyes Press, 1974), esp. pp. 118–19, 121–25; Michael Coffey, *Roman Satire* (London: Methuen and Co., 1976), pp. 100–103; and Charles Witke, *Latin Satire: The Structure of Persuasion* (Leiden: E. J. Brill, 1970), pp. 110–11.

a goal of the poem's first section—leaving aside, momentarily, its four-line *exordium* or introduction—is to make its audience aware of the enormity of the situation, aware of the pointlessness of all human actions when spiritual needs are neglected. To accomplish this, Donne's speaker turns to a favorite device of the Persian diatribist, a series of rhetorical questions or *percontationes*:

> Is not our Mistresse faire Religion,
> As worthy'of all our Soules devotion,
> As vertue was to the first blinded age?
> Are not heavens joyes as valiant to asswage
> Lusts, as earths honour was to them? Alas,
> As wee do them in meanes, shall they surpasse
> Us in the end, and shall thy fathers spirit
> Meete blinde Philosophers in heaven, whose merit
> Of strict life may be'imputed faith, and heare
> Thee, whom hee taught so easie wayes and neare
> To follow, damn'd? O if thou dars't, feare this;
> This feare great courage, and high valour is;
> Dar'st thou ayd mutinous Dutch, and dar'st thou lay
> Thee in ships woodden Sepulchers, a prey
> To leaders rage, to stormes, to shot, to dearth?
> Dar'st thou dive seas, and dungeons of the earth? (5–20)

As the rhetorician Thomas Wilson describes *percontatio* and its effect, "we do ask because we would chide, and set forth our grief with the more vehemency."[14] The above passage—like the lines Persius addresses to one in danger of straying from Stoic virtue—consists of just such "chiding" questions, questions that add "vehemency" to the argument. And Donne's satirist intensifies the emotiveness of the passage by shifting pronouns from *I* and *my* (1–3) to *we* and *our*—or, more often still, to *thou* and *thy*. A common feature of the diatribe style (and one that occurs throughout Persius's third satire, particularly in the passages quoted above), this second-person address endows the satirist with a public and indeed oratorical voice, a voice capable of stirring the passions and affecting the wills of his reading audience. Also of note in the passage is its allusion to the "merit / Of strict life" by which the "blinde Philosophers" could gain heaven: for it points clearly to the value Donne's speaker places on the strictness and the discipline of the moral philosophy his model espouses.

Dryden said of Persius's moral subject matter that "what he teaches might be taught from pulpits."[15] Persius's techniques are indeed those of the Stoic "preacher," and Donne, too, turns homilist when he exhorts his audience to know its "foes"—the "foule Devill," the "worlds selfe," and the "flesh" (33–42). Here the "medieval" subject matter, com-

---

14. Thomas Wilson, *The Arte of rhetorique* (1553), ed. Robert Hood Bowers (Gainesville, Fla.: Scholar's Facsimiles and Reprints, 1962), p. 184.

15. John Dryden, *A Discourse Concerning the Original and Progress of Satire* (1692), ed. W. P. Ker, in *The Essays of John Dryden*, 2 vols. (Oxford: Clarendon Press, 1926), 2:83.

bined with the satirist's manner of direct denunciation, evokes the distinctive tone of native homily and complaint—an effect culminating in the command, "Seeke true religion" (43). This tone of medieval complaint comes, however, to an abrupt end as the satirist, almost in defiance of his own exhortation, asks the question, "O where?":

> Seeke true religion. O where? Mirreus
> Thinking her unhous'd here, and fled from us,
> Seekes her at Rome, there, because hee doth know
> That shee was there a thousand yeares agoe,
> He loves her ragges so, as wee here obey
> The statecloth where the Prince sate yesterday.
> Crants to such brave Loves will not be inthrall'd,
> But loves her onely, who'at Geneva'is call'd
> Religion, plaine, simple, sullen, yong,
> Contemptuous, yet unhansome. As among
> Lecherous humors, there is one that judges
> No wenches wholsome, but course country drudges.
> Graius stayes still at home here, and because
> Some Preachers, vile ambitious bauds, and lawes
> Still new like fashions, bid him thinke that shee
> Which dwels with us, is onely perfect, hee
> Imbraceth her, whom his Godfathers will
> Tender to him, being tender, as Wards still
> Take such wives as their Guardians offer, or
> Pay valewes. . . .
> . . . .
> So doth, so is Religion; and this blind-
> nesse too much light breeds; but unmoved thou
> Of force must one, and forc'd but one allow;
> And the right. . . . (43–62, 68–71)

When Thomas Parnell, a minor Augustan poet and friend of Alexander Pope, "versified" Donne's third satire, he expanded line 43—"Seek thou religion primitively sound— / Well, gentle friend, but where may she be found?"—suggesting that the original text ushers in not only a change in tone but also a change in role for the satirist, from proponent to his own objector or *adversarius*.[16] Monologistic dialogue or this exchange between speaker and imaginary objector occurs in each of Persius's satires, and Donne,

16. *The Poetical Works of Thomas Parnell* (London: William Pickering, 1852), p. 119. "We display the inner thoughts of our adversaries as though they were talking with ourselves"; thus Quintilian describes *prosopopoeia*, one of the diatribe style's most characteristic figures (*Institutio Oratoria*, 9.2.29, trans. H. E. Butler, The Loeb Classical Library [New York: G. P. Putnam's Sons, 1933]). The Ramist rhetorician Omar Talon connects this figure with a broader rhetorical device, *subjectio*: "We discuss the objections which may be made against our case and reply to these ourselves . . . often using the form of *prosopopoeia* . . . to present the opposing argument as the direct speech of the opponent" (*Rhetorica*, 103ff.; quoted in Lee A. Sonnino, *A Handbook to Sixteenth-Century Rhetoric* [New York: Barnes and Noble, 1968], p. 174). As noted before, these and like figures are common features of monologistic dialogue.

too, uses the device throughout his criticism of the various stances toward religion.[17] This device allows Donne to introduce ways men have previously (and vainly) sought religious truth; by pointing out the failures of other men in this search, the imagined objector offers a counterpoint, as it were, to the satirist's argument. Equally important is the fact that the satirist, up to this point, has treated his spiritual subject matter with seriousness and due decorum; by mimicry of another's words, then, he can fall into a more irreverent and abusive manner of speech without undermining his own image of high seriousness. And there is something irreverent indeed in the imagery of those vignettes, as the proponents of each religion become comic suitors and the Churches the "wenches" they have courted.

The satirist interrupts the tirade of this objector, though, with the same abruptness that ushers it in; and as the satirist casts aside this more humorous and abusive strain, his rediscovered eloquence, his impassioned, second-person address, and his imagistic and extremely condensed manner of expression have an even greater emotive and, more importantly, persuasive effect:

> but unmoved thou
> Of force must one, and forc'd but one allow;
> And the right; ask thy father which is shee,
> Let him aske his; though truth and falshood bee
> Neare twins, yet truth a little elder is;
> Be busie to seeke her, beleeve mee this,
> Hee's not of none, nor worst, that seekes the best.
> To'adore, or scorne an image, or protest,
> May all be bad; doubt wisely, in strange way
> To stand inquiring right, is not to stray;
> To sleepe, or runne wrong is: on a huge hill,
> Cragged, and steep, Truth stands, and hee that will
> Reach her, about must, and about must goe;
> And what the'hills suddennes resists, winne so;
> Yet strive so, that before age, deaths twilight,
> Thy Soule rest, for none can worke in that night.
> To will, implyes delay, therefore now doe. (69–85)

The "huge hill, / Cragged, and steep" represents the mental pains and struggle of attaining truth, a struggle well expressed by the rambling circularity of the syntax itself: "and hee that will reach her, *about must*, and *about must* goe" (emphasis supplied). Here the figures of repetition imitate verbally the indirections of the ascent.[18] And the determination necessary for this search is expressed, once more almost mimetically, in the verbal repetition: "And what the'hills suddennes resists, *winne so*; / *Yet strive so*" (em-

---

17. Although Arnold Stein does not argue for Donne's use of these devices, he does point out that "rapidly shifting dialogues with undesignated speakers" form part of the tradition of satire that the Elizabethans inherited from Persius ("Donne's Obscurity and the Elizabethan Tradition," *ELH* 13 [1946], 98–118).

18. M. Thomas Hester has pointed out how syntax imitates the spiraling ascent in his "Donne's 'Hill of Truth,'" *ELN* 14 (1976), 100–105.

phasis supplied). The section as a whole is not easy to grasp on first reading, with its short, Senecan phrasing, its zeugmatic clauses, and its hyperbaton or avoidance of natural word order, all of which contribute to the brevity and concentration of thought; yet, while it evokes the Persian style in its concision, it generally avoids its model's penchant for obscurity. In this justly praised passage, then, Donne speaks not with Persius's "crabbedness" but with his concentration, seriousness, and persuasive vigor. Donne also speaks with Persius's symbolism. While Donne could have drawn on a number of sources for his Hill of Truth,[19] there are obvious parallels in theme and imagery between this allegory and Persius's own "steep path." It is arguable that Donne's "huge hill, / Cragged and steep" is a deliberate amplification of Persius's moral emblem; as a statement of general influence, one can say at the very least that Persius suggested to Donne the appropriateness of serious emblem and symbol in satire.

The abuse of temporal power in forcing religious conformity already received implicit criticism in the vignette on "Graius" and the personified Anglican Church (55–62); indeed, from line 89 to the end of the poem this abuse becomes the satirist's major concern: "Foole and wretch, wilt thou let thy Soule be tyed / To mans lawes?" (93–94). Persius states toward the end of his third satire, "It is too late to call for Hellebore when the skin is already swollen and diseased" (63–64); Donne returns to and extends this theme of urgency even to spiritual matters when, "At the last day" (95), cure is no longer possible for the soul, to say nothing of the flesh. But a Donnean poem that begins as an exhortation to examine one's conscience turns almost militant in its exhortation to scrutinize the rights and powers of temporal authority: "That thou mayest rightly'obey power, her bounds know" (100). Emblem and extended metaphor continue to play a significant role throughout this last section, but now it is the satirist's advice to his reading audience that most holds our attention: we find Donne's speaker urging not only a particular attitude on his reader but a course of action as well.

The full significance of this does not become clear until we compare "Satyre III" to other poems in the collection and recognize that the vituperation of "Satyre II" (that is, the speaker's Juvenalian invective against Coscus) and the dramatic, Horatian ironies of "Satyre I" and "Satyre IV" offer, at best, indirect methods of achieving social change—and that the satirist himself casts doubts on the moral efficacy of his first two poems. Though I initially passed over the opening of "Satyre III," it is here that the moral efficacy of formal satire—and the specific techniques of the classical models—becomes an immediate issue:

> Kinde pitty chokes my spleene; brave scorn forbids
> Those teares to issue which swell my eye-lids,
> I must not laugh, nor weepe sinnes, and be wise,
> Can railing then cure these worne maladies? (1–4)

19. W. Milgate assembles them in an appendix to his edition, *John Donne: The Satires, Epigrams and Verse Letters* (Oxford: Clarendon Press, 1967), pp. 290–92.

The satirist begins, suggestively, by denying the splenetic outbursts of hate and "just offense" that characterize the Juvenalian persona of "Satyre II": pity now "chokes" his spleen. At the same time he declares that he "must not laugh" at sins in the manner of a Horace. The satirist, in short, has discovered how difficult it is to find an appropriate response toward "sinnes": any of the reactions conventionally associated with the classical satirists would conflict with his own "kindness," his "bravery," or his "wisdom." It is not surprising, then, that his first question—"Can railing . . . cure these worne maladies?"—is left unanswered. But the reference to "cure" may surprise, for the word marks the first time in Donne's collection of satires that his speaker even alludes to the possibility of reform through this literary genre. And the possibility of curing sin gains greater significance when one recalls the cynicism that ends "Satyre I" and the sense of pessimism, in fact the admission of futility, that ends "Satyre II."

The "humorist," as the speaker suggests in the conclusion of "Satyre I," will remain constant but for "a while" (112), and thus "reformation by satire is left at the end of the poem as seemingly an impossible ideal."[20] At the end of "Satyre II," moreover, the speaker himself admits his inability to enact change: "But my words none drawes / Within the vast reach of th'huge statute lawes" (111–12). Hester notes "the ambiguous reference to 'none' in Donne's line (as a reference to himself as well as to those malefactors who go unpunished in spite of his revelation of their misdeeds)"—an ending that becomes, in fact, a "melancholic and ironic admission that his satire is ineffective (in that it does not bring about the prosecution of parasitic lawyers such as Coscus)."[21] Norman Knox observes that the term *railing*, in the usage of Donne's time, had thoroughly negative connotations.[22] So if by "railing" the satirist means a Juvenalian invective, the reader of "Satyre III" would already have reason to doubt the likelihood of serious "cure" or reform. But, as the satire progresses, the reader quickly finds that its persona utilizes a different method from the personal, bitter, and—as the speaker himself suggests—ultimately futile invective of "Satyre II": here is a persona who would reform through persuasion rather than attack. Much the same method of serious persuasion may be found in Donne's fifth satire, to which we now turn.

In "Satyre V" the poet's address to his patron, Egerton, and the stress on "Charity and liberty" are reminiscent of Persius's "Satyre V," addressed to the Roman's own great

20. Hester, *Kinde Pitty*, p. 32.

21. Hester, "The *Bona Carmina* of Donne and Horace," *Renaissance Papers, 1976*, ed. Dennis G. Donovan and A. Leigh DeNeef (Southeast Renaissance Conference, 1977), pp. 27, 28. "Satyre IV," which begins in a Horatian mode and, according to Hester, modulates into a more fiery, Juvenalian stance, likewise ironically disparages its ability to effect change. "Satyre V," on the other hand, attempts to effect social change through its direct address to a specific audience (Egerton); not surprisingly, Persius is the major stylistic influence on this protreptic and stylistically complex poem.

22. Norman Knox finds that the word had two possible meanings in the Renaissance, the first referring "simply to the act of verbal attack or criticism, without limits as to the method employed," and the second referring "specifically to angry invective." For both meanings, "the connotation of the word was highly unfavorable. . . . People who liked the witty invective of, say, a particular satirist usually preferred not to call it railing; people who did not used the word as a device of adverse criticism" (*The Word Irony and Its Context, 1500–1755* [Durham, N.C.: Duke University Press, 1961], pp. 190–91).

mentor, Cornutus, and devoted to the Stoic subject of *vera libertas*. These similarities, however, suggestive as they are, do not compel us to see Donne's fifth satire as an imitation of Persius's. Donne continues his use of a Persian manner and style through "Satyre V," but if the poem has a specific model, it is probably Donne's own "Satyre III." Beginning even with its *exordium*, "Satyre V" elaborates on this earlier, Christianized version of Persius, returning to its most distinctive qualities of persona, style, and satiric method; for the third satire's opening disavowal of spleen and laughter has inspired a similar, if more concise denial: "Thou shalt not laugh in this leafe, Muse, nor they / Whom any pitty warmes" (V, 1–2). As the persona of "Satyre V" develops his argument, the serious, homiletic tone again undermines the techniques of the Juvenalian and Horatian satirists; indignation and particularly laughter have been supplanted by other attitudes:

> . . . He which did lay
> Rules to make Courtiers, (hee being understood
> May make good Courtiers, but who Courtiers good?)
> Frees from the sting of jests all who'in extreme
> Are wreched or wicked: of these two a theame
> Charity and liberty give me. What is hee
> Who Officers rage, and Suiters misery
> Can write, and jest? . . . (2–9)

The "pitty" that warms this satirist may not be an attribute readers would readily associate with Persian satire, although it is a typically Stoic attitude toward the "insanity" of human sinfulness and error: the Stoic Epictetus, for example, devoted a diatribe to the theme that criminals should be pitied rather than hated (*Discourses*, 1.18). Donne's expressions of pity, nonetheless, amount to a Christian reorientation both of his Stoic model and of classical satire in general.

To so humane an emotion as pity the satirist adds the virtues "Charity" and "liberty," dual virtues that determine the satirist's attitude toward his dual subject, "Officers rage, and Suiters misery." The liberty is no doubt a fusion of Christian liberty and the *satirica libertas* claimed by poets in this genre, a freedom to discover and reprehend vice. What may surprise is that charity, the preeminently Christian virtue, here becomes an equally important quality of the satirist as well as a motivating force throughout the poem. Certainly the satirist's view of the interrelatedness of all men—that "all things be in all" (9)—is an attitude that derives from his charity and general concern for the whole of mankind. And perhaps a more militant expression of this *caritas* lies in the satirist's admonition to the "wrech'd" suiters, one that turns, finally, to an address of the Queen and the Lord Egerton:

> All men are dust;
> How much worse are Suiters, who to mens lust
> Are made preyes. O worse then dust, or wormes meat,
> For they do eate you now, whose selves wormes shall eate.

They are the mills which grinde you, yet you are
The winde which drives them; and a wastefull warre
Is fought against you, and you fight it; they
Adulterate lawe, and you prepare their way
Like wittals; th'issue your owne ruine is.
Greatest and fairest Empresse, know you this?
Alas, no more then Thames calme head doth know
Whose meades her armes drowne, or whose corn o'rflow:
You Sir, whose righteousnes she loves, whom I
By having leave to serve, am most richly
For service paid, authoriz'd, now beginne
To know and weed out this enormous sinne. (19–34)

Phrases like "All men are dust" introduce tones of homily and complaint into the satire, medieval elements that Milgate, for one, considers a blemish in the poem.[23] Yet these expressions of corruption (in the passage above, both literal and figurative) and homiletic tones blend naturally with the broader diatribe elements of the satire.

An impassioned, second-person address again forms part of Donne's rhetorical strategy; and if the repetition of "you" in the passage above (most obvious in lines 23–25) does not have the same power or emotive force as in "Satyre III" (in lines 17–28, for example: "Dar'st thou ayd mutinous Dutch, and dar'st thou lay / Thee in ships woodden Sepulchers"), still it shares the same purpose of engaging the poem's reading audience personally and of persuading them to initiate legal reform. In this regard the satirist's direct address to his monarch and to his political patron is also of great significance. I have suggested that Donne's Horatian and Juvenalian poems call into question their own methods of criticism and their potentials for causing change; here, by addressing Egerton particularly, the satirist discovers a means by which his words can truly influence his world. In his brief address to the Queen the satirist frees her of blame, since she, like the calm Thames, is ignorant of the actions of her tributary subjects. Egerton, on the other hand, "whose righteousnes she loves," and who is "authoriz'd" to act in the Queen's stead, can now "beginne / To know and weed out this enormous sinne" (31–34). These lines may be read as a statement of fact, that Egerton has begun the process of social and legal change; but within the argument of the poem one may easily read them as an imperative statement, an exhortation to Egerton that he undertake such action. In either case, here, more than anywhere else in the *Satyres*, poet and persona coalesce: in its address to Donne's patron, the Persian mask has now blended thoroughly and inseparably with Donne's own "public" voice.

"Satyre V" returns to many of the rhetorical techniques Donne utilized in "Satyre III," one of which is the use of elaborate image and symbol in the creation of argument; the Hill of Truth is an example already discussed, to which we may add the

---

23. See Milgate's Commentary to the *Satires*, p. 165.

symbolic presentation that "Satyre III" makes of the relationship between the individual and temporal power:

As streames are, Power is; those blest flowers that dwell
At the rough streames calme head, thrive and prove well,
But having left their roots, and themselves given
To the streames tyrannous rage, alas, are driven
Through mills, and rockes, and woods, and at last, almost
Consum'd in going, in the sea are lost:
So perish Soules. . . .

It is suggestive that "Satyre V," which also deals with the abuse of power, makes use of much the same imagery;

. . . Powre of the Courts below
Flow from the first maine head, and these can throw
Thee, if they suck thee in, to misery,
To fetters, halters; But if the'injury
Steele thee to dare complaine, Alas, thou goest
Against the stream, when upwards: when thou'art most
Heavy'and most faint; and in these labours they,
'Gainst whom thou should'st complaine, will in the way
Become great seas, o'r which, when thou shalt bee
Forc'd to make golden bridges, thou shalt see
That all thy gold was drown'd in them before;
All things follow their like. . . . (45–56)

We may remember Dryden's famous phrase that Donne "affects the metaphysics" in his satires. Here Donne expands and makes more abstract the analogy of "Satyre III," turning the relationship between suitors and officers into an elaborate conceit readers would not hesitate to call "metaphysical"; and the tendency toward abstraction and conceitedness operates throughout the poem. J. B. Leishman comments on "Satyre V" that "the particular abuse Donne professes to be satirizing is merely a topic for the display of his wit."[24] While this statement wrongly implies a lack of sincerity or commitment on the part of the satirist, it correctly notes the presence of a peculiarly Donnean wit in the poem, with its analogies between macro- and microcosm, between bodies of water, bodies politic, and human bodies—as in the following passage:

If all things be in all,
As I thinke, since all, which were, are, and shall
Bee, be made of the same elements;
Each thing, each thing implyes or represents.
Then man is a world; in which, Officers

24. J. B. Leishman, *The Monarch of Wit: An Analytical and Comparative Study of the Poetry of John Donne* (London: Hutchinson, 1951), p. 117.

Are the vast ravishing seas; and Suiters,
Springs; now full, now shallow, now drye; which, to
That which drownes them, run .... (9–16)

Hyperbaton and figures of repetition once again make for a tightly woven and complex argument; but here more important than the syntax is the abstruse and
"metaphysical" nature of the argument. We would search in vain for the same extended,
metaphysical analogies in Persius, for the analogies and conceits, like the Christian
concerns, are Donne's personal additions to the Persian mode: they are his transformation of a classical voice into a personal and contemporary style.

Having said this, we should remind ourselves that so sensitive a critic as George
Williamson traced Donne's penchant for "strong lines," and the development of his
mature, "metaphysical" style, to his early apprenticeship under Persius.[25] Persius evidently taught Donne much about concise expression and complexity of syntax, rigorous argumentation, abrupt transitions in thought, hyperbolic and catechretical imagery,
the drama and forcefulness of second-person address—much, in short, that readers have
associated with Donne's poetry in general. If in "Satyre III" or "Satyre V" we find poetry so obviously Donnean in thought and expression it is, as I have said, because
he has transformed his model into a truly English and personal voice. In so doing
Donne avoids the fault of those who "imitate servilely, as *Horace* saith, and catch at
vices, for vertue."[26] Rather, he adopts whatever there is of value in a style like Persius's,
at the same time altering or rejecting such idiosyncratic elements in Persius's style as
his "crabbedness" or obscurity. And what Donne does adopt from this model is, once
again, the protreptic zeal, the homiletic tone, and the emphasis on reform through
persuasion rather than through laughter or personal attack.

This distinction, we have seen, allows for a more Christian form of satire, the kind
that the Renaissance reformer of poetry, Lorenzo Gambara, suggests should be "without bitterness" and written "with the greatest sincerity, but without violating charity."[27]
And as recent articles on Donne have shown, charity is a key concept in the satires.[28]
Yet Donne's serious persuasions here have another, equally important effect. Ridicule
and invective targeted at specific individuals allow for a considerable distance between
the larger audience and the satiric criticism. Despite the argument that characteriza-

25. George Williamson, *The Donne Tradition: A Study in English Poetry from Donne to the Death of Cowley*
(Cambridge, Mass.: Harvard University Press, 1930), p. 43.

26. *Timber*, in *Ben Jonson*, ed. C. H. Herford and Percy and Evelyn Simpson, 11 vols. (Oxford: Clarendon Press, 1925–1952), 8:638.

27. "Satyrae sine amarulentia, dum in haeresim, vitiaque Poete sincerissimi salva charitate invehuntur"
(*Tractatio de perfectae poeseos ratione* [1576], trans. Bernard Weinberg, in *A History of Literary Criticism in the
Italian Renaissance* [London: University of Chicago Press, 1961], 1:308).

28. Emory Elliott claims, "The five poems present a probing examination of the ideal of Christian charity as a fundamental principle for a life of social action and reform" ("Narrative and Allusive Unity," p.
105). See also Clarence Miller and Caryl Berrey, "The Structure of Integrity: The Cardinal Virtues in Donne's
Saytre III," *Costerus* 1 (1974), 27–46; and A. F. Bellette, "The Originality of Donne's *Satires*," *UTQ* 44 (1975),
130–40.

tion and description in satire offer mirrors in which the reader sees reflections of his own vices (as Horace tells his reader, "Quid rides? Mutato nomine de te fabula narratur"; 1.1.69–70), it is the "humorist" that Donne's reader laughs at in "Satyre I," Coscus that he scorns in "Satyre II"—and not himself. But in Donne's imitations of Persius the speaker's direct address to his reading audience (of which Egerton, in "Satyre V," is a conspicuous member) makes this audience aware that the satirist's concerns are its own; and as he speaks to this audience directly he tries to influence it directly. In Persius, then, Donne discovered the broad outline of a deliberative and essentially public voice whose moral exhortations, much more than laughter or rage, could best result in reform.

8. TRADITION AND THE INDIVIDUALISTIC TALENT
Donne's "An Epithalamion,
Or mariage Song on the Lady Elizabeth . . ."

HEATHER DUBROW

> if I doe borrow any thing of Antiquitie,
> besides that I make account that I pay it to
> posterity, with as much and as good
> (Donne, "Metempsychosis")

Conscious of Donne's contempt for "the lazie seeds / Of servile imitation" (Carew, "An Elegie upon . . . D[r]. John Donne," 26–27),[1] readers long assumed that he disdained and discarded most of the generic traditions he had inherited. While a number of recent scholars have begun to challenge this view and to trace Donne's debts to his literary heritage,[2] we have yet to explore the relationship of his epithalamia to their genre. Because that literary type, like the very event it celebrates, is so influenced by convention, it offers a singularly good test case for the ways Donne approaches generic forms and norms. Especially illuminating is the wedding poem that he composed in 1613 to commemorate the marriage of Princess Elizabeth and the Elector Palatine: Donne's imaginative responses to the traditions of his genre are central to the success of this lyric.

Exemplified by such poems as Catullus LXI and codified by such rhetoricians as Scaliger, the norms of the epithalamium were well established by 1613.[3] In what is sometimes known as its "lyric" (as opposed to "epic") form, the genre typically celebrates a wedding by rehearsing its events in chronological order. An invocation to the gods, especially Hymen, generally opens the poem. The speaker then urges the bride to arise because the sun is already up, refers to the other wedding guests, details the religious ceremony and the ensuing communal festivities, notes the bride's bashfulness at the prospect of the wedding night, and offers a prayer for children. Certain wedding poems, such as the one in the Third Eclogues of Sidney's *Arcadia*, are set in the pastoral world, while others rely extensively on pastoral imagery. Also typical of the genre is its epideictic function, and the rhetoricians carefully enumerate instructions for praising the couple.

---

1. All citations from Carew are to *The Poems of Thomas Carew*, ed. Rhodes Dunlap (Oxford: Clarendon Press, 1949).

2. See, for example, Clayton D. Lein, "Donne's 'The Storme': The Poem and the Tradition," *ELR* 4 (1974), 137–63; and Barbara Kiefer Lewalski, *Donne's "Anniversaries" and the Poetry of Praise: The Creation of a Symbolic Mode* (Princeton: Princeton University Press, 1973), esp. chap. 1.

3. For summaries of those norms and the rhetoricians' commentaries on the genre, see especially Thomas M. Greene, "Spenser and the Epithalamic Convention," *Comparative Literature* 9 (1957), 215–28; Virginia Tufte, *The Poetry of Marriage: The Epithalamium in Europe and Its Development in England*, University of Southern California Studies in Comparative Literature, 2 (Los Angeles: Tinnon-Brown, 1970).

Behind these overt conventions, however, lie certain other characteristics of the epithalamium, characteristics that are often neglected by modern students of this literary type but seldom by Renaissance practitioners of it. First of all, poems in the genre are generally very concerned with time, a fact that may help to explain why the form appealed so much to Spenser and other Renaissance writers. Offering an image of "eterne in mutabilitie," lyric epithalamia characteristically play against each other two viewpoints on time, the linear and the cyclical. A linear perspective is provided by the chronological account of events. In some poems this perspective involves a disorderly, even chaotic, sequence of happenings—the bride sleeps too late, night does not come as quickly as the couple would hope, and so on. Counterpointed against this vision, however, is another one: the production of heirs can represent a cyclical notion of time and an implicit solution to mutability. The refrains that figure so prominently in many epithalamia mirror on the prosodic level the dual vision I am describing, for the way they shift from stanza to stanza parallels the linear movement of time, while the repetitiveness inherent in the very notion of a refrain echoes time's cyclical movement.[4]

An equally significant concern in epithalamia—and often an equally subterranean one—is the relationship between the demands of society and various natural forces, whether represented by the physical world itself or by the couple's own sexuality. The mere presence of this idea is hardly surprising: after all, weddings themselves mediate between social norms and sexual urges. What is striking is how frequently poets in the genre draw attention to the relationship between the social and the natural worlds and how characteristically each of them approaches that relationship. Thus, for example, Spenser's "Epithalamion" embodies a predictably ambivalent view of nature: if it joins in the wedding celebrations, it also threatens the couple with literal and metaphorical "tempestuous storms" (327).[5] But the threats of the physical world can be controlled ("Let not the shriech Oule, nor the Storke be heard," 345), much as the potentially anarchic demands of the speaker's own sexuality can be temporarily restrained. And that friend of established social and literary forms, Ben Jonson, declares that the wedding night will enable the couple to "know / All their Fathers, and their Mothers might / Of Nuptiall Sweets" ("Epithalamion . . . of . . . M^r. Hierome Weston," 146–48).[6] In other words, their passion in fact aligns them with their parents and thus with the social order as a whole, rather than distancing them from the com-

4. Spenser's "Epithalamion" renders this pattern, like so many other generic conventions, more complex: by associating each stanza with an hour of the day, he reminds us that the linear progress of time during the wedding day is also part of a diurnal cycle. For a different but not incompatible interpretation of time in the "Epithalamion," see, for example, Richard Neuse, "The Triumph Over Hasty Accidents: A Note on the Symbolic Mode of the 'Epithalamion,'" *UTQ* 61 (1966), esp. p. 168.

5. All citations from Spenser are to *The Minor Poems; Vol. 2*, in *The Works of Edmund Spenser: A Variorum Edition*, ed. Charles Grosvenor Osgood and Henry Gibbons Lotspeich (Baltimore: Johns Hopkins University Press, 1947).

6. The citation from Jonson is to *The Poems; The Prose Works*, vol. 8 of *Ben Jonson*, ed. C. H. Herford and Percy and Evelyn Simpson, 11 vols. (Oxford: Clarendon Press, 1947).

munity as it at least temporarily would in many other comedic genres. As we will see, Donne treats the interplay between sexuality and society, like so many other norms of the epithalamium, very differently from the ways Spenser and Jonson do.

Donne's opening lines—"Haile Bishop Valentine, whose day this is, / All the Aire is thy Diocis"—at once acknowledge a debt to the generic conventions I have been enumerating and announce an intention of reshaping them. Rather than omitting the opening invocation, as he had previously done in his "Epithalamion made at Lincolnes Inne," Donne is prominently incorporating it into his poem. But, not unlike the more conventional Christian humanists among his contemporaries, he is replacing pagan deities with a figure from the Christian calendar. He is also lowering the tone the invocation normally assumes in both pagan and Christian wedding songs; for example, the stanza ends on a note of good-humored raillery, "This day, which might enflame thy self, Old Valentine" (14). In this concluding line we encounter a parallel to one of the satiric patterns that recurs so often in the love lyrics, the mockery of a potentially imposing or threatening figure. Donne is, as it were, having his wedding cake and eating it: he is retaining the invocation that is so characteristic of his genre while typically avoiding the respectful subservience that invocation normally enjoins on the speaker.

The rest of the opening stanza incorporates the descriptions of nature that are so common in the genre:

> Thou marryest every yeare
> The Lirique Larke, and the grave whispering Dove,
> The Sparrow that neglects his life for love,
> The household Bird, with the red stomacher,
>   Thou mak'st the black bird speed as soone,
> As doth the Goldfinch, or the Halcyon;
> The husband cocke lookes out, and straight is sped,
> And meets his wife, which brings her feather-bed. (5–12)

This passage performs several functions. First of all, in referring to the folk custom that birds marry on St. Valentine's Day, Donne evokes a parliament of fowls.[7] Hence the conceit that he introduces in the next stanza, the marriage of the two phoenixes, is, like so many of the memorable images in this poem, a clever allusion to and extension of an established literary tradition. It is also suggestive that Donne domesticates the birds he describes (quite literally so in his references to "the household Bird" [8] and the "feather-bed" [12]) and thus links these anthropomorphized creatures to a human milieu. Behind these playful lines, then, we may perhaps see a hint of the way he approaches the natural world in "The Sunne Rising" and, indeed, in the final stanza

---

7. See *The Poems of John Donne*, ed. Herbert J. C. Grierson, 2 vols. (Oxford: Clarendon Press, 1912), 2: 92; *John Donne: The Epithalamions, Anniversaries and Epicedes*, ed. W. Milgate (Oxford: Clarendon Press, 1978), p. 114.

of the Palatine epithalamium: a source of neither awe nor fear, nature can be adapted to man's domain, tamed to man's needs. But Donne never loses touch with the physical realities behind his image: the birds are delightedly and delightfully realized. Since pastoral was evidently not one of his favorite modes, it is telling that he reacts to the generic convention of referring to the countryside by producing this carefully observed description. Here, as so often in this wedding poem, Donne meets the challenge of responding to a potentially uncongenial norm neither by skirting it nor by mocking it, but rather by skillfully working within it.

In his second stanza he confronts a generic convention that is far more hazardous than the practice of alluding to nature: the praise of the bride and groom. Even a glance at the other poems composed for the same wedding reminds us of how readily the relevant topoi degenerate into overt and cloying flattery. Wither, for example, addresses the bride as "O most true majestik creature" ("Epithalamion")[8] and continues at length in that vein. It is primarily by comparing the couple to the phoenix that Donne avoids the sycophancy into which Wither's poem and so many other works on this wedding descend. When first introducing the figure, he simultaneously elevates the bride and bridegroom to a mystical and mythical status and links them to the world of nature, to the more homely birds described in stanza 1 and briefly evoked here:

Till now, Thou warmd'st with multiplying loves
    Two larkes, two sparrowes, or two Doves,
      All that is nothing unto this,
For thou this day couplest two Phœnixes. (15–18)[9]

A higher compliment is also implicit in the image: the phoenix is often associated with Christ, a link later foregrounded by the line, "Bee thou a new starre" (39). But even when highlighted by that subsequent allusion, the reference to Christ is so subterranean and so playful that the most sober of Donne's readers would hesitate to accuse him of blasphemy.

Above all, however, the phoenix image fulfills the epideictic functions of its genre by effecting a comparison between Princess Elizabeth and Queen Elizabeth, who was often associated with that mythical bird.[10] As Heywood's treatment of the same compliment indicates, an overt comparison between the two Elizabeths runs the risk of sounding coy or sycophantic:

To none I better may compare
Your sweet selfe then one so rare:

---

8. Wither, *Epithalamia* (London: for E. Marchant, 1612), sig. C1ᵛ. All citations from Wither are to this edition.

9. Wesley Milgate comments perceptively on the ways Donne moves between the natural and supernatural in this poem (*Epithalamions*, pp. xxiii–xxiv).

10. On the association between Elizabeth and the phoenix, see Frances A. Yates, *Astraea: The Imperial Theme in the Sixteenth Century* (London and Boston: Routledge and Kegan Paul, 1975), pp. 58–59, 65–66, 78, 83.

>   Like grac't you are from above,
>   You succeed her in her love.
>   As you enjoy her name:
>   Likewise possesse her fame.
>   For that alone lives after death;
>   So shall the name *Elizabeth*. ("A Marriage Triumphe")[11]

By relying on his reference to the phoenix to link the two Elizabeths, Donne is able to bestow praise more tacitly—and hence more tactfully.

Also present in the second stanza is Donne's sole allusion to what is so central a theme in most epithalamia, the production of heirs: "Where motion kindles such fires, as shall give / Yong Phœnixes, and yet the old shall live" (25–26). Other poets in the genre typically place their references to the couple's children in the climactic final stanzas of the poem. Thus in his poem about the Palatine wedding Henry Peacham concludes: "And let me live to see betweene you twaine, / A *Caesar* borne as great as *Charlemaine*."[12] Donne's decision to assign a less prominent position to the allusion implies that he is comparatively uninterested in the idea. Moreover, it is suggestive that his poem literally separates the prayer for children from his lengthy description in stanzas 7 and 8 of the couple's sexual union. The very structure of the epithalamium mirrors its author's attitude to sexuality: sex is separable from procreation, not a mere means to an end but an end in itself. In short, Donne is not wholly discounting this social aspect of the marriage—he does refer to children, however briefly—but he is subordinating it to what he considers more important, the sexual bond between the couple.

His decision to play down the dynastic ramifications of the wedding also figures in a broader pattern. Throughout the entire poem, Donne virtually ignores the political significance of the event; indeed, his sole acknowledgment that this is a royal marriage is his brief reference to Elizabeth as a "Great Princess" (38). The political issues that Donne chooses to neglect were important ones. Though she had been courted by several Catholics, including King Philip of Spain, Elizabeth was marrying a Protestant. Moreover, that marriage strengthened James I's position with the Protestant German princes (an alliance he had cause to regret in 1619–1620 when, participating in an ill-fated rebellion, the Count Palatine assumed the title of King of Bohemia).[13] Predictably enough, most of the poets who celebrated the wedding emphasize its political ramifications:

11. The citation from Heywood is to *A Marriage Triumphe* (London: for E. Marchant, 1613), sig. E1ᵛ.

12. The citation from Peacham is to *The Period of Mourning . . .Together With Nuptiall Hymnes* (London: for J. Helme, 1613), sig. G3.

13. On Elizabeth's previous suitors, see G. P. V. Akrigg, *Jacobean Pageant, or, The Court of King James I* (Cambridge, Mass.: Harvard University Press, 1962), p. 142; David Harris Willson, *King James VI and I*, The Bedford Historical Series (1956; rpt. London: Jonathan Cape, 1959), pp. 282–83. On the political ramifications of the marriage, see especially Akrigg, *Jacobean Pageant*, chap. 27; Willson, *King James VI and I*, pp. 286–87, 408–31.

Happy they, and we that see it,
For the good of *Europe* be it.
And heare Heaven my devotion,
Make this *Rhyne* and *Thame* an *Ocean*:
That it may with might and wonder,
Whelme the pride of **Tyber* under. (Wither, "Epithalamion," sig. C2ᵛ)

By disregarding the issues that Wither raises, Donne again implies that what is most important about the wedding is the personal relationship between his two phoenixes.[14] Here, as so often in the annals of literary history, what a writer chooses not to do is quite as revealing as what he does.

The third stanza opens,

Up then faire Phœnix Bride, frustrate the Sunne,
    Thy selfe from thine affection
    Takest warmth enough, and from thine eye
All lesser birds will take their Jollitie. (29–32)

The phrase "frustrate the Sunne" (29) signals yet another transformation of a generic norm. The author of "The Sunne Rising" again disarms a potentially powerful figure: characteristically, he avoids the respect for "the worlds light giuing lampe" ("Epithalamion," 19) expressed by Spenser and many of his followers in the genre. Reshaping the generic convention that the bride must get up because the sun has done so, Donne substitutes a combative bride who will rival and even surpass that celestial body. But the very lines that establish this deviation from one tradition also evince Donne's debt to another one. The word "Jollitie" (32) appears nowhere in Donne's works save this passage and a similar one in the "Epithalamion made at Lincolnes Inne"; in both instances he is surely echoing—and perhaps even alluding to—a line from Spenser's "Epithalamion," "With joyance bring her and with jollity" (245).[15]

Later in the stanza Donne's speaker addresses the bride by means of a series of imperatives:

    Up, up, faire Bride, and call,
Thy starres, from out their severall boxes, take
Thy Rubies, Pearles, and Diamonds forth, and make
Thy selfe a constellation, of them All,
    And by their blazing, signifie,

14. In addition, one effect of ignoring the political significance of the wedding is to direct attention away from the bridegroom. It is conceivable that Donne did so in part because he had reservations about the match; we do know that Robert Drury, with whom Donne was closely associated at the time he composed the poem, publicly expressed his disapproval of the Elector Palatine (see R. C. Bald, *Donne and the Drurys* [Cambridge: Cambridge University Press, 1959], pp. 102–3, 122). Given the lack of firm evidence, however, this hypothesis must remain speculative.

15. See Homer Carroll Combs and Zay Rusk Sullens, *A Concordance to the English Poems of John Donne* (Chicago: Packard and Co., 1940), s.v. "jollity."

> That a Great Princess falls, but doth not die;
> Bee thou a new starre, that to us portends
> Ends of much wonder; And be Thou those ends. (33–40)

Throughout these lines, the monarch of wit employs the imperative mood to estab-lish the nature of his relationship to the royal princess.[16] That mood can express a plea, and on one level the speaker is indeed entreating the bride to awake, to dress, and so on. But it can also express a command, and on another and more prominent level the speaker is giving orders to the internal audience of the poem, instructing her quite as confidently as, say, his counterpart in "Valediction of the booke" instructs his mistress. Hence Donne's imperatives define the speaker at once as a respectful sub-ject who must entreat the bride and as a knowledgeable guide who can and will com-mand her.

"Bee thou a new starre" (39) relies on these and other equivocations. On a first reading, the line may seem to be a resonant and unqualified compliment. But Donne is in fact delimiting the force of that compliment in several ways and in so doing en-suring that it stops far short of sycophancy. First of all, the line highlights the power of the poet who writes it almost as much as the power of the princess who figures in it. As we have seen, in a sense he is commanding her to become a star. And the reader is aware that he is transforming her into one through the very metaphor he creates (poetic transformations mirror the many other metamorphoses in this poem). Also, the phrase carries with it a suggestion that in "being" a star the bride is merely assuming a role, playing a game. Stylistic analyses of Donne's work often dwell ex-clusively on certain aspects of his grammar, such as his knotty syntax or his logical connectives. The artful imperatives he uses throughout this stanza, like the surprisingly straightforward language in some of the verse epistles to male friends, remind us that Donne could "our stubborne language [bend]" (Carew, "An Elegie . . . upon D^r. John Donne," 50) to achieve a whole range of different effects as well.

The allusion in stanza 4 to the marriage ceremony further illuminates Donne's at-titudes to both literary and social conventions: "Goe then to where the Bishop staies, / To make you one, his way, which divers waies / Must be effected" (51–53). These lines downplay the religious ceremony in two ways. First of all, virtually the only reference to that ritual or the church in which it occurs is this brief and vague passage (Spenser's "Epithalamion," in contrast, devotes two detailed stanzas to the ceremony). And the fact that Donne writes "Goe" (51) rather than "Come" is also telling. Con-sistently employing proximal deictics such as "here" and "this," elsewhere in the poem he stresses his speaker's proximity to the events of the wedding: "*Come* forth, *come* forth" (43), "*here* he staies" (57), "Staies he new light from *these* to get?" (59), "*Here* lyes a shee Sunne, and a hee Moone *here*" (85), and so on (emphasis supplied). Hence the word "Goe" (51) represents a significant deviation. It suggests that the speaker is

16. For a summary of these varying usages of the imperative, see Otto Jespersen, *A Modern English Grammar on Historical Principles* (Copenhagen: Ejnar Munksgaard, 1940), 5:467–70.

physically—and, by implication, emotionally—more distant from the rite in the church than from the other events he evokes.

One way of understanding why Donne establishes that distance is to compare passages from other epithalamia:

> Open the temple gates unto my love,
> Open them wide that she may enter in,
> And all the postes adorne as doth behove,
> And all the pillours deck with girlands trim,
> For to recyve this Saynt with honour dew, (Spenser, "Epithalamion," 204–8)

> Weelcome! but yet no entrance, till we blesse
> First you, then you, and both for white successe.
> Profane no Porch young man and maid, for fear
> Ye wrong the *Threshold-god*, that keeps peace here:
> (Herrick, "The Entertainment: or, Porch-verse, at the Marriage
> of Mr. Hen. Northly, and . . . Mrs. Lettice Yard," 1–4)[17]

As these lines suggest, buildings, whether churches or houses, feature prominently in a number of wedding poems. One reason is that the figurative threshold that the couple is crossing can be aptly symbolized as a physical threshold. Another reason, though, is that the buildings function as synecdochic versions of the society into which that couple is being welcomed, the social constructs they are accepting and gracing: in entering its buildings they are in effect reentering the whole society, assuming in it a more stable and more central role than they had enjoyed before their marriage. By playing down the church building, then, Donne once again plays down the community itself, the social codes that it embodies and transmits.

But the brevity of his allusion to the wedding ceremony evidently reflects his responses not only to the social aspects of the marriage but also to the specifically religious ones. The future Dean of St. Paul's does not, of course, ignore the religious ramifications of the event completely; after all, his refrain focuses not on echoing woods or a softly running river but rather on Bishop Valentine. On the other hand, as we have seen, that luminary is greeted with less respect than he might have earned from another poet, much as the religious ceremony he performs seems to be mentioned almost in passing. For Donne wishes instead to emphasize the "divers waies" (52) the couple will be joined—especially their emotional and sexual union. If the marriage bed is indeed a marriage temple, as the speaker in "The Flea" so solipsistically but so engagingly asserts, then what happens in the actual temple inevitably loses some of its significance.

Catullus and many of his followers express some impatience with the social rites and customs that precede the wedding night. But no one dismisses these events more thoroughly or more wryly than Donne:

17. The citation from Herrick is to *The Poetical Works of Robert Herrick*, ed. L. C. Martin (Oxford: Clarendon Press, 1956).

> The feast, with gluttonous delaies,
> Is eaten, and too long their meat they praise,
> The masquers come too late, and'I thinke, will stay,
> Like Fairies, till the Cock crow them away.
> . . . .
>   What meane these Ladies, which (as though
> They were to take a clock in peeces,) goe
>   So nicely'about the Bride;
> A Bride, before a good night could be said,
> Should vanish from her cloathes, into her bed. (65–68, 73–77)

In these comments on the masquers we may perhaps detect an undertone of criticism of the lengthy and lavish festivities associated with the wedding (one seventeenth-century writer records that the marriage cost the bride's father £93,294).[18] But Donne's customary emphasis on the privacy of love and lovers is surely the main explanation for these passages: the celebrations of the masquers and the ministrations of the matrons, he implies, are not central to an occasion that centers on the relationship, especially the sexual union, of the couple themselves.

It is that union that he stresses in the final section of the poem:

> And by this act of these two Phenixes
>   Nature againe restored is,
>   For since these two are two no more,
> Ther's but one Phenix still, as was before. (99–102)

Here and in the preceding stanza Donne totally abandons the generic convention of the modest and reluctant bride. Instead, he characteristically portrays sex as a source of mutual and equal pleasure for both of his phoenixes.

Equally characteristic is the way these stanzas relate to the preoccupation with time that, as I suggested earlier, is very common in epithalamia. Donne is no less concerned with a cyclical temporal movement than other writers in the genre are (indeed, by both opening and concluding his poem on an allusion to the rising sun, he draws attention to the cycles in nature itself). But, unlike other authors of epithalamia, he suggests that it is the couple, not the children they will produce, who effect a cyclical pattern of rebirth and rejuvenation: "And by this act of these two Phenixes / Nature againe restored is" (99–100).

Later in the final stanza, however, Donne again draws attention to his indebtedness to the conventions of his genre. The lines "wee . . . will stay / Waiting, when your eyes open'd, let out day" (103–5) remind us that the very term *epithalamium* signifies "at the bridal chamber" and that the genre is rooted in folk rituals and ceremonies that took place by the couple's door. But the same lines also serve to underscore Donne's

---

18. William Sanderson, *A Compleat History of . . . Mary Queen of Scotland and . . . James the Sixth* (London: for Humphrey Mosely, Richard Tomlins, and George Sawbridge, 1656), p. 405. On the cost of the wedding and the elaborate festivities associated with it, also see Akrigg, *Jacobean Pageant*, pp. 145–56.

idiosyncratic approaches to that genre. To be sure, the image bodies forth the two forces with which epithalamia are so concerned, sexuality and society, and suggests their literal and figurative proximity. The community is present by the couple's chamber, much as the demands of society have been acknowledged throughout the poem. But Donne again assigns a distinctly secondary role to society: the bride and groom are the sun, controlling the world rather than being controlled by it.

Throughout this epithalamium, then, the attitudes Donne's speaker advises the couple to assume toward the social codes of the wedding are not unlike the ones Donne himself assumes toward the literary codes of the wedding poem. The bride and bridegroom do, of course, participate in the social rituals involved in their marriage— as we have seen, the final image draws attention to the presence of the wedding guests —but the dictates of their own, private relationship qualify and subsume that participation. Similarly, the author himself participates fully in the generic traditions he inherited, ignoring comparatively few of them. The others he plays on and plays with, skillfully adapting them to the predilections of his sensibility. In the process he does not fail to remind us of the dangers inherent in both social and literary codes—witness the intrusive revelers—but he also demonstrates a range of strategies for combating those dangers, such as the ways "Bee thou a new starre" (39) preserves the speaker's self-respect.

The epithalamium evidently attracted Donne for one of the same reasons the verse letter and the epicede did: all these literary types offer appropriate forums for responding to the demands of the patronage system. But our reading of the Palatine epithalamium hints at another and no less important reason the form appealed to him: he wrote epithalamia not in spite of but rather because of the many conventions with which the genre is laden. He appears to have relished the opportunity of adapting a genre some of whose norms were uncongenial to him, to have welcomed the challenge of playing the traditions of that genre against the demands of his individualistic talent.

Admittedly, in the two wedding poems outside the scope of this essay, Donne's responses to that challenge are not always felicitous. In the "Epithalamion made at Lincolnes Inne," his ambivalence about Spenser's "Epithalamion" produces an uneven and inconsistent poem.[19] He approaches many generic traditions imaginatively in the epithalamium he composed in 1613 for the marriage of Frances Howard and Somerset —witness the clever antipastoral eclogue, which both extends and undercuts the pastoral elements of the genre. Other conventions, however, he treats mechanically, at times merely repeating interpretations of them he had developed shortly before in the Palatine epithalamium: "Let every Jewell be a glorious starre" (155). But even the less

19. For an elaboration of this point, see my article, "Donne's 'Epithalamion made at Lincolnes Inne': An Alternative Interpretation," *SEL* 16 (1976), 131–43. In this essay I attempt to rebut David Novarr's contention that the poem is a parody written for mock nuptials at the Inns of Court ("Donne's 'Epithalamion made at Lincoln's Inn': Context and Date," *RES* 7 [1956], 250–63).

successful passages in these two poems testify to their author's knowledge of and interest in generic norms. And the Palatine epithalamium, as we have seen, unmistakably confirms his engagement with those norms, his desire to work with and within them. Rosalie Colie's observation is an apt summary of the ways Donne approaches generic conventions as he writes the poem: "Certainly for the period in which Shakespeare lived and worked, one *can* have it both ways: just as there was no possibility that any author or artist could 'make it new' by abandoning inherited forms, so also there was an insistence on outdoing and overgoing earlier achievements, each man newly creating out of and against his tradition."[20] For in the Palatine epithalamium, as in so many of his mature poems, Donne discards that "servile imitation" (27) to which Carew's elegy refers not in favor of total iconoclasm and deracination but rather for a type of creativity and originality that is rooted in the conventions of his genre.

---

20. Rosalie Colie, *Shakespeare's Living Art* (Princeton: Princeton University Press, 1974), p. 5.

SOULES EXHAL'D WITH WHAT THEY DO NOT SEE

9. "LA CORONA"
Donne's Ars Poetica Sacra

PATRICK F. O'CONNELL

John Donne began his career as divine poet by explicitly recognizing and success-fully dealing with the special demands of the religious lyric.[1] "La Corona," a sequence of seven linked sonnets, is often regarded by critics as a series of rather unremarkable meditations on the life of Christ, a rather bloodless experiment not particularly con-genial to Donne's temperament.[2] Yet the sequence, considered as a single unified work, is not simply a detached, objective presentation of the Christian mysteries, but the vehicle for a careful investigation of the meaning of human activity, and in particular of the vocation of the Christian artist, in the light of these mysteries.

The method we might expect when a master of love poetry, especially love po-etry so often charged with religious imagery and associations, turns to religious verse is a synthesis of sacred and profane, a fusion of religious subject matter with the forms of secular verse. Such an approach is suggested by the very title of the sequence, which refers both to the *corona di sonnetti*, a form borrowed from Continental love poets in which the last line of one sonnet is repeated as the first line of the next, and also to the variant of the rosary known as the corona, which provides the meditative framework.[3]

Yet such a synthesis, Donne realized, is more a tantalizing possibility or vexing prob-lem than a readily available technique. In secular verse, the poet is in complete control of his universe and can create and people a world as close to or as far from the world of reality as he wishes. To achieve a "higher truth" he can forego historical and bio-graphical accuracy. But a poet does not have the same freedom to create when he

---

1. "La Corona" can still plausibly be considered the first important Divine Poem, though a date of July 1607 or shortly before, assigned by Helen Gardner in her edition of *John Donne: The Divine Poems* (Oxford: Clarendon Press, 1952; 2d ed., 1979), p. xlix, is almost certainly inaccurate. See David Novarr, "The Dating of Donne's *La Corona*," *PQ* 36 (1957), 259–65, and my "The Successive Arrangements of Donne's 'Holy Sonnets,'" *PQ* 60 (1981), 334–37.

2. See, for example, J. B. Leishman, *The Monarch of Wit: An Analytical and Comparative Study of the Poetry of John Donne* (1951; London: Hutchinson, 1962), pp. 257–58: "His attitude, whatever it may actually have been, appears in these poems strangely external and detached. . . . They are essentially religious exercises – Donne is exercising his faith, whipping it up, trying to make himself feel and experience what he has apprehended intellectually." This idea goes back to Herbert Grierson's 1912 edition of Donne, in which "La Corona" was first assigned to the Mitcham period, before 1611 (*The Poems of John Donne*, 2 vols. [Ox-ford: Oxford University Press, 1912], 2: lii, 226), and has generally survived Gardner's redating of the "Holy Sonnets" to this period as well. Gardner's own contention is that "'*La Corona*' has been undervalued as a poem by comparison with the 'Holy Sonnets', because the difference of intention behind the two sets of sonnets has not been recognized. The '*La Corona*' sonnets are inspired by liturgical prayer and praise – oral prayer, not by private meditation and the tradition of mental prayer" (*Divine Poems*, p. xxiii). In *The Poetry of Meditation* (New Haven: Yale University Press, 1962), Louis L. Martz suggests a difference of meditative traditions as basis of the difference of styles (p. 110). Neither mentions the specifically aesthetic concern of the poem.

3. Martz, *Poetry of Meditation*, pp. 107–8.

is writing of, or to, Christ, nor the same capacity to name when he is addressing the one whose name, insofar as it is known, is known only as a gift, a revelation. Divine poetry cannot be "imitation" in the same sense as love poetry without falling into the trap of taking God's name in vain. To write a poem that is only an imitation, with only a formal resemblance to prayer, is to subordinate the religious to the aesthetic and so to "use" God for one's own ends. Prayer is thereby reduced to a laboratory for poetic effects as the poet focuses his own, and the reader's, attention not on God but on the speaker. The poem becomes a feigned prayer, but it is a feigned prayer to a real God. To make prayer a means to the end of poetry is in effect to indulge in "idolatry," to elevate self over God.

The very real dangers of religious verse are perceptively analyzed by Andrew Marvell in his own poem "The Coronet":

And now when I have summ'd up all my store,
    Thinking (so I my self deceive)
    So rich a Chaplet thence to weave
As never yet the king of Glory wore:
    Alas I find the Serpent old
    That, twining in his speckled breast,
    About the flow'rs disguis'd does fold,
    With wreaths of Fame and Interest.[4]

For Donne as for Marvell, the crown of poetry and that of piety are not easily woven into one. In the course of the first sonnet appear not one but five crowns, and their proper relationships are not perceived until the final couplet of the entire sequence, when we "arrive where we started / And know the place for the first time."

A revaluation of "La Corona" must begin with the recognition that the poem does not start out to be a meditation on the life of Christ. Rather, the shift to the external pattern, which comes only in the second sonnet, involves a change in focus determined by what we may call "dramatic" exigencies. Apparently beginning with no prior awareness of the complexities of religious verse, the speaker soon becomes so entangled in what Marvell calls the "wreaths of Fame and Interest" that in effect he has to begin all over again. Yet a deeper continuity underlies and motivates this change: for even the apparent impersonality of much of the sequence is actually a necessary part of the speaker's journey toward self-discovery, which depends for the Christian on the prior awareness of the identity of Christ. This discovery of the real Christ makes possible a genuine relationship with him: that is, it leads to authentic prayer.

A crucial distinction should be made here. While the poem's speaker does not know in what direction his meditation will lead him, it is evident that John Donne himself is quite aware where the poem is going, and why. Although the speaker is at the out-

---

4. Andrew Marvell, *Complete Poetry*, ed. George deF. Lord (New York: Modern Library, 1968), pp. 7–8, lines 9–16. See Frank J. Warnke's analysis of the poem in *Versions of Baroque: European Literature in the Seventeenth Century* (New Haven: Yale University Press, 1972), pp. 144–46.

set obviously confused, undisciplined, ready to settle for the appearance rather than the reality of resolution, on another level the poem reveals a thematic development and tonal modulation of the utmost precision. The significance of this "double consciousness" is at the heart of the poem's meaning:[5] the speaker's sense of his own identity is quickly revealed to be inadequate, a projection of his own desires and delusions. Because it sees itself as the center of reality, this persona is of necessity false, invented. But in the course of the sequence, the speaker progressively recognizes the illusory nature of this self, so that when the poem actually becomes the offering of "prayer and praise" it is intended to be, the two levels of consciousness have merged. The distinction between the poet and his speaker is transcended in the single voice of genuine prayer. As readers, we are able to share both the knowledge of Donne and the experience of the speaker, to undergo the process of transformation and to reflect on the meaning of that process, an opportunity singularly appropriate in a poem whose last line, being also its first, is an invitation to read over again with deepened insight.

The opening sonnet begins with the naive assumption that the divine poet can proceed just as a love poet would: "this crown of prayer and praise" (1) is of course a religious analogue to the crown of posies, both flowers and poems, that a love poet presents to his mistress to honor her and win her favor. Yet this shift from secular to sacred is radically unsuccessful. Even as he presents his crown, the speaker senses his audacity in offering his own creation to the Creator of all reality, "Thou which of good, hast, yea art treasury, / All changing unchang'd Antient of dayes" (3–4). Here is no easily flattered mistress or patron, but the Aristotelian Unmoved Mover, the apocalyptic Judge of the Book of Daniel. This first view of God as the eternal, all-powerful one can only serve to emphasize the insignificance of the poet's own offering, as well as to call into question the whole enterprise of modeling religious verse on profane. The analogy falters, for what can be given, what added, to the infinite source of all good?

Yet the speaker's own expectations are far from trivial:

But doe not, with a vile crowne of fraile bayes,
Reward my muses white sincerity,
But what thy thorny crowne gain'd, that give mee,
A crowne of Glory, which doth flower alwayes.... (5–8)

5. In *John Donne's Poetry* (Cambridge: Cambridge University Press, 1971), Wilbur Sanders's failure to make this distinction results in a total misreading of the poem: "one is bound to take note, in the *Divine Poems*, of a studious attempt to repress the idiosyncratic, and an effort, sometimes very visible, to bend an individualist temper to bear the yoke of a common faith. The poetic effect, as might have been predicted, is often to give us the idiosyncratic, oddly distorted by the strains of self-abasement, wreathed in strange distracting shapes around the familiar doctrines—like a serpent round a crucifix. The most palpable case is 'La Corona', where the serpent is doubly distracting in that he appears to believe himself invisible" (p. 121). This kind of impressionistic criticism, which provides no corroborating evidence—"La Corona" is scarcely mentioned again—attempts to convey the idea that the critic knows more about the poem than the poet himself, a demonstrably false assumption in this case. The snake is as visible here as in Marvell's

Where there was one crown, suddenly there are four.[6] This multiplication is not merely verbal ingenuity but Donne's way of calling attention to the central problem of the poem: what is the value of human activity, and artistic creativity in particular, in the context of man's ultimate destiny? In terms of the image itself, what relationship is there between the crown the poet gives (the work of art) and the crown he hopes to get (eternal life)? The answer seems to be that there is no intrinsic relationship. To win a heavenly crown by offering a crown of poetry would be to gain salvation by one's own efforts, and thus to reduce Christ to the status of exemplar: what "thy thorny crowne gain'd" for you, may my poetic crown gain for me. Yet if the poet accepts the orthodox answer that the heavenly reward is gained for all men, including the speaker, by Christ's own "thorny crowne," symbol of his redemptive suffering, then the poet's gift can add nothing of merit to what Christ has already won, and thus becomes supererogatory, completely unconnected to the crown he desires. Thus the shift to Christ as the basis for analogy is unsuccessful as well.

The speaker's immediate solution, to link the reward not to the product but to the intention behind it (his "muses white sincerity"), only complicates matters further by its presumption of innocence and disinterestedness, while implicitly relegating the poem itself to a strictly mundane level. Unless some valid link can be established between the thorny crown of Christ's passion and his own gift-crown, then the act of writing poetry, and by extension any human offering to God, must remain earthbound, as frail as the bays the poet now scorns.

Though the emergence of the figure of Christ will in the course of the sequence be recognized as the solution to the speaker's dilemma, at this point he is perceived only as a deepening of the problem:

The ends crowne our workes, but thou crown'st our ends,
For, at our end begins our endlesse rest,
The first last end, now zealously possest,
With a strong sober thirst, my soule attends. (9–12)

Human and divine economies are perceived to work in radically different ways. From an earthly perspective, "The ends crowne our workes": either the completed work itself is its own fulfillment (the weaving of the crown is its own reward), or, more pragmatically, the work obtains the fruits for which it was undertaken (the reward, at best, of a crown of bays, or some other form of remuneration). In contrast, "thou crown'st our ends": Christ rewards not works but ends, both motives and the end of a person's life; more profoundly, he himself *is* the crown, the final cause for which man was created and toward which he is drawn, "The first last end" in the deepest sense. Thus the succession of crowns in the octave is matched here by an even more

poem on the same topic, and as consciously intended: it is precisely the process of exorcism that determines the structure and movement of the entire poem.

6. The contrast between perishable and imperishable crowns is found in 1 Corinthians 9:25, but in the context of athletic competition.

bewildering variety of ends: yet the full meaning of crown and end, both initially used by the speaker to describe his own work, is finally appropriated to the person of Christ. Not even the images the speaker has chosen can be kept distinct from the divine reality.

Unsuccessful in his efforts to discover the significance of religious poetry as an offering to God, the poet seeks to find a justification for his art by turning outward in the final couplet, only to be frustrated once again: "'Tis time that heart and voice be lifted high, / Salvation to all that will is nigh" (13–14). But it just does not work: the apparent resolution remains unconvincing, aesthetically and religiously, because it fails to address the problems raised earlier. The speaker finds a new audience instead of, not because of, his personal confrontation with God. Rather than being called to proclaim the good news, he has assumed the role as a solution to his own problem of justifying religious poetry. The poem is now conceived not as prayer and praise but as exhortation, a disembodied didacticism preaching a message that has not been learned. In fact, we cannot even be sure how the proclamation is to be taken: in what sense is salvation near "to all that will"? Unless qualified, such a phrase is open to the same Pelagian interpretation as the earlier request for the crown of glory. Furthermore, the final couplet, far from resolving difficulties, has raised another, the relationship of the reader to the poem.

Any lingering doubts about the failure of the first sonnet to arrive at a satisfactory resolution are swept away as the second sonnet opens. The exhortation is repeated only to be left hanging, grammatically, with only the most tenuous connection to the following sentence of which it is nominally a part. The "all" of the poet's new audience is dwarfed by "That All, which alwayes is All every where" (16). His new strategy falters once again before the inescapable figure of the God-man. So the poet now turns to the life of Christ because he has no other choice. He is compelled to recognize that the central figure in a Christian poem is not the poet but Christ himself, so that his primary concern must be not his own aesthetic role but rather his relationship as a human person to Christ. This relationship, as yet unclear, becomes the object of the speaker's meditative quest throughout the course of the sequence.

Yet by removing himself and his original problem from the center of attention, the speaker has in effect taken the first step toward its resolution. In fact, the rest of the sequence recapitulates the material of the first sonnet, but from a different starting point and in a different context. The questions of God's omnipresence, man's ability to give gifts to God, the human being's relationship to God, to self, and to others, and the place of art in the life of the spirit all reappear in turn and are successfully dealt with, not as independent topics but as aspects of the mystery of the Incarnation and Redemption.

Already in the second sonnet, "Annunciation," the relevance to the speaker's dilemma of Christ's coming is implicit. The initiative of bringing God within man's reach, in art as in life, belongs not to man but to God himself, who has in fact graciously undertaken it: "That All, which alwayes is All every where, / . . . yeelds himselfe to lye / In prison, in thy wombe" (16, 19–20). The speaker's initial insight, the crux of his difficulty as religious poet, was that there is no room for a reality separate from God. But now it appears that God himself makes that room, limiting his infinity to the dimensions of a human being so that other human beings can approach him. The paradox of the Incarnation, God in human flesh, undergirds the paradox of religious poetry, the Word in human words. Because the Almighty humbled himself to such an extent as to become human, he can be brought within the confines of human words and art, not by human power but by cooperation with this divine gift. Thus the paradoxical role of Mary, model for all believers, can be seen as a paradigm for the Christian poet in particular:

> thou art now
> Thy Makers maker, and thy Fathers mother,
> Thou'hast light in darke; and shutst in little roome,
> Immensity cloysterd in thy deare wombe. (25–28)

Christ willingly allows himself to be "made" by his own creature, to be shut "in little roome."[7]

While the speaker does not make the connection between Mary's role and his own in "Annunciation," in the "Nativity" sonnet that follows he attempts, somewhat hesitantly, to discover a place for himself in the events being narrated. He realizes that Christ's freely chosen weakness makes Christ not only available but also vulnerable. The challenge of his presence, which elicits "*Herods* jealous generall doome" (36), naturally evokes a response from the speaker:

> Seest thou, my Soule, with thy faiths eyes, how he
> Which fils all place, yet none holds him, doth lye?
> Was not his pity towards thee wondrous high,
> That would have need to be pittied by thee?
> Kisse him, and with him into Egypt goe,
> With his kinde mother, who partakes thy woe. (37–42)

Here the poet reflects on the unique relationship of man to Christ: the speaker can indeed give pity to the Christ-child, born in poverty and threatened by the powerful, but this ability, properly understood, is itself a divine gift. The dilemma of the crowns again presents itself, but it is now treated with deeper spiritual insight. The speaker's pity is contingent and limited, dependent on God's own pity for him, but it is nonetheless real. Man is able to give something to God, even something of which he, as the newborn infant Jesus, "would have need." Clearly we have come a considerable way in understanding in what sense human activity can be given to God. Man does not stand outside the process of salvation as an independent agent, as the speaker ini-

---

7. The phrase recalls "We'll build in sonnets pretty roomes" ("The Canonization," 32).

tially attempted to do, but responds to the prior act of God that makes his gift possible. The analogies between human and divine take on new life, but now their origin is seen to be the divine act, not the human.

But the speaker has not quite learned his lesson. We should not be surprised – the Incarnation demands a more radical and mature response from man than pity. As in the first sonnet, the final couplet leaves us uneasy and dissatisfied. For the poet has suddenly taken over the primary role. If he can claim that the Virgin partakes of *his* woe on the flight into Egypt, his priorities remain confused.

Repeated as the opening line of "Temple," the fourth sonnet, the verse "with his kinde mother who partakes thy woe" is more appropriately addressed to Joseph, whose sorrow at losing the child Jesus is shared by his wife. Thus a sense of due proportion is restored, but the speaker is once again observer rather than participant. For it is not only the infant Christ, helpless and speechless, whom man must encounter. Like Joseph, the speaker is forced to "turne backe" (44) to find Jesus on his own terms. In this, the central sonnet of the sequence, Christ reveals himself to be both human and divine, and first assumes responsibility for his mission.[8] He sits in the Temple,

> Blowing, yea blowing out those sparks of wit,
> Which himselfe on the Doctors did bestow;
> The Word but lately could not speake, and loe
> It sodenly speakes wonders, whence comes it,
> That all which was, and all which should be writ,
> A shallow seeming child, should deeply know? (45–50)

Reversing roles with the doctors, Jesus both enkindles and surpasses their powers of intellect, of which he himself is the origin and final cause. Here Jesus is definitively presented as the center; he is not only in the midst of the doctors but is also the center of the poem and the center of history. He reveals himself as master of the Old Law and the New, the fulfillment of all that has gone before and the initiator of all that is to come.

But the centrality of Christ is no longer the threat it seemed to be earlier, for it does not exclude the speaker. Rather, there is a suggestion that Christ already looks toward him: "all which should be writ" refers in context to the New Testament, but in a wider sense the phrase encompasses all human creations, including the very poem now being written. Without realizing it, the speaker has been incorporated into the scene, though not by his own efforts. It is not the speaker's search for Christ, but

---

8. In "The Meaning of the 'Temple' in Donne's *La Corona*," *JEGP* 59 (1960), A. B. Chambers quotes from the traditional glosses on Luke 2:42–52 to show that "the 'Temple' appears in a poem of prayer and praise upon the life of Christ not as an extraneous element but as a thematic part which is in effect a précis of the whole" (p. 217). The relevent glosses "make it possible to see that the subject matter of the fourth sonnet looks back to the human frailty of the birth of Jesus, signifies the first manifestation of his divinity, marks his entrance into the ministry, and forecasts the end for which he came" (p. 217). All these interpretations are supported by details from the sonnet itself.

Christ's search for the speaker, that will draw them together. Moreover, the speaker like the doctors owes his own "sparks of wit" to Christ, who is thus the source of the creative power producing the poem. The speaker's identity as man and poet is therefore intimately bound up with the person and mission of Christ, so that the moment of definitive encounter will also be a moment of self-discovery.

Such a moment comes in the following poem, "Crucifying," which begins with the recognition that a detached, uninvolved attitude toward Christ is impossible. People can either admire and imitate Christ in humble submissiveness, being weak as he is weak (32), or take advantage of his weakness for their own purposes:

> By miracles exceeding power of man,
> He faith in some, envie in some begat,
> For, what weake spirits admire, ambitious, hate . . . (57–59)

The dramatic urgency of this choice is emphasized by the change from the narrative past tense of the first four lines to an anguished present, marking a return to the highly affective tone of "Nativity," but with added insight into Christ's mission and its demands on each person:

> But Oh! the worst are most, they will and can,
> Alas, and do, unto the'immaculate,
> Whose creature Fate is, now prescribe a Fate,
> Measuring selfe-lifes infinity to'a span,
> Nay to an inch. . . . (61–65)

The imagery describing this rebellion shows it to be a monstrous distortion of Christ's own intent in becoming human. If Mary "shutst in little room, Immensity," Christ's tormentors pervert this freely willed limitation to their own ends. What God has begun in love, his creatures complete in hatred.

While the present tense and emotional exclamations give the impression of an eyewitness account, the rather stylized description of the events has the effect of universalizing the crime: "the worst are most" not only in first-century Jerusalem but in every age, including the one in which the poem is being written. Thus it is natural and necessary that the speaker once again enter his poem as a participant, to choose how he will respond. For the first time since the introductory sonnet, he speaks directly to Christ:

> Now thou art lifted up, draw mee to thee,
> And at thy death giving such liberall dole,
> Moyst, with one drop of thy blood, my dry soule. (68–70)

This adaptation of Jesus' own words, "And I, if I be lifted up from the earth, will draw all men unto me" (John 12:32), represents the speaker's surrender to the Lordship of Christ. The journey that culminates in this petition is recognized to have its impetus in Christ himself, who draws others to him by his sacrificial love. Refusing to take advantage of Christ's self-imposed weakness to assert his own autonomy, at the cross the speaker is able to respond to Christ directly, to acknowledge responsibility for his initial estrangement, and to move into a new dimension in which the spurious identity of gift-giver is replaced by the authentic identity of redeemed sinner. While the figure of Christ was a threat to the first identity, it is in fact the ground of the new identity. Only in the light of the cross does man see himself as he is, both sinful and redeemed: in finding Christ he also discovers himself. Yet his prayer is in no sense individualized: he asks only to be included among "all men" whom Christ draws to himself. Finally the distinction between the speaker within the poem and Donne himself is no longer necessary or meaningful, for the words of the prayer can be spoken without reservation by both. The cross is in the end the source of reconciliation of self with self, as well as with God and with other people.

If the crucifixion is depicted as the convergence of the individual with Christ, the two final sonnets of the sequence show that there need be no subsequent separation. The most remarkable thing about "Resurrection" is that it deals primarily not with Christ's resurrection but with that of the speaker himself, both his rebirth from the spiritual death of sin and his anticipated rising into glory at the Last Judgment. While this may at first seem to be a regression to the poet's earlier preoccupation with self, it is actually just the opposite. The resurrections he speaks of are not something other than the resurrection of Christ, but the speaker's participation in the Easter mystery (compare Colossians 2:12–13). Man's true vocation is thus to realize in his own space and time the once-for-all saving event of Christ.[9]

Once again the technique of repetition establishes an angle of vision on the new sonnet. Here, for the first time in the sequence, the grammatical structure of the repeated verse is altered from one sonnet to the next. The imperative of the speaker's prayer ("Moyst, with one drop of thy blood, my dry soule") becomes adjectival: "Moyst with one drop of thy blood, my dry soule / Shall . . . bee / Freed" (71–74). The effect is of course to affirm that the prayer will be heard, that Christ's death is indeed fruitful. The change in meaning reflects the passage from death to life for the speaker, as well as for Christ.

The dominant tense of this sonnet is future, another break in the established pattern, and the emphatic form *shall*, used repeatedly, testifies to the speaker's faith in Christ's transforming power. His confident tone and far-ranging perspective, able to confront even the thought of his own death and dissolution without alarm, are compelling evidence that Christ has already heard his prayer. The repetition of the word *death* has the effect not of inspiring horror or foreboding but of showing the word, and the thing itself, to be harmless. The "first last end" of the opening sonnet, Christ

9. Irene Simon, in "Some Problems of Donne Criticism," *Revue des Langues Vivantes* 19 (1953), comments: "Whereas Sonnet 5 dealt with Christ, then with 'mee,' here Christ and 'mee' are really inseparable; though little feeling is expressed, yet we gather that the poet is deeply involved" (p. 38). Simon's reading of the poem is generally excellent but does not consider the question of poetry as prayer.

himself, has definitively overcome the "Feare of first or last death" (77). The perspective is that of eternity, as the speaker prays now to the glorified Christ who enrolls the names of the elect in "thy little booke" (78; compare Revelation 3:5). The act of writing that will gain the speaker an eternal crown is now acknowledged to be Christ's, not his own. Beginning within time with the transformation of the soul, the sonnet concludes beyond time with the transformation of the body, the end of physical death:

> May then sinnes sleep, and deaths soone from me passe,
> That wak't from both, I againe risen may
> Salute the last, and everlasting day. (82–84)

Easter itself is "the last and everlasting day" for Christ, but the completion, the full effect of the resurrection, will take place only when his glory is shared by all the faithful.

Since the fullness of the Christian communion is the union with Christ, not of the individual believer alone, but of all the redeemed, the sequence rightly concludes by widening its perspective to incorporate others in an explicit way. This unity was implied from the very moment the speaker discovered himself at the foot of the cross, praying that Christ's promise to draw all men to himself might be fulfilled in his own life. Thus when he turns outward in "Ascension" to speak directly to his audience, the effect is completely different from the attempt at the close of the first sonnet to justify his own status as a divine poet by rhetorical exhortation, addressed to no one in particular. He speaks here to those who have also known the experience of sin and redemption, "Yee whose just teares, or tribulation / Have purely washt, or burnt your drossie clay" (87–88). They are not simply an audience of his poem but fellow participants in the drama of salvation. In summoning them to witness "the last and everlasting day," the final triumph of Christ, the speaker calls attention not to himself but to the Lord, with the confidence that the vision he presents is not a product of his own imagination but has its source in an experience of Christ that is available to all.

Thus the introduction of other persons results not in a diffusion of focus but actually in its intensification, since Christ is shown to be the center, not only of the speaker's life, but of the lives of all the faithful. Just as in "Resurrection" the speaker no longer sought a separate identity for himself but considered his own rebirth in the light of Christ's resurrection, so the method of merging the redemptive acts of Christ with their eschatological fulfillment is employed here on a wider scale. The saving pattern established by Christ is extended to all, his ascension being the promise and prefiguring of the entrance into heaven of the whole company of the saved. Thus, in the first quatrain, "the'uprising of this Sunne, and Sonne" (86) is first of all the Last Judgment, with its sun that will never set and the second coming of Christ; but the uprising of the Son also suggests Easter itself, the paradigm of that day when each person's body rises incorruptible. The image makes the two events in some sense inseparable, each the beginning of eternity.[10]

10. Thus "La Corona" shows precisely the "analogical kinship between the personal-moral, the personal-

Conversely the second quatrain seems to return speaker and audience to the Mount of Ascension, but the description is equally applicable to the Vision of Christ leading the assembled faithful into glory: "Behold the Highest, parting hence away, / Lightens the darke clouds, which hee treads upon" (89–90). These convergences reach their climax in the elliptical compression of the final two lines of the octave: "Nor doth hee by ascending, show alone, / But first hee, and hee first enters the way" (91–92). The meaning depends not only on the distinction between "first hee" and "hee first" but also on the correspondingly different senses of "alone." In the first sense, Christ not only ("alone") *shows* the way to salvation but in his own ascension is also the first in time ("first hee") to enter upon it. The second sense looks forward to the fulfillment of this promise: Christ does not show the way by himself, unattended ("alone"), but is the first, in precedence and leadership ("hee first"), of the whole multitude of the faithful to enter the way.

This integration of past, present, and future, of the saving events of Christ and their recapitulation in the life of each believer, both spiritually now and eschatologically at the end of time, brings the poem to its culmination. As the initial self-conscious alienation of the speaker from Christ, from others, and from his true self has given way to the recognition of his true identity, so the prayer of the final sestet, a colloquy of striking balance and simplicity, is available to speaker and reader alike:

O strong Ramme, which hast batter'd heaven for mee,
Mild lambe, which with thy blood hast mark'd the path;
Bright Torch, which shin'st, that I the way may see,
Oh, with thy owne blood quench thy owne just wrath . . . (93–96)

No hint of "my muses white sincerity" here, but for all that these lines have the tone of authentic prayer.

It is only after the whole journey of redemption has come to fruition in this intimate prayer that the speaker turns back, briefly but conclusively, to the relevance of all this for his own art: "And if thy holy Spirit, my Muse did raise, / Deigne at my hands this crowne of prayer and praise" (97–98). Once again he presents to God his gift-crown, but with literally a world of difference. He now offers his gift not in order to gain anything but in loving response to what the cross of Christ has already gained. The aftermath of Christ's ascension is of course Pentecost, the outpouring of the Spirit promised by Christ, and the poet finally locates the proper place for his art as one of the gifts of the Spirit, one of the ways in which the Spirit speaks to God and to other men through a human instrument.[11]

---

historical, and the personal-divine life of the soul in its ascent to the Beatific Vision" that M. M. Ross, in *Poetry and Dogma* (New Brunswick, N.J.: Rutgers University Press, 1954), calls the "historical concrete" and considers to have been gradually lost in the weakening sacramentalism of the Anglican Church (p. 88).

11. While Judah Stampfer, in *John Donne and the Metaphysical Gesture* (New York: Funk & Wagnalls, 1970), rightly sees the communal dimension of this sonnet, he misses the concluding point of complete reliance on God, which is the solution of the aesthetic problem raised in the first sonnet, by reversing subject and object in the penultimate line: "As angry soldiers once hoisted Christ's body to a death, so his muse

While it is creation that makes a poet, redemption restores the proper relationship of this talent, of any human activity, to Christian life. By allowing Christ to assume the rightful and necessary place as the center, indeed the totality, of his world, the poet is able to discover the true meaning and purpose of his own creativity. The problems have all been resolved, not directly, but in the process of coming to accept Christ. Indeed the process itself, including the failures, the premature resolutions, and all, is an integral part of the overall pattern that makes up the gift-crown. "La Corona" is both a series of meditations on the life of Christ and a record of the personal appropriation of that life through dying and rising with Christ. As such, it provides a paradigm and interpretive key for the entire body of Donne's religious poetry, the principal subject of which is the possibility, and the difficulty, of self-transcendence (that is, prayer) in a world where the self has assumed a degree of independence unknown in previous centuries. Donne's end in the Divine Poems is the traditional one of expressing dependence on and potential union with God; his innovation is in starting from a new point—self-centered individualism, which he identifies with sin and alienation from God and the true self. This autonomous self is "the God-subverting element in Man,"[12] which must be transcended to discover not only God but also one's own true identity.

Hence we can discover in "La Corona" a valid and helpful model for the religious lyric. When a poem depicts the failure of this process of self-transcendence, as in the first sonnet here, the speaker remains alienated, separated from Christ and consequently from others, and the reader remains an observer of his isolation, which exemplifies the sinful state. But when the process is successful, as it finally is in "La Corona," the speaker has become a representative figure whose relationship with Christ typifies that of the Christian believer. This movement from spurious autonomy to self-definition as one who shares in the life of Christ and of the Church invites a corresponding shift in the reader from observer to participant. All divisions are overcome, including that between fictive and real worlds, as the perspective of the speaker merges with that of the poet and the words of the poem become genuine "prayer and praise" for poet and reader alike. The gift that the poet finally presents to God in "La Corona" is the divine image itself, at once Christ and the Christian conformed to him, an image presented at the same time to the reader, not merely to admire but to make one's own.

---

raises the Holy Spirit to life (1. 13). So the opening prayer ineluctibly returns, but now as the joyous hymn of an equal" (p. 238). Such a reading totally misconstrues the meaning of the entire poem.

12. The phrase is that of William H. Halewood, in *The Poetry of Grace: Reformation Themes and Structures in English Seventeenth-Century Poetry* (New Haven and London: Yale University Press, 1970), p. 32.

10. "FANTASTIQUE AGUE"
The Holy Sonnets and Religious Melancholy

ROGER B. ROLLIN

... Agues physicke are.
—"The First Anniversary," 21.

"Oh, to vex me," complains the speaker of Donne's sonnet-cycle, "contraryes meete in one." Vexation, however, has also been an *effect* of these poems for many readers, who have found them to be difficult, discomfiting, or both. Scholars, moreover, continue to be vexed by problems of the sonnets' dating, sequence, possible autobiographical content, and, certainly, interpretation.

Such problems shall not be solved here, though they may be rendered somewhat less vexing by this essay's conclusion—that the Holy Sonnets, like so many of Donne's secular poems, seem to be written mainly for their shock effect (or, in this case, as shock treatment). That is, they seem to be deliberately intended to vex readers, to "afflict [them] with mental agitation or trouble; to make [them] anxious or depressed; to distress [them] deeply or seriously" (*OED*, s.v.3). Whereas a trifle like "Goe, and catche a falling starre," with its comic portrait of the rejected lover-turned-amatory Jacques, is obviously intended merely to entertain, the Holy Sonnets prove to be vexatious poems in part because they are sick poems in the service of preventive medicine, intended to instruct as well as entertain. They are not so much "private ejaculations," highly personalized confessional works, as they are "sacred poems," public demonstrations of (in this case) spiritual malaise meant to be exemplary to disease-prone readers. They succeed in creating this effect by presenting readers with a kind of composite portrait of one suffering from what Renaissance psychology classified as "religious melancholy" (and what modern psychiatry understands as a form of "affective disorder").

Seen from this perspective the Holy Sonnets become a kind of case study in a disease of the times, and thus as much a negative lesson in holy living as the *Devotions upon Emergent Occasions* is a positive lesson in holy dying. For Donne to have thought of his religious poems in this way is more likely than for him to have regarded them as *cris de coeur* or catharsis. As one scholar has pointed out, even the young Milton "viewed poetry as a form of ministry and emphasized the close relationship between the art of poetry and the art of pulpit oratory." Milton's view is in fact representative: "The concept of the poetic vocation and the recognition of the law of *caritas* indicate that seventeenth-century devotional poetry is *public, not private*, that the poet is not confessing his sins but is functioning much like the minister in diagnosing spiritual diseases and prescribing remedies."[1]

1. Elaine B. Safer, "On the Morning of Christ's Nativity," *A Milton Encyclopedia*, ed. William B. Hunter, Jr., et al., 8 vols. (Lewisburg: Bucknell University Press, 1979), 6: 27; and the abstract of Frances M. Malpezzi, "*Ministerium Verbi*: The Christian Aesthetics of the Renaissance and the Seventeenth-Century Tuning Poets," *DAI* 34 (1974), 7713A (Nebraska), in *SCN* 34 (1976), 113, italics added. For their generous and helpful

The sense that the psychological phenomenon of religious melancholy is important to the very nature and function of the Holy Sonnets is clearly present in Helen Gardner's suggestion that in the sonnets "The 'low devout melancholie' of '*La Corona*,' the 'dejection' of 'A Litany,' are replaced by something darker. . . . The two poles between which [the soul] oscillates [in the Holy Sonnets] are faith in the mercy of God in Christ, and a sense of personal unworthiness that is very near to despair. The flaws in [the] spiritual temper [of these poems] are a part of their peculiar power." Gardner, however, proceeds to examine the psychological tension of the Holy Sonnets in mainly religious terms because, in her view, Donne regarded melancholy as a sin.[2] She says little more about the "peculiar power" these poems seem to have for the modern reader.

This essay, then, will attempt to take up where Gardner leaves off but will approach the problem of Donne's collection from a different, dual perspective, that of seventeenth- and twentieth-century psychology. From that perspective the Holy Sonnets begin to look like not so much a sonnet sequence as a kind of anti-sequence, one whose main ordering principle is disorder, and specifically mental disorder.

I

Two of the chief tendencies of modern scholarship on the Holy Sonnets have been to regard Donne's poems as constituting a more or less traditional sonnet sequence and to identify the thoughts and feelings expressed in them with the mental states of their author. Both of these approaches have caused at least as many problems as they have solved.

To conceive of the Holy Sonnets as belonging to the genre made fashionable by *Astrophel and Stella* and the *Amoretti* is reasonable, given the common form of these poems and, to a lesser extent, their content and provenance. But when such a conception goes hand in hand with a formalistic bias, that rage for order that characterizes so much modern scholarship, the result tends to be a grim search for the "unity" and "coherence" of Donne's collection. This tendency is exemplified by the editorial efforts of Gardner herself and by the work of such critics as Douglas Peterson and Don Ricks.[3] But unity and coherence can make up a Procrustean bed upon which meaning is wrenched and nuance and affect are simply lopped off.

Although it can be helpful to think of Donne's poems as constituting a traditional

advice, I wish to thank John Idol (Clemson University), Lucy W. Rollin (The Graduate Institute of Liberal Arts, Emory University), and Donald K. Freeman, M.D., Winston-Salem, North Carolina.

This essay is dedicated with respect and affection to another student of the Holy Sonnets, Professor Shonosuke Ishii of Soka University, Tokyo, Chairman of the Renaissance Institute (Japan).

2. *John Donne: The Divine Poems*, ed. Helen Gardner (Oxford: Oxford University Press, 1952), pp. xxxi, xliii.

3. Douglas L. Peterson, "John Donne's *Holy Sonnets* and the Anglican Doctrine of Contrition," *SP* 56 (1959), 504–18; see also Peterson's *The English Lyric from Wyatt to Donne* (Princeton: Princeton University Press, 1967); and Don M. Ricks, "The Westmoreland Manuscript and the Order of Donne's 'Holy Sonnets,'" *SP* 63 (1966), 187–95. For a response to this method, see John N. Wall, Jr., "Donne's Wit of Redemption: The Drama of Prayer in the Holy Sonnets, *SP* 73 (1976), 189–203.

sonnet sequence, it would have been difficult for most readers of his own time to have appreciated them as such until the first edition of 1633. Prior to that date seventeenth-century readers were in rather the same position as are most contemporary readers who experience the Holy Sonnets only in anthology selections. If it can be assumed that Donne himself was at least as conscious of the likely effects of his poems on his readers as other poets of his time, prudence dictates that criteria associated with the sonnet sequence not be applied to his collection with Puritan rigor.

Likewise, the tendency of an earlier school of critics and of the new school of psychobiographers to read these poems as nearly straightforward autobiography merits scrutiny.[4] Whether an exercise in fashionable antifeminism like "The Indifferent" is more or less autobiographical than the idealism of "A Valediction: forbidding mourning" or whether the Divine Poems are more or less autobiographical than the Songs and Sonets cannot likely be known and if known would only add to our store of literary gossip. Although Donne did diagnose himself as suffering from melancholia and although symptoms of that disease seem to be expressed with some frequency in his writings, Peterson's warning that "it is rash to assume from the subject matter and emotional quality of [the Holy Sonnets] that their author was a victim of over-wrought religiosity" is well taken.[5] Thus, in this essay I will confine myself to a consideration of religious melancholy as a psychological phenomenon and as a controlling *fiction* of the Holy Sonnets.

II

Like a number of commentators on the Holy Sonnets, Gardner tries to explain their "superiority" and "power" in terms of a thematic unity arising out of their participation in the tradition and technique of the formal meditation. This explanation is rejected by Ricks and by Peterson, for whom the governing principle of the collection is that of contrition. John L. Wall, Jr., views the poems as "an exploration of the paradoxes of Christian life on earth."[6] But such hypotheses offer no satisfactory explanation as to why the Holy Sonnets seem to have been sufficiently compelling to that religiously contentious age as to be included in seven editions of Donne's collected poems between 1633 and 1669. Nor do they go very far toward explaining the peculiar power these poems continue to have in the twentieth century, when even an acknowledged Christian critic like Douglas Bush admits that the religious experience they dramatize is "so narrowly and concretely fundamentalist that . . . a modern reader may not find enough of the common ground needed for full imaginative participation." Perhaps, as Michael Steig has suggested, the apparent universality of the

4. In the category of psychobiographical critics I place John Stachniewski, on the basis of his essay "John Donne: The Despair of the 'Holy Sonnets,'" *ELH* 48 (1981), 677–705; and John Carey, on the basis of his study, *John Donne: Life, Mind and Art* (New York: Oxford University Press, 1981). Both read the Holy Sonnets as if each poem were a versified treatment of an actual event in Donne's psychological life.

5. Peterson, "Anglican Doctrine of Contrition," p. 158.

6. Gardner, *Divine Poems*, p. xxix; Ricks, "The Westmoreland Manuscript," p. 187; Peterson, "Anglican Doctrine of Contrition," pp. 505–6; and Wall, "Donne's Wit of Redemption," p. 191.

Holy Sonnets has its locus elsewhere, in the psychological forms and contents of these poems.[7]

Let us then consider the possibility that in these poems Donne manages to do on a limited scale what Burton's *Anatomy of Melancholy* attempts on the grandest possible scale, to hold a mirror up to human psychological nature. But, whereas Burton develops a taxonomy of melancholy, Donne limits himself to portraying what the *Anatomy* classifies as a subdivision of love melancholy, religious melancholy.[8] Thus, as I will suggest, readers of the Holy Sonnets, late Renaissance readers or contemporary readers, Anglicans or agnostics, encounter an archetypal human crisis that they themselves have experienced or that they could imagine themselves experiencing—the individual's struggle to establish some kind of efficacious relationship with God. For anyone beyond the state of spiritual innocence, such a struggle must be fraught with anxiety-inducing possibilities. These possibilities are displayed, indeed maximized, in the Holy Sonnets, regardless of which scholar's ordering of the poems one follows—or even if one follows no authorized order to speak of, as in an anthology selection.

Democritus, Jr., "writ of melancholy, by being busy to avoid melancholy" (p. 16). Whether John Donne did likewise can only be conjectured. But to the reader able to identify with the speaker of his Holy Sonnets, Donne might say, with Burton, "Thou thyself are the subject of my discourse" (p. 11). Moreover, if he would have agreed with his fellow divine, Burton, that "A good Divine is or ought to be a good physician, a spiritual physician at least" (p. 29), Donne could have hoped that he had been able to present religious melancholy in particular, as Burton presented melancholy generally, "that it may be the better avoided . . . to do good" (p. 101).

III

Bibliographical problems aside, the Holy Sonnets offer readers what all sonnet cycles, whether tightly or loosely organized, offer—a distinctive speaker whose characteristic "voice" issues forth from the poems' rhetoric and whose composite "personality" is the medium and sometimes the message of the reading experience. Such a speaker can exhibit a variety of moods, sometimes contradictory ones, and can express a variety of attitudes, also sometimes contradictory. Readers encounter him during that limited phase of his fictional "life" that transpires between the first sonnet and the last. Such is the theoretical form of the English sonnet sequence generally, one to which the Holy Sonnets can be seen loosely to conform. The speaker, not the "story," is the unifying principle in those collections of sonnets that continue to interest us. It is he who blocks or facilitates reader-identification and involvement with the poetry.

As a psychological process, identification with a literary character entails both "pro-

---

7. Douglas Bush, *English Literature in the Earlier Seventeenth Century, 1600–1660*, rev. ed. (Oxford: Oxford University Press, 1962), pp. 140–41; and Michael Steig, "Donne's Divine Rapist: Unconscious Fantasy in Holy Sonnet XIV," *Hartford Studies in Literature* 4 (1972), 52–58.

8. *The Anatomy of Melancholy*, ed. Floyd Dell and Paul Jordan Smith (New York: Tudor Publishing Co., 1927). Subsequent citations will be identified parenthetically in my text.

jection" and "introjection," that is, "taking in from the character certain drives and defenses that are really objectively 'out there' and . . . putting into him feelings that are really objectively our own, 'in here.'"[9] Such identification can take place under the most unlikely circumstances, even when a literary character is of a different age or gender than the reader. It is an aspect of that uniquely human process wherein we deliberately "split" our egos, a process known in literary study as "the willing suspension of disbelief." Thus, achieving identification with a victim of religious melancholy, temporarily introjecting characteristics of his into our own consciousness and projecting our qualities into him, is in no wise unusual. The doctors regard all of us as neurotics: "There is no health; Physitians say that we / At best, enjoy but a neutralitie" ("The First Anniversary," 91–92). "Who," asks Democritus, Jr., "is free from melancholy?" (p. 32).

Certainly not the speaker of the Holy Sonnets. "Contraryes" meet in him; his only consistency is his "Inconstancy"; he is changeable, "humorous," "distempered," swinging wildly between hope and fear—in a word, sick: "So my devout fitts come and go away / Like a fantastique Ague" ("Oh, to vex me, contraryes meete in one"). It would be Burton's diagnosis that he has brain fever, triggered perhaps by an overheated imagination:

> If the imagination be very apprehensive, intent, and violent, it sends great store of spirits
> to or from the heart and makes a deeper impression and greater tumult . . . so that the first
> step and fountain of all our grievances in this kind is a distorted imagination, which, misinforming the heart, causeth all these distemperatures, alterations, and confusion, of spirits
> and humors. . . . I may therefore conclude with Arnoldus: great is the force of the imagination, and much more ought the cause of melancholy to be ascribed to this alone, than to
> the distemperature of the body. (p. 219)

Scholars, poets, and divines, Burton notes, are most susceptible to this malady.[10] That the speaker of the Holy Sonnets is apprehensive, intense, even violent (at least linguistically) has not, of course, gone unnoticed by critics. Gardner refers to his "exaggeration," "near . . . despair," and "moral intensity." A. L. French notes elements of wavering, worry, and confusion in the poems, indeed sees a "confusion of thought and feeling as their salient characteristic." And, according to Carey, "Donne's

---

9. Norman N. Holland, *The Dynamics of Literary Response* (New York: Oxford University Press, 1968), p. 278.
10. Here it might be noted that Burton, as is his wont, has his psychology both ways. On the one hand, he seems to see melancholy as a "perturbation" of the mind rather than as a "distemperature" of the body—see the description of "accidental melancholy" (which is not due to physiological causes) in Lawrence Babb, "Melancholy and the Elizabethan Man of Letters," *HLQ* 4 (1941), 249. On the other hand, the imagination as it is described by Burton seems intimately linked to human physiology, suggesting a "psychology that may be almost behaviorist: a rigorous physical determinism" to Patrick Crutwell, in "Physiology and Psychology in Shakespeare's Age," *Journal of the History of Ideas* 12 (1951), 85. During the last two decades modern psychiatry itself has been divided between affective and biochemical theories of the etiology of mental disorder. On the susceptibility of scholars, poets, and divines to melancholy, see "Love of Learning" (1.2.3.15).

'Holy Sonnets,' like his love poems, are torn by conflicts. They are full of sound and fury, and hang together by the makeshift expedients of passionate argument."[11] The "alteration" of "spirits and humors" to which Burton refers is seen by Gardner as fundamental to the personality of Donne the man, whose "problem was to come to terms with a world which alternately enthralled and disgusted him, to be the master and not the slave of his temperament."[12] However speculative, this analysis may have some validity: what is more certain is that the speaker of the Holy Sonnets is highly susceptible to alterations of spirit and humor: he is one who "durst not view heaven yesterday" but "to day / In prayers, and flattering speaches" courts God, and then fully anticipates that tomorrow he will "quake with true feare of his rod" ("Oh, to vex me, contraryes meete in one").

Plus ça, change, plus c'est la même chose. Modern psychiatry confirms Burton's establishment of a link between piety taken to its limits and alternating moods of depression and elation. Clinical literature documents cases in which individuals undergo episodes of mania, wherein "the predominant mood is either elevated" ("valiantly I hels wide mouth o'rstride") or "irritable" ("If serpents envious / Cannot be damn'd; Alas why should I bee?"). These are then followed by episodes of major depression, characterized by "loss of . . . pleasure" ("And all my pleasures are like yesterday") as well as by "feelings of worthlessness and guilt" ("Weaker I am, woe is mee, and worse then you") and "thoughts of death" ("Oh my blacke Soule! now thou are summoned / By sicknesse, death's herald and champion").[13] Additional clinical features of this condition (one of the "bipolar affective disorders") include psychomotor agitation, metaphorically suggested in the Holy Sonnets by such lines as "I runne to death, and death meets me as fast," and that condition's opposite, psychomotor retardation: "I dare not move my dimme eyes any way, / Despair behind, and death before doth cast / Such terrour." Fearfulness is frequently present, "but my'ever-waking part shall see that face, / Whose feare already shakes my every joint," as is brooding, "How shall my mindes white truth by them be try'ed?"

The clinical picture, then, has not changed appreciably over the centuries. As one scholar has noted:

> Melancholy was a state that included violent opposites in feeling and behavior, from total dejection and apathy to hysterical outbursts and frenzy, with swings from one to the other, as the Queen suggests in her description of Hamlet's supposed "fits" (V.1.279–82). Lemnius described the variety of melancholy moods and behaviors, the changes (depending upon

11. Gardner, *Divine Poems*, pp. xxx, xxxi, xxxvii; A. L. French, "The Psychopathology of Donne's *Holy Sonnets*," *The Critical Review* 13 (1970), 123, 121; and Carey, *Life, Mind and Art*, p. 146.

12. Gardner, *Divine Poems*, pp. xxxv, xxxvi.

13. See Mortimer Ostow, "Religion and Psychiatry," and Edward A. Wolpert, "Major Affective Disorders," in *Comprehensive Textbook of Psychiatry / III*, ed. Harold I. Kaplan et al., 3d ed., 3 vols. (Baltimore: Williams and Wilkins, 1980), 3: 3199; 2:1323–24, respectively. The sonnets cited in this paragraph are, respectively: "If faithfull soules be alike glorifi'd," "If poysonous mineralls," "Thou hast made me, And shall thy worke decay," "Why are wee by all creatures waited on," "Oh my blacke Soule," "Thou hast made me, And shall thy work decay," "This is my playes last scene," and "If faithfull soules be alike glorifi'd."

whether the humor was hot or cold) from mirth to sadness, and Bright also gave an account of such diversified moods:

> The perturbations of melancholy are for the most parte, sadde and fearful . . . sometimes furious, and sometimes merry in apparaunce, through a kind of Sardonian, and false laughter, as the humor is disposed that procureth these diversities.[14]

"Diversities" are indeed to be encountered in the Holy Sonnets: as readers work their way through Grierson's text or Gardner's—or even the *Norton Anthology*'s—from poem to poem they are exposed to the speaker's "violent opposites in feeling and behavior," from "dejection and apathy" ("This is my playes last scene") to "hysterical outbursts and frenzy" ("At the round earths imagin'd corners"). Mood swings such as these can also occur within individual sonnets. "If faithfull soules," for example, begins elatedly, with the speaker portraying himself as the Christian hero, triumphing over the world, the flesh, and the devil:

> If faithfull soules be alike glorifi'd
> As Angels, then my fathers soule doth see,
> And adds this even to full felicitie,
> That valiantly I hels wide mouth o'rstride.

This self-image of a Colossus of Faith, however, holds up only as far as line 5, at which point there arises the possibility of some discrepancy between the speaker's appearance of salvation and the reality of his inner insecurity. In bipolar disorders "self-esteem is inflated during a manic episode [but] as the activity level increases, the feelings about the self become increasingly disturbed."[15] Donne's speaker reveals his anxiety by conjecturing how his "mindes white truth" might be assessed in heaven, then partially displaces his fear by cataloging a variety of religious hypocrites. The poem concludes ambivalently, with the same soul that was implied to be faithful in line 1 now being characterized as "pensive" and requiring instruction: "Then turne . . . to God." The pattern is typical of the Holy Sonnets: though the mood swings of the melancholy persona are a major source of the collection's dramatic power, the same religiosity that triggers these moods is also a force for their control. This paradox is explained by one clinician as follows: "Religion provides mechanisms for both intensifying guilt and alleviating it. It creates guilt by setting up high standards of behavior and pointing up transgressions. It provides a number of methods for alleviating guilt: confession, prayer, acts of good work, and charity. These two directly opposite, separate mechanisms do not cancel each other out. Working alternately, they tend to bring the person under the influence of religious authority and its natural ally, the person's superego."[16]

The adaptive capacity of the superego, that is, as a source of strategies that can be consciously employed to alleviate psychic stress and promote adjustment, is illus-

---

14. Bridget Gellert Lyons, *Voices of Melancholy: Studies in Literary Treatments of Melancholy in Renaissance England* (New York: W. W. Norton, 1971), p. 93.
15. Wolpert, "Major Affective Disorders," p. 1325.
16. Ostow, "Religion and Psychiatry," pp. 3200–3201.

trated in such poems on Last Things as "Death be not proud." Here the speaker wards off the threat of destruction by bringing to bear the doctrine so cheerfully proclaimed by Burton: "The world shall end like a Comedy, and we shall meet at last in heaven and live in bliss together" (p. 963).

Burton also observes, however, that "Continual meditation of God's judgments troubles many" (p. 940), and in "At the round earths imagin'd corners" Donne's speaker seems to invite trouble. The sonnet preceding this one (in both Grierson's and Gardner's orderings) is "This is my playes last scene." Thus a poem dealing with the speaker's imminent death is followed by one in which he calls for the death of the world itself. The latter opens busily and stridently, with the issuance of rapid-fire imperatives: "blow," "arise," "goe." Indeed, readers must be forgiven if initially they assume that the speaker is the Almighty himself. Considering, however, that Donne's speaker is a mere mortal—how "mere" he is ever fond of telling us—taking upon himself to command what only Divine Providence can ordain, his presumption is breathtaking. His progressive multiplication of items in lines 5–8 requires that they be read with increasing rapidity, thus intensifying the manic quality of the octet. The sudden shift of mood with line 9 is almost histrionic: "But let them sleepe, Lord, and mee morne a space." Grandiosity gives way to guilt: "For, if above all these, my sinnes abound, / 'Tis late to aske abundance of thy grace." Burton notes that the "main matter which terrifies and torments" victims of religious melancholy is "the enormity of their offenses" (p. 951). Although Donne's speaker admittedly only considers the possibility that he is preeminent among sinners, that consideration smacks of a kind of perverse egotism that is merely the inverse of the hubris that marks the sonnet's opening lines.[17] He is not that truly world-class sinner, Milton's Satan, and thus he is wrong in assuming that God's grace has a time limit. Burton is more conversant with common theological knowledge: quoting "St. Austin," he says to his reader, "Comfort thyself, no time is over-past, 'tis never too late" (p. 955).

"Teach me how to repent" is the murmuring of one who has only just ceased to issue orders to the Almighty and his angels. That repentance is a kind of skill that needs to be taught is yet another instance of the confusion of Donne's persona. Somehow he has failed to understand that, as Burton puts it, "A desire to repent, is repentance itself, though not in nature, yet in God's acceptance; a willing mind is sufficient" (p. 195).

What most marks the confusion of Donne's speaker, however, is his claim that learning how to repent will be "as good / As if thou'hadst seal'd my pardon, with thy blood." The conditional mood used here is shocking if not heretical. There is no need to cite church doctrine to confirm that Christ has indeed sealed all pardons: readers can hear

---

17. Other readers have remarked on this sonnet's oddity. Wall, "Donne's Wit of Redemption," suggests that the speaker achieves reconciliation with the deity but then retreats from it (p. 198). French, "The Psychopathology of Donne's *Holy Sonnets*," regards the entire poem as "confused" and sees its speaker as "bluffing" (p. 115). Carey, *Life, Mind and Art*, comments on the "characteristic display of egotism" in the poem (p. 229).

the speaker's own voice proclaim (in "Oh my blacke Soule!"): "wash thee in Christs blood, which hath this might / That being red, it dyes red soules to white." Paradoxically, the theological confusion of Donne's speaker makes it clear that intellectualization, and specifically the doctrinal interpretation of life situations, is his primary coping strategy. No matter that he sometimes *mis*interprets: so long as a concept increases his ability to adjust to his situation it serves its purpose for the speaker—as well as for any reader who fails to notice its invalidity. This adaptive (conscious) strategy is complemented in this sonnet by a defensive (unconscious) strategy: implicit in the speaker's rhetoric is the replacement of an untenable power fantasy, in which he presides over the world's destruction, by a more appropriate fantasy of submission, in which he represents himself as suppliant, student, and criminal.

Yet another fantasy, this time of intellectual dominance, is embodied in "If poysonous mineralls." However it, too, collapses under the onslaught of the speaker's superego. His question concerning the damnation-proof creatures implies, as French points out, a "vehement protest at the world-order that makes him a man and therefore damnable; and that in turn implies a criticism of God." But the speaker's argument is specious, based on a false analogy between different levels of the great chain of being. It is not the inadequacy of his logic, however, that causes the sudden alternation of the speaker's mood in the sestet, but an attack of anxiety arising out of his recollection that God is capable of "sterne wrath" as well as mercy. The speaker's response to this fear is submission and a plea that God forget him, which, as French notes, "is scarcely the same as exercising that mercy which is so easy and so glorious."[18] The idea of Omniscience forgetting, besides being yet another indication of the speaker's theological ineptitude, concludes the sonnet with what might pass as wit, but, given the tone, seems more like spiritual confusion. Even more importantly, the speaker's impulse toward oblivion, reflecting so different a mood from that with which the poem began, suggests that he is sinking into depression. He seems perilously close to despair, and "this kind of persons," observes Burton, for the most part "make away with themselves" (p. 949). In such a state, reading—or writing—*Biathanatos* could be dangerous.[19]

IV

As has been suggested above, it is hardly possible to read more than a few of the Holy Sonnets without encountering marked alternations of mood between as well as within individual poems. "As due by many titles," for example, opens with a quiet recitation of doctrinal commonplaces that establishes the speaker's total dependency on and submission to the deity. On the surface, the poem's octet suggests not only the speaker's understanding and acceptance of his relationship with God but also an easy compatibility between his ego and his superego. On the other hand, the legalistic

18. French, "The Psychopathology of Donne's *Holy Sonnets*," pp. 111, 112.
19. Carey, *Life, Mind and Art*, remarks, "In Donne's day the natural outcome of religious despair was suicide. It was the devil's masterpiece" (p. 54).

and mercantile metaphors employed here may reveal a latent tension that is eventually expressed in the anguished outburst of the sestet's first line: "Why doth the devill then usurpe in mee?" The concluding mood of the poem is one of depression so profound as to verge on hysteria: "Oh I shall soone despaire."[20]

In Grierson's ordering the next poem in the sequence is "O Might those sighes and teares," classified by Gardner as a "penitential sonnet." Here Donne's speaker, though he is in the grip of strong emotions, is able to make spiritually productive use of his "holy discontent." In Gardner's ordering, however, "As due by many titles" is followed by "Oh my blacke Soule," which reverses the bipolar pattern of its predecessor. The passivity of the speaker in "As due by many titles," neglected (he alleges) by God, possessed, even ravished by the Devil, is present as well in the opening lines of "Oh my blacke Soule" in the summoning of the hapless speaker by imperious sickness, "deaths herald, and champion."[21] Contrition, however, rather than near hysteria is the predominant mood here. Donne's speaker feels guilt more than abandonment, associating himself with traitors and thieves. Guilt, according to contemporary psychiatric theory, "signals superego protest and, therefore, indicates tension between the ego and the superego" (the kind of tension, as mentioned above, implicit in the octet of the previous sonnet). "[Such guilt] normally elicits the desire to conciliate the superego and whatever parental or community authority may share the influence of the superego at the moment."[22] Thus the shift of mood in the sestet—"Yet grace, if thou repent, thou canst not lacke"—is clinically as well as poetically predictable. Once more Donne's

20. "As due by many titles" is one of the poems on which Stachniewski focuses in order "to establish a strong Calvinist influence on Donne's 'Holy Sonnets'" ("The Despair of the 'Holy Sonnets,'" p. 677): "The doctrinal base of the poem is decidedly Lutheran and Calvinist" because it implies that God intervenes only arbitrarily on behalf of individuals (p. 701). One of the difficulties with Stachniewski's reading of this sonnet and of the collection as a whole is that he assumes—indeed asserts—that the speaker of the Holy Sonnets is no less and no more than John Donne himself. This claim is made in spite of the fact that in none of the sonnets does Donne invite an autobiographical reading by supplying specific cues—as he does in the case of such divine poems as "Goodfriday, 1613. Riding Westward" and "A Hymne to Christ, at the Authors last going into Germany." By identifying Donne the man with the sonnets' speaker, Stachniewski is forced to adopt the viewpoint that everything the speaker says is a "true" representation of Donne's personal beliefs—even as he is forced to acknowledge that in his sermons Dr. Donne could attack Calvinist interpretations (p. 701). What we are being asked to accept then, apparently, is that Donne was a closet Calvinist.

But Stachniewski's colleague, John Carey, takes a less extreme view, suggesting that Donne was "deeply influenced by Calvinism" but was an admirer of Aquinas, too, and in the end adhered to the more "moderate" (Aquinian) view (*Life, Mind and Art*, pp. 240, 242). The present essay adopts a yet more conservative view—that, in the Holy Sonnets, Donne creates a speaker who often errs (as speakers in his Songs and Sonets often err) and who thus, like the erring characters of the drama, takes on interest and serves as something of an object lesson. The latter approach would seem to have the additional benefit of preserving the traditional sense of the Holy Sonnets as the product of the genius of a recent Catholic and future Dean of St. Paul's.

21. Stachniewski observes that "extreme passivity is a strikingly consistent feature of the sonnets" ("The Despair of the 'Holy Sonnets,'" p. 699) and sees such passivity as another indication of the collection's Calvinist tendencies—that modification of the doctrine of prevenient grace that holds that God often denies such grace because he has not willed to save the majority of mankind. But Stachniewski's analysis of "Oh my blacke Soule" as an example of such passivity glosses over the sonnet's last four lines, in which a marked shift in mood takes place.

22. Ostow, "Religion and Psychiatry," p. 3200.

speaker performs a psychological adaptation, consciously bringing doctrine (in this case, correct doctrine, that of the Atonement) to bear on his spiritual state. As one of the cures for religious melancholy, Burton recommends "hearing, reading of scriptures, good Divines, good advice and conference, applying God's words" (p. 950). In the case of the sonnet in question, such therapy seems to work: the passive verbs of the poem's octet give way to active ones—"make thy selfe," "wash thee"—as the depression of the opening lines gives way to the positive prospect of a soul dyed newly white by Christ's blood.

At this point it may be recalled that the blood of Christ also figured importantly in the octet of "As due by many titles." Thus the reader following Gardner's order will have come full circle, in the space of but twenty-eight lines encountering pious resignation, near despair, profound guilt, and preparation to receive God's grace. In Grierson's ordering the reader must respond to even more marked alternations in mood, from the near hysteria that characterizes the conclusion of "As due by many titles" to the achieved state of contrition with which "O Might those sighes and teares" begins. Donne is always a demanding poet, but perhaps nowhere more emotionally demanding than in the Holy Sonnets.

V

One argument against the thesis proposed by this essay is that bipolarity or mood swings are characteristic of the sonnet form itself, its traditionally reflexive structure, with sestets reversing octets, couplets turning upon quatrains. This generalization is belied, however, by at least five of Donne's own sonnets, poems that exhibit a high degree of internal consistency in mood and theme. "This is my playes last scene," for example, is the Christian "comedy" described by Burton, a miniature religious drama with a happy ending: "For thus I leave the world, the flesh, and devill." Although Donne's speaker experiences one difficult moment, when he envisions seeing "that face, / Whose feare already shakes [his] every joynt," the mood of the poem as a whole is composed. The piling-up of metaphors, near-clichés really, for death in the octet defuses the anxiety normally attendant on dying, and the sestet's mood is marked by a conviction of salvation. To call this sonnet manic would be to go too far, but it does exhibit some of that state's symptoms, a mood that is "elevated" and "expansive" and a mind set tending toward the "flight of ideas"—"Then, as my soule, to'heaven her first seate, takes flight."[23]

Similarly, "Spit in my face, yee Jewes," for all the theatrics of its octet, never wavers from the commonplaces of Christian dogma and, as a consequence, largely sustains a mood of spiritual confidence. Again, there is an almost manic quality to the poem. So melodramatic is its adherence to the principle of the Imitation of Christ that new readers might well infer that the outburst of lines 1–2 is being voiced by the Savior himself. Though the next line and the rest of the octet feature a role reversal—the

---

23. Wolpert, "Major Affective Disorders," p. 1323.

speaker now imitating the impious Jews—this procedure, too, is doctrinally correct: man's sinfulness, though inevitable, is inevitably painful to Christ. The speaker's insistence that he is a more grievous sinner even than Christ's historical tormentors is a variation on the strain of inverse narcissism to be encountered elsewhere in the Holy Sonnets, but it is consistent with the speaker's identifying himself with the martyred god-figure of lines 1–2. ("Loosened associations" and "inflated self-esteem," it should be noted, are also characteristic of manic episodes.)[24] Indeed, this sonnet well illustrates the "overdetermination" so characteristic of Donne's poetry (and of complex literature generally): at the deepest levels of its psychological structure this poem provides its readers with materials not only for the evocation of unconscious narcissistic fantasies but also for sado-masochistic fantasies (torturers/victim) and for Oedipal fantasies (surrogate son supplanting surrogate father).[25]

In marked contrast to the aesthetic and psychological patternings of "Spit in my face, yee Jewes" is another of Donne's less reflexive sonnets, "What if this present were the worlds last night?" In the octet of this meditation Donne's speaker wittily converts the convention of the catalog of beauties into an enumeration of the facial features of the tortured deity and the logic of love's religion into doctrine: "This beauteous forme assures a pitious minde." For French this line reduces the Christian paradox of an "infinitely merciful and loving being who can yet send people to eternal damnation" into "a piece of sophistry," and for Carey its effect is "gruesome" and it constitutes "blasphemy."[26] But, as was noted above, as a phenomenon psychological adaptation does not demand intellectual rigor: whatever may be effective in warding off anxiety— "can that tongue adjudge thee unto hell, / Which pray'd forgivenesse for his foes fierce spight?"—will serve. The poem's shift of subject from its re-creation of the Crucifixion in its composition-of-place stage to its analysis of love's philosophy does not also entail a radical shift in mood. Burton, of course, distinguishes between love melancholy and religious melancholy, but he tentatively classifies the latter as a subdivision of the former (p. 886). (At the age of twenty-three, we recall, Jack Donne had his portrait painted as a love-melancholiac.)

Religious melancholy could be "counter-poised," according to Burton, by "comfortable speeches, exhortations, arguments" (p. 950). This remedy seemingly proves effective in three other "unipolar" sonnets: "Why are wee by all creatures waited on," "Wilt thou love God, as he thee," and "Father, part of his double interest." None of these is predominantly manic or depressive. All are "wholsome meditations" that provide the reader of any text of the Holy Sonnets with respites from the intensity and the mood swings of other poems in the sequence. In these three sonnets there is no discernible tension between the speaker's ego and superego, and no radical shift in mood between octet and sestet. Both "Wilt thou love God, as he thee" and "Father, part

24. Ibid., p. 1323.

25. Carey refers to a "hunger for pain" that is "clamorously explicit" in "Spit in my face, yee Jewes," a poem that begins, he says, in "ecstatic masochism" (*Life, Mind and Art*, p. 48).

26. French, "The Psychopathology of Donne's *Holy Sonnets*," p. 113; and Carey, *Life, Mind and Art*, p. 47.

of his double interest" are notable for their father-son motifs. For Freud, of course, the concept of God was "a cosmic projection of the Father of our childhood," and it is a commonplace of modern psychiatry that, in Mortimer Ostow's words, "The prospect of depression frequently motivates a person to attach himself . . . to a parental protector . . . or may take the form simply . . . of a filial, devotional attitude toward God."[27] The two sonnets in question, then, constitute "comfortable speeches" because, for all their literary and theological sophistication, in psychiatric terms they license a regression into an earlier state, that of a nurturing childhood. In these poems (as so often in life) such regression has positive effects, providing the ego with its required reinforcement and placating the usually unrelenting superego.

VI

Serving to counteract the three "wholsome meditations" and thus to destabilize readers of the Holy Sonnets — as the sonnets discussed in section III destabilize by radical mood swings *within* their fourteen-line structures — is another group of poems whose consistency resides in their moods of almost unrelieved depression. The speaker of these sonnets is well described in Burton's terms as one of "those poor distressed souls" whose bodies seem "predisposed by melancholy," who are "religiously given," and who are excessively afflicted by "tender consciences" (p. 940). Three centuries after the publication of the *Anatomy*, Freud described the superego in language ("the severity of this agency," "its cruelty")[28] that recalls Burton's characterization of the conscience: "A continual testor to give in evidence, to empanel a Jury to examine us, to cry guilty, a persecutor with hue and cry to follow, a baliff to carry us, a Serjeant to arrest, an Attorney to plead against us, a gaoler to torment, a Judge to condemn, still accusing, denouncing, torturing, molesting" (p. 943).

Three of the Holy Sonnets in particular present this image of the superego as moral tyrant: "Thou has made me," "I am a little world made cunningly," and "O Might those sighes and teares returne againe." In Grierson's ordering these poems are interspersed with mood-swing sonnets ("As due by many titles," "Oh my blacke Soule'); in Gardner's they are together, a trilogy of depression preceded by "Father, part of his double interest," a "wholsome meditation," and followed by the reflexive "If faithfull soules be alike glorif'd." Belonging with these, but separated from them in both orderings is "Batter my heart, three person'd God." All four sonnets allow the reader "no ease." All four illustrate an ego generating anxiety in response to guilt, and in each the corollary of emotional trauma is a passivity (conveyed by a number of intransitive verbs and passive voice constructions) reminiscent of the state labeled "psychomotor retardation" in modern psychiatry.

In "Thou hast made me" the speaker is all but catatonic: "I dare not move my dimme

---

27. Freud, *The Standard Edition of the Complete Psychological Works of Sigmund Freud*, ed. James Strachey et al., 24 vols. (London: Hogarth Press, 1964), 3:128; and Ostow, "Religion and Psychiatry," p. 3199.

28. See Freud's "The Dissection of the Psychical Personality," in *Complete Psychological Works of Freud*, ed. Strachey et al., 22:61–62.

eyes any way"; "not one houre I can my selfe sustaine." In his rhetoric he reduces him-self to an artifact: "Thout has made me"; "thy worke"; "Repaire me." If he is man, he is a hollow man, with "febled flesh," or he is but a sack of sin, wholly dependent on outside forces to prevent his plummet into hell. Such spiritual impotence is also to be found in "I am a little world made cunningly" and "Batter my heart, three per-son'd God." At the same time, both poems are fraught with aggression – but aggression that Donne's speaker calls down on himself. Steig has observed that "images of sex and violence are closely intertwined" in "Batter my heart, three-person'd God,"[29] and such is also the case with "I am a little world made cunningly," in which rather routine sins like "Lust and envie" call forth apocalyptic action – "Drowne," "burne" – directed not at the macrocosm but at the microcosmic "me." The materials for masochistic fan-tasy are so far from being latent in both poems that they have been known to make even experienced scholars wince. More pertinent here, however, is the curious fact that, though both poems display major depression, their energy levels are nothing less than manic. They are dynamic poems about paralysis.

"O Might those sighes and teares returne againe" is more conventional, a sonnet whose mood of depression is relieved only by the oxymoron "holy discontent." The phrase implies that the speaker understands, with Burton, that "affliction is a School or Academy, wherein the best Scholars are prepared to the Commencement of the Deity" (p. 965). But such, finally, is not the case with Donne's speaker. Though he is repentant, grief is his past, his present, and his future, "Th'effect and cause, the pun-ishment and sinne." Regretful for his lapse into love melancholy – "In mine Idolatry what showres of raine / Mine eyes did waste" – he is too full of self-pity, "(poore) me," to recognize that he has fallen prey to religious melancholy.

"That there is such a distinct species of Love-melancholy," says Burton, "no man hath ever doubted; but whether this subdivision of Religious Melancholy be warrant-able, it may be controverted" (p. 866). Yet the organization of the *Anatomy* aligns its author with those who "do not obscurely make a distinct species of it, dividing Love-Melancholy into that whose object is women; & into the other, whose object is God" (p. 867). Donne's "Since she whome I lovd" is likewise ambivalent: its speaker implies that it is only since his "good" has died that his commitment to "heavenly things" has been total, yet he also claims that his earthly love "did whett" his mind to seek God. The actual subject of this sonnet, however, is not love but the speaker's religious melan-choly, made manifest in his "inordinate desire that God provide him with further in-dications of his love, some assurance that he is in a state of grace."[30] Burton affirms that religious melancholy can be brought on by such "dismal accidents" as the "loss of friends" (p. 939), but Donne's speaker seems reconciled to his loss. He is even capable of self-diagnosis, acknowledging that God's gift of perfect and complete love should cure his "holy thirsty dropsy." That knowledge does not prove therapeutic, however,

29. Steig, "Donne's Divine Rapist," p. 54.
30. Peterson, "Anglican Doctrine of Contrition," pp. 515–16.

and in the poem's last four lines the speaker's ego unconsciously attempts to defend against anxiety by projecting that anxiety onto God, attributing to the Omniscient some uncertainty as to whether he (the speaker) will ultimately attain salvation.

Anxiety is also present, but less obviously so, in "Show me deare Christ, thy spouse." In "Satyre III" the admonition to "Seeke true religion" (line 43) is directed toward a silent auditor, apparently a young ne'er-do-well; here Donne's persona is himself the seeker. And despite all this apostrophe's outward and visible signs of control—its historical perspective, its satire, and its wit—the speaker's anxiety, not unmixed, perhaps, with latent hostility, is suggested in its concluding metaphor of Christ as Pandarus to the pious and the True Church as his Holy Whore, "Who is most trew, and pleasing to thee, then, / When she is embrac'd and open to most men." Those "several Oppositions, Heresies [and] Schisms" abroad in the world, complains Burton, both exemplify and cause religious melancholy: they "dementate men's minds" (p. 912).

By placing "Oh, to vex me, contraryes meete in one" last in Donne's sequence, editors may effect their own wish-fulfillment fantasy, providing the Holy Sonnets with, if not exactly a happy ending, at least an ending that is ego-reinforcing and thus therapeutic. Although this poem will not make it easy for readers to transform Donne's collection into a divine comedy, neither will it readily lend itself to serving as the denouement of some Christian tragedy. For it may be that in this sonnet Donne's speaker comes closest to an accurate diagnosis of his own religious melancholy, his mind diseased, and thus he becomes more capable of ministering unto himself. For one, he acknowledges his mood swings: "Inconstancy unaturally hath begott / A constant habit; that when I would not / I change in vowes, and in devotione." Moreover, he seems to recognize that his condition is a chronic one: "As humorous is my contritione / As my prophane Love, and as soone forgott: / As ridlingly distemperd, cold and hott." He seems aware that the remedy may lie in his understanding that, though his "fitts come and go away," they are "devout fitts," due to an "excess" rather than a "defect" of piety, as Burton explains; it is the malady of those who "do go astray, are zealous without knowledge, and too solicitous about that which is not necessary" (p. 873). Coping with such an affliction is, paradoxically, facilitated by the very strength of the affliction. To be vexed by contraries, according to Burton, may even be a sign of divine intervention in one's case: "God often works by contrarieties, he first kills, and then makes alive, he woundeth first, and then healeth, he makes man sow in teares, that he may reap in joy; 'tis God's method" (p. 967). It may be no delusion then to conclude that "Those are my best dayes, when I shake with feare."

A "fantasique ague" like religious melancholy can never be wholly cured. Even with modern chemical techniques the recovery rate averages only 65 percent.[31] Nevertheless, the kind of incipient control implied in "Oh to vex me, contraryes meete in one" may warrant an optimistic prognosis. This traditional conclusion of the Holy Sonnets, then, may be seen as pointing readers of Donne toward his *Devotions upon Emer-*

---

31. Wolpert, "Major Affective Disorders," p. 1326.

gent Occasions. In the morality-play structure and orthodoxly Christian content of this prose work they will encounter adaptational and defensive strategies so successful that neither the ravages of spotted fever nor the residues of religious melancholy are capable of undermining the ego of a human being wholly bent upon holy dying.

In the final analysis, the impact of the Holy Sonnets on readers depends neither on the collection's supposed "plot" nor on that plot's ultimate mood. For they are, in the main, poems meant to vex, to be as unsettling in their own modest scale as Shakespeare's portrayal of the melancholy prince. Whether *Hamlet* or the Holy Sonnets ever prevented or cured an affective disorder may be doubted. What can scarcely be doubted is that they constitute powerful dramatizations of how deeply rooted melancholy is in human nature and in the human condition.

11. CONVERSION OF THE READER IN DONNE'S "ANATOMY OF THE WORLD"

KATHLEEN KELLY

Since Louis Martz first lifted them up for modern critical attention, John Donne's *Anniversaries* have attracted sufficient scholarship to help us deal with the major obstacles readers of the poems have traditionally encountered. Especially troublesome has been "The First Anniversarie: An Anatomy of the World," with its apparent breaches of decorum, its illogical causality, and its mixed genre. Readers have wondered how Elizabeth Drury could be worthy of such exorbitant praise, how her death could be said to be the "cause" of the world's fall from original grace, and how an elegy praising this girl relates to what seems to some to be the real concern of the poem, a complaint against the corruption of the world. Of all that has been offered, perhaps Barbara K. Lewalski's comprehensive study of the poem's literary and intellectual contexts best helps us with these questions.[1] Yet, even seeing the poem in relation to its precedents, the reader may still feel uncomfortable with the "Anatomy." Lewalski has pointed out that her work, by focusing on theme and structure, excludes other elements in the experience of the poem and that, for all our understanding, the "poems may continue to repel or antagonize us as readers."[2] Perhaps this is because, to borrow a phrase from Stanley Fish, critics have been doing less "focusing on the mind in the act of making sense, . . . than on the sense it finally (and often reductively) makes."[3] Of course, even without explicitly saying so, much good criticism of the poem has illuminated the reader's mind "in the act of making sense." But, on the whole, critics have fo-

---

1. Barbara K. Lewalski, *Donne's "Anniversaries" and the Poetry of Praise: The Creation of a Symbolic Mode* (Princeton: Princeton University Press, 1973). For a summary of the critical approaches to the question of how Elizabeth may be understood as object of such hyperbolic praise, see Lewalski, pp. 108-11. On the issue of causality, see especially Earl Miner, *The Metaphysical Mode from Donne to Cowley* (Princeton: Princeton University Press, 1969), pp. 63-66; and Harold Love, "The Argument of Donne's *First Anniversary*," *MP* 64 (1966), 125-31. On the issue of genre, see the summary note in Lewalski, p. 11, but especially Rosalie L. Colie, "'All in Peeces': Problems of Interpretation in Donne's Anniversary Poems," in *Just So Much Honor: Essays Commemorating the Four-Hundredth Anniversary of the Birth of John Donne*, ed. Peter Amadeus Fiore (University Park: Pennsylvania State University Press, 1972), pp. 189-218; see as well W. M. Lebans, "Donne's *Anniversaries* and the Tradition of Funeral Elegy," *ELH* 39 (1972), 545-59, and Paul A. Parrish, "Poet, Audience, and the Word: An Approach to the *Anniversaries*," in *New Essays on Donne*, ed. Gary A. Stringer (Salzburg: Institut für Englische Sprache und Literatur, 1977), pp. 110-39. For an annotated bibliography of writings on the *Anniversaries*, 1942-1972, see Louis L. Martz, "Donne's *Anniversaries* Revisited," in *That Subtle Wreath: Lectures Presented at the Quartercentenary Celebration of the Birth of John Donne*, ed. Margaret W. Pepperdene (Atlanta: Agnes Scott College, 1973), pp. 29-50.

2. Lewalski explains her focus thus: "I have concentrated upon theme and structure. . . . As a result of this focus the pyrotechnics of wit and language-play in these brilliant works may receive somewhat short shrift" (*Donne's Anniversaries*, p. 7). I argue here that the relation between reader and speaker might also bear more attention. Regarding the poems repelling us, Lewalski goes on to say that Donne "exploits for literary effect the slight shock and tension which even the informed reader must experience; . . . this tension will be found to be a source of [the poems'] special power" (pp. 219-20); but, so far as I can determine, she does not demonstrate how.

3. Stanley E. Fish, *Self-Consuming Artifacts: The Experience of Seventeenth-Century Literature* (Berkeley:

cused not on the reader of the poem but on the person or audience whom the speaker states or implies he is addressing.[4] Yet it is precisely because there is often a great distance between dramatic audience and reader, as well as between speaker and poet, that the problems with decorum, causality, and genre arise. By looking closely at the introduction to the "Anatomy," I hope to demonstrate that Donne creates a speaker who is initially distanced from both poet and reader, demanding that we be an audience we initially cannot be. But, by insisting that despite our resistance we are his audience, the speaker draws us into the anatomy, and there causes us to undergo a conversion to his world: eventually poet, speaker, audience, and reader join in celebrating both Elizabeth and our own hopes for a spiritual life.

In considering the relations among poet, speaker, audience, and reader, we are entering territory well marked by Earl Miner, who has studied seventeenth-century poetry largely in these terms, using them to define the public, private, and social modes. The primary distinction between the public or social mode and the private, according to Miner, is that in the private mode the speaker and his dramatic audience are considerably detached from the reader: reader and speaker have distinct, sometimes antagonistic values. But in the public and, though less so, social modes, a dramatic audience does not separate speaker from reader: speaker and reader share proper norms and a common history that permit the use of allusion and public detail. Miner describes the effects on the reader of shifts in these relations: On the one hand, "the extent to which [speaker and person addressed] are fictional divides the poet from his speaker and the dramatic audience from the reader. On the other hand, . . . to the degree that the speaker and the poet move closer together, . . . the reader as audience . . . is set at greater distance. And to the degree that the reader is addressed, the dramatic audience grows distant." Miner discusses Donne specifically: "The remarkable thing about Donne's poetry is that in it he shifts the audience addressed, or its distance from him and from the reader, with such astonishing ease."[5] The "Anatomy," however, is an exception to Miner's observation because, although it is full of such shifts, it is thereby both more

---

University of California Press, 1972), p. xii. I am aware of the pitfalls of speaking of "the reader's" experience, as if there were only one informed reading. This article is an attempt to persuade the "interpretive community" (to borrow another phrase from Fish) of what I think is one possible "informed" reading.

4. Lewalski is characteristic in this regard. She raises the question of how we are to understand the several "worlds" the speaker addresses (the "sicke" world, the "dead" world, the "new" world), makes intelligent distinctions among them, and then suggests that the speaker identifies his auditory sometimes with one and sometimes with another of these worlds (*Donne's Anniversaries*, pp. 240–43). But the question of how the reader goes along with these identifications imposed by the speaker remains open. O. B. Hardison, Jr., identifies the dramatic audience exclusively with Elizabeth's admirers and so neglects the speaker's overtures to a larger, more public audience (*The Enduring Monument: A Study of the Idea of Praise in Renaissance Literary Theory and Practice* [Chapel Hill: University of North Carolina Press, 1962], pp. 173–74). Finally, those who read the *Anniversaries* as a private meditation concentrate on defining the experience of the speaker, identifying him with the poet, rather than on the experience of the reader: see Louis L. Martz, *The Poetry of Meditation: A Study in English Religious Literature of the Seventeenth Century*, rev. ed. (New Haven: Yale University Press, 1962), pp. 211–48; and Carol M. Sicherman, "Donne's Timeless *Anniversaries*," *UTQ* 39 (1970), 127–43.

5. Miner, *The Metaphysical Mode*, pp. 18, 20.

astonishing and less easy. Whereas usually in Donne's poetry we know where to stand in relation to the speaker and audience addressed, in the "Anatomy" our relation with the speaker is extremely difficult.

In contrast to the "Anatomy," Donne's other elegiac poems, for example, address a public or social audience with which we can readily identify. Speaker and reader share a common sense of the subject's significance and relevance to the world. Even amid such apparently complicated shifts as that in "Elegie on Mris. Boulstred," in which the speaker begins by addressing death as a dramatic audience and then turns to the reader, we need not be confused about our relation to the speaker:

> Death I recant, and say, unsaid by mee
> What ere hath slip'd, that might diminish thee.
> Spirituall treason, atheisme 'tis, to say,
> That any can thy Summons disobey.
> Th'earths face is but thy Table; there are set
> Plants, cattell, men, dishes for Death to eate.
> In a rude hunger now hee millions drawes
> Into his bloody, or plaguy, or serv'd jawes. (1–7)

In line 6, the speaker shifts from directly addressing death to referring to "Death" in the third person and thus turning to the reader as the person addressed. But we can readily accept this invitation to become his audience, for, although the speaker has been apostrophizing a monstrous personification of death, we can assent to this depiction of death's rapaciousness. We can become his audience because we share a common sense of the world.

Conversely, in many of Donne's lyrics, the speaker alienates his reader by creating an audience role the reader must refuse to play, but both poet and reader understand this. Often it is in this very divergence that the wit of the poem lives. At the end of Donne's lyric "Communitie," for example, the speaker directly addresses the audience with a rhetorical question:

> Chang'd loves are but chang'd sorts of meat,
> And when hee hath the kernell eate,
> Who doth not fling away the shell? (22–24)

This question invites the audience's participation, but the proposition of the argument, that mistresses are to be enjoyed then flung away, forces us to distance ourselves from the audience addressed. From this distance we can be amused by this cavalier's inventive casuistry, but we do not assent to his version of the world.

Regardless of whether the speaker and reader are distanced or close, what both these elegiac and lyric examples have in common with most of Donne's other poetry is that the message to the reader is clear. Either the speaker is following the norms of the community or he is not. In the "Anatomy," however, the message is very mixed, the speaker seeming to speak with two voices. On the one hand he appeals to a common concern for the good in a reasonable, Christian vocabulary; on the other hand he refers to earthquakes and cataclysms and seems to speak from an extremity outside the bounds of ordinary human community. Yet he insists we see the world as he does. He at once forces the reader away from him and yet strongly pulls him close. This push and pull is most evident in the introduction, lines 1–90, where speaker and reader must first establish their relations. If we chart the reader's progress through the introduction, we see that the reader's major difficulties with decorum, causality, and genre arise out of this insecure relation with the speaker. Yet in provoking this fitful, often antagonistic relation with the reader, Donne sets the stage for the anatomy proper, where the speaker's strange and alien world becomes the reader's own. The introduction calls up a world of decorum and causality that the anatomy itself obviates.[6]

In his title—*An Anatomy of the World. Wherein, By occasion of the untimely death of Mistris Elizabeth Drury the frailty and the decay of the whole World is represented*—the speaker's voice is reasoned and objective: a death is to be considered an "occasion" for reflection, in this case an "anatomy," that will represent the decay of the world. We expect perhaps a somber memento mori, perhaps a controlled elegy, certainly a well-ordered public dissection of a subject.

Yet the first lines tell us this is no reasoned public demonstration, but one for an intimate audience: "When that rich soule which to her Heaven is gone, / Whom all do celebrate, who know they'have one" (1–2). Presumably all public readers know they have souls, but very few know of Elizabeth Drury, much less consciously celebrate her soul. Thus the public reader is immediately excluded from the audience addressed in favor of those readers who have known Elizabeth Drury. It seems O. B. Hardison was right when he declared that the rules of decorum require the audience to be Elizabeth's acquaintances and admirers.[7] We are distanced observers as the speaker addresses an intimate audience.

Yet, before this speaker allows us to draw the line between his world and ours, he makes room for us:

(For who is sure he hath a soule, unlesse
It see, and Judge, and follow worthinesse,
And by Deedes praise it? He who doth not this,
May lodge an In-mate soule, but tis not his.) (3–6)

Anyone who seeks worthiness, the speaker claims, qualifies as a celebrator of Elizabeth; as readers we may yet find in this anatomy some direct message for ourselves. While we will not say that this speaker entirely appreciates our world—his introduction presumes too much our intimacy with his subject—yet we have evidence that he is concerned not to lose a public reader.

6. Readers may recognize the "self-consuming" nature of this interpretation. For a different and very fine article in the same self-consuming vein, see Ruth A. Fox, "Donne's *Anniversaries* and the Art of Living," *ELH* 38 (1971), 528–41.

7. Hardison, *The Enduring Monument*, p. 174.

The speaker has thus in the same breath broken and repaired the rules of decorum, and, as if aware that our energies are spent defining our relation to him, without finishing his sentence he begins again with another "when" clause:

> When that Queene ended here her progresse time,
> And, as t'her standing house, to heaven did clymbe,
> Where, loth to make the Saints attend her long,
> Shee's now a part both of the Quire, and Song,
> This world, in that great earth-quake languished;
> For in a common Bath of teares it bled,
> Which drew the strongest vitall spirits out. . . . (7–13)

But again he has broken decorum. The allusion to "that great earth-quake" excludes us from his active audience; we simply do not share that experience in common. That the earth mourns the loss of a beloved is a conceit allowed pastoral figures and grieving lovers, families, and friends, but to say the earth mourned Elizabeth "in a common Bath of teares," to say the entire world was animated exclusively by her and died when her soul left it, is to imply that she was a great public figure.[8] The fact that she is an obscure girl forces us to step out of the world the speaker had just accommodated to us, or else, as several critics have attempted, to read into the poem instead of Elizabeth Drury some more illustrious personage—Queen Elizabeth, St. Lucy, Wisdom, The Blessed Virgin.[9]

Subsequent lines only contribute to our confused relation with the speaker. Following the same pattern of exclusion then accommodation, in lines 14–24 the speaker still claims that the world is desperately affected by the loss of Elizabeth, yet he allows us the appearance of normalcy:

> But succor'd then with a perplexed doubt,
> Whether the world did loose or gaine in this,
> (Because since now no other way there is
> But goodnes, to see her, whom all would see,
> All must endeavour to be good as shee,)
> This great consumption to a fever turn'd,
> And so the world had fits; it joy'd, it mourn'd.
> And, as men thinke, that Agues physicke are,
> And th'Ague being spent, give over care,
> So thou, sicke world, mistak'st thy selfe to bee
> Well, when alas, thou'rt in a Letargee. (14–24)

Insofar as Elizabeth was an innocent child, we can agree with the speaker that "all must endevour to be good as shee" (18), but his claim that the world is deathly ill because of Elizabeth's death belongs in the same category as his claim for earthquakes.

---

8. On the "nature reversed" or "world upsidedown" commonplace in epideictic poetry, see ibid., pp. 116–17.
9. See Lewalski's summary of this critical approach, *Donne's Anniversaries*, p. 108.

These may be the speaker's private, subjective experiences, but they are not our own. Again, however, before he loses us entirely the speaker makes a concession to our perception of the world. True, he tells us, the world does not look sick, but we think ourselves to be well only because we are "in a Letargee." Apparently the speaker is aware that our perceptions differ from his and is concerned that we do not therefore dismiss him. Here he has us caught. If we do not agree that Elizabeth's death made the world sick, it is because we are so sick we do not even realize we are.

Having given us enough to wonder about, the speaker leaves off addressing us directly and, in lines 22–62, dramatically addresses the "sicke world" that he claims is ours. During this address nothing essentially new happens to resolve our ambiguous relations: we still observe with consternation and detachment, but also with curiosity and mounting seriousness, a speaker strange to our world, referring to cataclysmic losses and addressing us as if we need to care and are one with him in this. What now becomes much stronger is the speaker's anger, his outrage, and his urgency that his truth be made known. Addressing the sick world, he harangues it:

> Her death did wound, and tame thee than, and than
> Thou mightst have better spar'd the Sunne, or Man;
> That wound was deepe, but 'tis more misery,
> That thou hast lost thy sense and memory.
> T'was heavy then to heare thy voyce of mone,
> But this is worse, that thou art speechlesse growne.
> Thou hast forgot thy name, thou hadst; thou wast
> Nothing but she, and her thou hast o'rpast. (25–32)

It begins to seem as if the reason the speaker resists the usual rules of decorum is that he is possessed of a truth so radical he has no energy to sustain the usual courtesies. Like the prophet calling "repent," he turns from us to his vision of a corrupt world, and back to us again, alternating horror with exhortation, and foreshadowing the movement of the anatomy itself.

In addition to the mounting anger and urgency that bid us to take him seriously, what also now comes to the fore is a suggestion as to why the speaker insists we share his experience of the world's earthquake:

> Some moneths she hath beene dead (but being dead,
> Measures of times are all determined)
> But long shee'ath beene away, long, long, yet none
> Offers to tell us who it is that's gone. (39–42)

The audience, the speaker has argued, must see the world the way he saw it when Elizabeth died, the vital spirits run out. Now we can begin to understand why, for with "Measures of times are all determined," the speaker suggests that the way the world appeared to him at Elizabeth's death is, in fact, what the world has truly been since Adam. Here is adumbrated the problem with causality that the reader will encounter full-force when the anatomy proper begins. How can Elizabeth cause the death of a world that has been corrupted since the fall of the angels? Critics have tried to excuse what they see as Donne's confusing sense of time or continual lapse of memory.[10] Rather than a flaw, however, this inconsistency is central to understanding our relations with the speaker. For to explain the inconsistency we must recognize that when the speaker tells us that Elizabeth's recent death has "caused" the death of the world, he is referring to his subjective experience at her death of "nature reversed" or the "world upsidedown." According to this topos, the grieving poet imposes his despair on the external world, seeing everything as out of joint. But, when Donne's speaker now tells us that the world has *always* been corrupt, he is referring to what he has come to realize is not the world of subjective despair but is, rather, objective reality. Before Elizabeth's death, because of her virtue, he was distracted from realizing the world's corruption. But now that this distraction is gone, he sees, and believes we also must see, our true condition. (In the anatomy proper the reader will hear him argue that Elizabeth's virtue gave heart and life to, and gilded into beauty, what in truth had always been an abhorrent carcass.) In this complicated permutation of the pathetic fallacy, Donne's speaker demands that we see what has recently become so obvious to him: that his subjective, desperate vision of the world caused by Elizabeth's death is in fact our real condition. He demands that we share his experience of Elizabeth's loss because we must all become mourners in this dead world.

In a final apparent concession to the reader's skepticism, the speaker attempts to demonstrate that he understands why no one has acknowledged the significance of Elizabeth's death, why no one has offered "to tell us who it is that's gone." We deny our world is dead, according to the speaker, out of fear: Mankind "Thought it some blasphemy to say sh'was dead" (51). And he explains why an anatomy is necessary:

> Her Ghost doth walke: that is, a glimmering light,
> A faint weake love of vertue and of good
> Reflects from her, on them which understood
> Her worth:
> . . . . . .
> Yet, because outward stormes the strongest breake,
> And strength it selfe by confidence growes weake,
> This new world may be safer, being told
> The dangers and diseases of the old:
> For with due temper men do then forgoe,
> Or covet things, when they their true worth know. (70–73, 85–90)

10. See, for example, Martz in *The Poetry of Meditation*: "A central inconsistency . . . defeats all Donne's efforts to bring its diverse materials under control" (p. 229); or Miner, *The Metaphysical Mode*, who identifies Elizabeth Drury as the "formal cause" for the earth's decay, which thus, according to Miner, makes chronology irrelevant: even though the world's consumption began long before Elizabeth, with the Fall, "it did not much matter to Donne that one part of his praise should be that her death should be made the cause of 'This great consumption' (19) of the world" (pp. 63–66).

This sounds like genuine concern for the reader's question: If Elizabeth is so important, why has no one before remarked her death? Yet the explanation raises the very questions it pretends to answer. Who understands Elizabeth's worth? In what sense can the world be said to have died? The speaker has only apparently answered the reader's objections, seeming to obey the familiar courtesies of discourse, trying again to keep us in his audience. The familiar Christian vocabulary also appears: we are "weedeless Paradises" (82), there are "serpents" (84), "storms," and "dangers and diseases" in this world that we must avoid. If we choose to identify ourselves with the speaker's remnant, we are promised "due temper" to know things for their "true worth." With such language the speaker again equates every Christian with the celebrators of Elizabeth's soul and suggests that we cannot afford *not* to be in his audience.

At the end of the introduction, then, where is the reader in relation to the speaker, particularly regarding the problems of decorum, causality, and genre? The difficulties can all be seen to arise from the speaker's claims that his subjective experience represents the objective world. Clearly, the speaker has broken the rules of decorum, praising an obscure girl as if she were queen or in some other way the fabric of the whole state. Yet, for all that, if we consider the speaker to have experienced crushing grief at the loss of the girl — and his nature reversed or world-upside-down conceit suggests this — we may be inclined to overlook the breach of decorum, especially since he seems so insistently to know some truth thereby.

As for causality, for how Elizabeth may be said to have stopped "Measures of times," so that, although recently dead, "long shee'ath beene away, long, long," so that somehow her death has caused the ruination of the world since the beginning of time, again we can only understand this in the context of the speaker's experience of Elizabeth's death. For the speaker, she sustained the illusion that this world had value. Now the illusion is gone and the truth revealed. It remains for the speaker to convince us of this truth.

Finally, regarding the question of genre, what is the connection between on the one hand the speaker's concern to praise Elizabeth and on the other his urgent need to convince us the world is corrupt? Again we look to the speaker to hold together these two intentions. Only the power of Elizabeth's virtue allowed him to experience what satisfaction he has had on this earth and, at her death, to realize the corruption of the world. While discussion of the world's corruption might well go on without discussing Elizabeth's death, in his experience the two subjects are bound together: to tell of his horror at the world is to tell of the world's loss of her virtue.

Thus, as long as we acknowledge Donne's fiction of a speaker affected desperately by grief, as long as we separate the poet and ourselves from the speaker, the difficulties with decorum, causality, and genre are greatly mitigated. To criticism of his hyperbolic praise of Elizabeth, Donne reportedly responded that he "described the Idea of a Woman and not as she was."[11] In the same respect he may be said to have repre-

---

11. Ben Jonson, *Conversations with William Drummond of Hawthornden*, lines 47–48, in *Ben Jonson*, ed. C. H. Herford and Percy and Evelyn Simpson, 11 vols. (Oxford: Clarendon Press, 1925–1952), 1:133.

sented in the person of his speaker the Idea of Grief and not as it was for him. By creating the fiction of a speaker bereaved at Elizabeth's death, Donne separates himself from his speaker and his speaker from his reader.

What is the advantage of this sometimes tortuous relation between speaker and reader? Maintaining the fiction of bereavement explains the speaker's passionately felt insight into the human condition and the urgency with which he argues it to all Christians. But does not that very privacy separate speaker and audience so that his urgency is lost to us? This is where both the speaker's introductory overtures to the public reader and, most profoundly, the anatomy itself serve to bring speaker and reader together.

Although the speaker's introduction has made us skeptical of his version of reality, it has also demonstrated his urgent concern for our souls. And this concern has now brought us to the anatomy itself, in which the speaker becomes more persuasive. Hardison has observed that in the anatomy Donne shifts the eulogy's standard sequence of praise, lament, and consolation to begin with the lament, and only then to praise and console.[12] For good reason. The lament or complaint section of each of the anatomy's five segments forces the reader to see a world decayed and atrophied on its own terms, objectively, regardless of the death of Elizabeth and the subjective experience of the speaker. The topical allusions, the wit, and the amplitude of the complaint speak directly to the public reader. It is essential for the poem's effect that there be none of the pathetic fallacy in these descriptions of our world, for no matter how possessed the speaker may be with anger and grief, his insistence that his loss is our loss depends on his ability to convince us that, Elizabeth or no, we do indeed share a common world of decay.

When the speaker does, then, after each of the five lament sections, move to praise Elizabeth, we may not accept her as the source for our own experience of coherence and virtue, but we do accept her as the source of the speaker's superior awareness and, through the speaker, our own. The passionate concern with which he urges us to realize that our world is decayed was born in him by the contrast that Elizabeth's death caused in his own private world. And, because of Elizabeth, he now compels us to undergo our own sort of "earth-quake," our own "Bath of teares," tears that bleed "the strongest vitall spirits out." In this sense we, too, lose what is for the speaker the equivalent to Elizabeth Drury. Insofar as we accept the picture of the world that the speaker urges upon us (and the power of the anatomy says that we must), we acknowledge the strength of Elizabeth to precipitate so powerful a vision, to reveal so startlingly by her absence our enormous deficiency.

By the time he reaches his conclusion, the speaker has transformed us into the audience we had initially refused to be. We mourn because we have lost all that we thought valuable in the world in the same way that the speaker mourns the loss of Elizabeth. And we praise Elizabeth at least insofar as her absence was able to precipi-

---

12. Hardison, *The Enduring Monument*, pp. 178–79. As for the structure of the anatomy as a whole, whether they see five, four, or three major divisions (Martz, Lewalski, and Hardison, respectively), most critics illuminate significant structures and themes.

tate the true vision of the world that the speaker has conveyed to us. Whereas initially it seemed that Donne had created a confusion of audiences no genre could make orthodox, it now becomes clear that Donne found, in the congruence between a private mourner's grief and the attitude every Christian should have toward the world, the means of rendering Elizabeth Drury consummate praise. As Elizabeth showed the speaker, so he has shown us: we must live in the world but not of it, pursuing that "faint weake love of vertue and of good," creating a new world.

In concluding, Donne's speaker alludes to his invasion of the prophetic office: "Such an opinion (in due measure) made / Me this great Office boldly to invade" (467–68). It is not only that the speaker plays the role of biblical prophet. We also play the role of the biblical prophet's audience, at first skeptical of his authority, initially unable to share his vision. Only when the prophet persists in establishing his authority — through his compelling sense of urgency, through his claim to a higher source of wisdom, through his holy indignation — only then does the community finally begin to embrace his vision, to become his audience. By creating the fiction of a speaker possessed of a sacred experience, Donne's "Anatomy" truly unites speaker and poet, audience and reader, the fate of a mere girl and every Christian soul.

12. JOHN DONNE AT PLAY IN BETWEEN

ANNA K. NARDO

Even in such a self-consciously witty age as the seventeenth century, Donne's poetry and prose stand out as exceptionally playful. The word play of his puns, equivocations, and paradoxes; the role play of his mercurial personae; the sacred play in his fanciful use of typology and analogy; and the metaphysical play of his conceits—all this fooling around at every level of technique and content is the special Donnean trademark, and critics have long acknowledged its curious power to puzzle and move readers. Some evaluate Donne's play as frivolous, aimed at cocky self-display or at debunking conventions. Others argue that it is significant, accomplishing serious poetic or religious goals. And a few find it sometimes frivolous (and thus to be criticized) and other times significant (and thus to be praised).[1] Donne himself ruefully acknowledged his almost obsessive playing: in a letter, he confessed to having "a ridling disposition,"[2] and in a sermon, to punning involuntarily even while praying (10.1.567–68). Acutely self-conscious though he was, he never said why he played or what he gained. Donne played, I think, because play is always in-between—the precise location his poetic speakers and his preaching persona need to occupy.

His lyric poetry expresses a radical contradiction: simultaneous fears of separation from and possession by a beloved object—whether a woman or God. To find this con-

---

1. Some critics merely note, without evaluation, that Donne plays: T. S. Eliot, "Donne in Our Time," in *A Garland for John Donne: 1631–1931*, ed. Theodore Spencer (1931; rpt. Gloucester, Mass.: Peter Smith, 1958), p. 12; Paul N. Siegel, "Donne's *Paradoxes and Problems*," *PQ* 28 (1949), 511; and Evelyn M. Simpson, *The Sermons of John Donne*, ed. George R. Potter and Evelyn M. Simpson, 10 vols. (Berkeley: University of California Press, 1962), 10:3. Quotations from sermons will follow this edition, cited parenthetically by volume, sermon, and (where appropriate) line numbers in arabic numerals.
Critics who emphasize Donne's frivolity include Pierre Legouis, *Donne the Craftsman: An Essay upon the Structure of the Songs and Sonnets* (1928; rpt. New York: Russell and Russell, 1962), pp. 29, 37, 68–69; J. B. Leishman, *The Monarch of Wit: An Analytical and Comparative Study of the Poetry of John Donne* (1951; rpt. London: Hutchinson, 1969), p. 96; Clay Hunt, *Donne's Poetry: Essays in Literary Analysis* (New Haven: Yale University Press, 1954), pp. 88, 135; and Richard E. Hughes, *The Progress of the Soul: The Interior Career of John Donne* (New York: William Morrow, 1968), pp. 37, 49.
Critics who stress the serious intent of Donne's play include Charles Monroe Coffin, *John Donne and the New Philosophy* (Morningside Heights, N.Y.: Columbia University Press, 1937), pp. 114, 294; A. Alvarez, *The School of Donne* (1961; rpt. New York: New American Library, 1967), p. 26; Arnold Stein, *John Donne's Lyrics* (1962; rpt. New York: Octagon, 1980), pp. 90, 101; Joan Webber, *Contrary Music: The Prose Style of John Donne* (Madison: University of Wisconsin Press, 1963), p. 131; Michael McCanles, "Paradox in Donne," *Studies in the Renaissance* 13 (1966), 266–87; N. J. C. Andreasen, *John Donne: Conservative Revolutionary* (Princeton: Princeton University Press, 1967), pp. 7–14; Murray Roston, *The Soul of Wit: A Study of John Donne* (Oxford: Clarendon Press, 1974), pp. 74, 80, 95; and John S. Chamberlin, *Increase and Multiply: Arts-of-Discourse Procedure in the Preaching of Donne* (Chapel Hill: University of North Carolina Press, 1976), pp. 28, 33–34, 158.
Critics who alternately praise and blame Donne's play include A. J. Smith, *John Donne: The Songs and Sonnets* (London: Edward Arnold, 1964), p. 35; and Wilbur Sanders, *John Donne's Poetry* (Cambridge: Cambridge University Press, 1971), pp. 23, 33, 45, 48, 55.
2. Quoted in Evelyn M. Simpson, *A Study of the Prose Works of John Donne* (Oxford: Clarendon Press, 1924), p. 298.

tradiction embodied in his art, we need not assume that his personae always speak for Donne, the man. That he creates such compelling voices for these fears; that poems and prose works whose voices, critics assume, speak for Donne himself clearly manifest the same fears; and that he returns to themes of both desiring and fleeing union again and again—such evidence is sufficient to establish that this contradiction moved Donne profoundly.[3]

Certainly, he does return to these themes, repeatedly. The speakers of his love poems often seek total union with the beloved, body and soul: the couple becomes two hemispheres of one globe ("The good-morrow"), pictures in one another's eyes ("The Extasie"), even a phoenix, the "one neutrall thing [to which] both sexes fit" during intercourse ("The Canonization," 25). Almost one-fifth of the Songs and Sonets (not to mention the elegies and several sermon and poetic farewells to earthly life) are valedictions—farewell poems in which the poet probes and salves the wounds of breaking union with his beloved.[4] On the other hand, a substantial number of Donne's love poems are mock-serious paeans to promiscuity ("Confined Love"), cynical justifications for the rake's life ("Communitie"), or disillusioned renunciations of love ("Love's Alchymie"). Here, the antifeminist, Ovidian, or Propertian speakers seek escape from a stifling union that threatens either to possess them and their means or to trap them into fidelity.

These contradictory fears of both separation and union reappear with less distanced personae in poems about Donne's relationship to God. The Holy Sonnets argue God's property rights over him ("As due by many titles"), ask God to be the adamant to draw his iron heart ("Thou hast made me"), and even command God to imprison, enthrall, and ravish him because he is powerless to overcome his separation from divine unity ("Batter my heart"). The last (and most grave) sin he confesses in "A Hymne to God the Father" is "a sinne of feare, that when I'have spunne / My last thred, I shall perish on the shore" (13–14)—the fear of eternal separation from God. Just as frequently, however, in his divine poems the speaker willfully runs away from love and grace abounding. In the same hymn, he feels that God has already forgiven the manifold sins he confesses: each "Wilt thou forgive . . . ?" is followed by the assumption of forgiveness, "When thou hast done. . . ." Nevertheless, the speaker lacks faith—repeatedly finding more and more sins, pushing mercy (he thinks) to the limit, and making God chase this slippery sinner down.

Even more clearly, in "Good Friday, 1613. Riding Westward," the perverse traveler turns his back on the cross, the source of God's love and grace to man. He both fears

3. For Donne's fear of separation, see Evelyn Hardy, *Donne: A Spirit in Conflict* (London: Constable, 1942), p. 244; D. W. Harding, "Coherence of Theme in Donne's Poetry," *Kenyon Review* 13 (1951), 431–32; and John Carey, *John Donne: Life, Mind and Art* (New York: Oxford University Press, 1981), pp. 37–38, 59, 61–62. On his fear of being possessed, see Hughes, *Progress*, p. 44. For the concept of "voice," see Sanders, *John Donne's Poetry*, p. 8; and Walter J. Ong, S. J., "Voice as Summons for Belief: Literature, Faith, and the Divided Self," in *The Barbarian Within* (New York: Macmillan, 1962), 49–67.

4. Richard W. Bollman, S.J., "Saying Goodbye: Essays on Donne's Poetics of Departure," Ph.D. Diss., SUNY-Buffalo, 1975, pp. 5, 8.

to look on "Gods face," whose "selfe life" would annihilate him (17), and longs to be restored to God's image. Like the equally perverse speakers of "A Hymne to God the Father" (16) and "Batter my heart" (2), who doubt the efficacy of the shining Son, the speaker of "Good Friday" both does and does not want the fulfillment of the blessing God commended to Aaron: "The Lord make his face *shine* upon thee . . . The Lord lift up his countenance upon thee" (Numbers 6:25–26, emphasis mine). He both does and does not want God's shining countenance to "burn(e)" him into newness ("Good Friday," 40; "Batter my heart," 4).

This image of looking into the face of the beloved—an image crucial to Donne's poems of sacred and profane love—provides a clue to the typical source of conflicting fears of separation and engulfment. The need for face-to-face encounters recalls the earliest and most important face to a child—the mother's. As the mother and child exchange awareness of the other's self, mutual smiles that confirm the other's self, and communication of joint need and gratification, this reflexive recognition creates a substitute for the primal oneness from which the child was originally separated at birth.[5] Inevitably, this face-to-face union is broken as the child either unwillingly confronts the mother's absence or begins to desire independence for himself. In either case, the child discovers that he is not one with the source of nurture, that the self is separate from the other. This universal experience causes conflict because the child wants to experience secure wholeness and immediate gratification, but at the same time he wants to explore the world independently, beyond the mother's presence or control.[6] These contradictory desires, which survive in some form in all adults, marked Donne's poetic representation of intimacy.

One way to mediate this conflict between separation and union may be found in play. Through play, a child may learn to bridge the gap between self and other—a gap that can be experienced as a terrifying abyss of isolation and alienation unless the child finds some way to connect what he feels and needs with the unyielding reality of fact, some way to unite the in-here with the out-there. Neither wholly internal, like dreaming or hallucinating, nor wholly external, like the environment so far beyond his control, play arises in the potential space between self and other. Into this "play space," the child gathers odds and ends of external reality (a blanket, crayons, a wooden stick, clay, a stuffed monkey) and transforms them to suit some facet of his inner reality. In between the in-here and the out-there, the playing child can experience a realm where he is separate, but not alienated; he is connected to, but not engulfed by, the world. As the child plays peek-a-boo and later hide-and-seek to comprehend separation and return, the adult may play at witty valedictory verse. Play can fill up a nearly infinite space of separation as the playing child matures into *homo ludens*.[7]

5. Erik Erikson, *Young Man Luther* (New York: W. W. Norton, 1958), pp. 115–19. See also Sanders, *John Donne's Poetry*, p. 67.

6. Erik Erikson, *Childhood and Society*, 2d. ed. (New York: W. W. Norton, 1963), pp. 72–85.

7. Donald Woods Winnicott, *Playing and Reality* (New York: Basic Books, 1971), pp. 41, 51, 108.

Paradoxically, play both connects and distances self and other because it is a framed activity. Defined structurally, play is a context, a frame, or a stance players adopt toward a source, almost any source—such as an object when toying with a pencil, or a person when teasing a friend, or a role when acting Macbeth, or an activity when playing war. The text produced by this context alludes to, purports to imitate, and transforms the source of the play.[8] So, when one otter playfully nips another otter, the nip both is and is not a bite, and the ballerina who dances *Swan Lake* both is and is not a swan. In short, the transforming frame of play creates an inherently in-between reality: what occurs inside it is simultaneously both real and not real, true and not true. As a result, players need never fear engulfment in the kind of relationships established by the play world. Because play relationships are based on play selves put on for the limited time and space of the play world, no real consequences need occur. For example, kisses during a game of spin-the-bottle are not exactly real kisses (but they are not non-kisses either). The defining frame, "This is just play," insures that all selves and all actions inside the frame be somewhat distanced from real selves and real actions.

Because of its inherently in-between reality, play became Donne's characteristic mode of mediating contradictory fears of separation and union. In order to create unity despite apparent disunity, he plays with witty images: a departing lover's tears, which reflect his beloved's face, become whole worlds and seas like those through which he must sail ("A Valediction of weeping"), a "ragged bony name" scratched in a window will bring the muscle and sinew of its body home again ("A Valediction of my name, in the window," 23), and two feet that make a single compass represent lovers who, although "two souls," "are one," joined at a point above the earthly movement that separates the roaming from the fixed foot ("A Valediction forbidding mourning," 21). The images and objects Donne uses in the valedictions to deny the total separation of the lovers are perhaps comparable, in psychoanalytic parlance, to "transition objects"—portable substitutes, such as a blanket or stuffed monkey, for the nurturing presence that allow the child to be physically separate, but not cut off from that presence.[9] Although in the valedictions and elsewhere Donne's play yokes self to other, the union only lasts in the fragile play-world of his wit, and he knows it.

Whether exalting union or fleeing it, he is always self-consciously playing. Often, the tone of even Donne's most serious poems is uncertain. Does the arrogant speaker of "The Sunne Rising" really expect the sun to revolve around his bed? Isn't there something almost waggish about the speaker of "Good Friday," who cleverly transforms

---

8. Gregory Bateson, *Steps to an Ecology of Mind* (New York: Ballantine Books, 1972), pp. 33–37, 177–93; Erving Goffman, *Frame Analysis: An Essay on the Organization of Experience* (New York: Harper and Row, 1974), pp. 40–82; Helen B. Schwartzman, *Transformations: The Anthropology of Children's Play* (New York: Plenum Press, 1978), p. 330.

9. Winnicott, *Playing and Reality*, pp. 1–14, 38–52. Bollman has also noted the almost "sacramental" quality of these images to embody the presence of the absent lover ("Saying Goodbye," pp. 12–13, 24, 33n.36).

turning his back on God into a submission to correction, and who coyly refuses to face God until he is assured of acceptance? Likewise, when the speaker of "A Hymne to God the Father" ends two stanzas (ruefully or gleefully?) with "When thou hast done, thou hast not done, / For I have more" (5–6, 11–12), isn't he playing catch-me-if-you-can with God? All the while these ingenious speakers find ways to transcend separation from the beloved or God, their playful tone keeps the object of their longing within reach, but not attained. By placing his poems in the paradoxical play frame (by its nature in-between), Donne can have union and distance simultaneously.

Although Donne's play in his lyrics and *Devotions upon Emergent Occasions* is apparent and frequently examined, the ludic spirit of his sermons may be less evident. When he assumed his public role as a man of God and preacher of the Word, his fundamental concerns were not changed, only refocused. As a preacher he understood the needs of his congregation, indeed of all mankind, in terms of the same contradictory desires for union and distance that had marked his more personal poetry.

No theme so fired Donne's preaching as the blessedness of union with God—a union frequently imaged as the beatific vision.[10] Whereas once the face-to-face encounters of his love lyrics had figured forth the wholeness sought in profane love, now he defines blessed union as the sight of God's radiant face. He exults that in heaven,

> I shall have an uninterrupted, an un-intermitted, an un-discontinued sight of God; I shall looke, and never looke off; not looke, and looke againe, as here, but looke, and looke still . . . my soule shall sleep, not onely without trouble, and startling, but without rocking, without any other help, then that peace, which is in it selfe; My soule shall be thoroughly awake, and thoroughly asleep too. . . . I shall see this light in his face, who is all face, and yet all hand, all application, and communication, and delivery of all himselfe to all his Saints. (9.4.719–61)

The images of rocking, waking sleep, and nurture suggest the bond between mother and child. Such union with God requires complete surrender because "Love," says Donne, "delivers over him that loves into possession of that that he loves . . . it changes him that loves, into the very nature of that that he loves, and he is nothing else" (1.3.56–59). Since Donne understood the fear of such engulfment of the self, even into the godhead, he suspected that his parishioners shared his perverse desire to ride the other way: "We pretend to be sayling homewards, and yet we desire to have the winde against us; we are travelling to the heavenly *Jerusalem*, and yet we are loath to come thither" (3.8.601–4). Fallen, sinful man yearns toward God, but wants Him at a distance.

So Donne came to preach about life in-between because this was man's lot—caught between contradictory fears of separation and engulfment, between flesh and spirit,

---

10. Winfried Schleiner, in *The Imagery of John Donne's Sermons* (Providence, R.I.: Brown University Press, 1970), pp. 65–66, has argued that the images and themes in Donne's sermons are rooted in Christian tradition and, therefore, can tell us little about Donne's frame of mind. Carey, however, has pointed out that Donne's principle of selection from among the great varieties of traditional themes and images is revealing (*Life, Mind and Art*, p. 219).

between the kingdom already but not yet come. Donne, the preacher, realized that being human meant being in-between. At his ordination he anchored himself to the sign of all men's radical in-betweenness by taking a new *impresa*: the god-man raised up between two worlds on a cross shaped like an anchor. After his ordination, Donne preached that the cross must become man's playground:

> A fundamentall joy, a radicall joy, a viscerall, a gremiall joy, . . . arises out of the bosome and wombe and bowels of the tribulation it selfe . . . when as cold and dead water, when it comes to the fire, hath a motion and dilatation and a bubling and a kind of dancing in the vessell, so my soule, that lay asleep in prosperity, hath by this fire of Tribulation, a motion, a joy, an exaltation. (3.16.404–29)

In man's inevitable suffering, the soul learns to dance, to play in the space between earth and heaven. Donne joins the dance of Wisdom who plays before the face of the Father for all eternity (Proverbs 8:27–31; "*Ludens coram eo omni tempore*," in the Vulgate), bringing to preaching the skills of a player par excellence that he mastered in his more personal poetry. The job suited him perfectly for three reasons: it was inherently in-between, its traditions justified displays of wit, and it was dramatic.

As an Anglican priest, Donne's public identity was as a man who—by his clothes, his position in a raised pulpit, and his Christian life—was conspicuously set apart from this world in order to lead men to the next. His poem "To Mr. Tilman after he had taken orders" emphasizes a priest's in-between position as an "Embassadour to God" from man, even "a blest Hermaphrodite" (38, 54). In sermons, Donne often characterizes the preacher as the nurse of God's children: he begs that God not give him "*dry breasts*; that you may always suck pure milk from us" (6.3.391); and he hopes that through him God will rain on his congregation the "dew . . . honey . . . Manna . . . Oyle . . . Balsamum" of consolation (7.4.600–606). When he feeds his flock with this consolation, he is amazed that he is fed in return: "For, when I have given that man comfort, that man hath given me a Sacrament / . . . Lord, when I went, I was sure, that thou who hadst received me to mercy, wouldst also receive him, who could not be so great a sinner as I; And now, when I come away, I am sure, that thou who art returned to him . . . wilt never depart from mee" (8.10.448–59). In between pulpit and pew, heaven and earth, God's presence is given, received, and by its reception returned to the giver—thereby multiplying to a triple presence of preacher, sinner, and God in a holy interchange of selves.

The second reason Donne's job suited him is that the mediating presence he feeds to his flock is the Word, the perfect medium for his wit. In the *ars praedicandi* (art of discourse) of the Church Fathers, Donne found a tradition remarkably congenial to his skills as a player. Augustine's justification of finding multiple transferred meanings in biblical texts, so long as they conduce to faith, and the emphasis on memory as the key to salvation produced a sermon style in which the preacher played out the significances of his text, weaving an intricate, often fanciful, network of associations. One word of the text might bring to mind other biblical texts that might lead to still other allegorized meanings so that several facets of the Word were polished and re-volved in the memory of the listeners. Playing thus with the Word, the preacher brought the congregation into his sacred game, which one reader of Donne's sermons has called "play that is delightful and redemptive."[11]

A typical example of Donne's play with "the plenty, and abundance of the *holy Ghost* in the *Scriptures*, who satisfies us as with marrow, and with fatnesse, to induce the *diverse senses* that the Scriptures doe admit" (3.17.178–81), is the first half of his 1619 sermon on Matthew 21:44: "Whosoever shall fall on this stone, shall be broken; but on whomsoever it shall fall, it will grinde him to powder" (2.8). Because biblical metaphor suggests that God dwells with man and "builds upon" him, Donne concludes that the stone in the text is Christ. He is the foundation stone on which life must be built (1 Corinthians 3:11), the cornerstone that unites and reconciles (Isaiah 28:16), the stone of rest that Jacob used for a pillow when he dreamed of the ladder to heaven (Genesis 28:10–12), the stone in David's sling that killed Goliath (1 Samuel 17:40–50), and the rock that both gave the Israelites water in the desert (Numbers 20:11) and is a dwelling place unmoved by tempests (Isaiah 42:11). Each of these significa-tions is played out using allegory (Jacob's ladder becomes the steps toward holy rest), typology (David's sling prefigures the cross by which Christ slew the true giant, sin), and metaphoric associations that circle back on themselves (the rock that gave the Is-raelites water and in which Christians dwell reminds Donne that the father whose son asks for bread will not give him a stone [Luke 11:11]; yet, he adds, all Christians pray for "daily bread" [Matthew 6:11] which is Christ in the sacrament of the Church which is the stone that both nourishes and provides a safe dwelling). The same fertile wit that animates this lively sermon once produced so many far-fetched associations on a name scratched in a windowpane that the reader wonders how long the game can go on. Only now Donne's wit has found a tradition and a God that redeems his compelling passion to play.

The third reason his job suited him was its potential for high drama. Since in the *ars praedicandi* tradition the Christian was a neotype, reenacting Christ's fulfillment of the Old Testament types, Donne could preach a life of play. By training the hear-er's memory to revolve the multifaceted Word in his mind, the preacher provided a manifestation of the Christ within.[12] Donne tells the listener that he has the Bible without book: "He hath a *Genesis* in his memory; he cannot forget his *Creation*; he hath an *Exodus* in his memory; he cannot forget that God hath delivered him, from some kind of *Egypt*, from some oppression; He hath a *Leviticus* in his memory; hee cannot forget, that God hath proposed to him some Law, some rules to be observed" (2.2.73–78). But the Word must not remain in the memory alone; the hearer must write it in his life. At the end of an allegorization of the aspects (called "characters")

11. Chamberlin, *Increase and Multiply*, p. 28. For Donne's reaction against Ramistic preaching and his consequent return to the older Augustinian tradition, see pp. 95–108. See also Dennis Quinn, "Donne's Christian Eloquence," *ELH* 27 (1960), 276–97.

12. Chamberlin, *Increase and Multiply*, p. 34.

of Simeon's life, Donne reminds his hearers to become actors: "I shall onely have time to name the rest of those characters; you must spell them, and put them into their syllables . . . their words . . . their Syntaxis, and sentences; that is, you must pursue the imitation" (7.11.371–75). Donne's congregation must enact the script written first in the Bible, then in their memories, then in their lives in order to effect a new incarnation — the Word made flesh again in human lives lived as a theater staged by Christ for the angels (3.9.429–33).

For all his skill at using the traditional *ars praedicandi* to join preacher, hearer, and Word into a triple presence, Donne's wit sustains their in-between status. His word play often takes the same odd forms in his public sermons as in his private poetry. In a Lenten sermon on penance, a simple paradox becomes a comic cadenza: "I must not be alone with my selfe; for I am as apt to take, as to give infection; I am a reciprocall plague; passively and actively contagious; I breath corruption, and breath it upon my selfe; and I am the Babylon that I must goe out of, or I perish" (9.13.545–48). Can a true penitent play so wittily? Nor can he resist, even at a funeral, an equivocation worthy of Hamlet on the legal language of divorce bills: "For, though [the soul and body] be separated *à Thoro & Mensa*, from Bed and Board, they are not divorced; Though the soule be at the *Table of the Lambe*, in Glory, and the body but at the table of *the Serpent, in dust*" (7.10.19–22). Were Sir Aston Cokayne's grieving friends amused? Finally, his logic can be more clever than convincing: somewhat altering the proverb "Truth and oyle are ever above,"[13] he proves that, even in tribulations (so often symbolized by water), God's mercy (imaged as oil) will triumph because, when mixed, oil always rises above water (7.14.229–36). Donne's sermon play is as complex as his poetic play; it both brings the congregation to the Word and distances them by his own witty words.

The distance is further emphasized because Donne framed his sermons as dramatic performance. Despite his frequent warnings against "ostentation, and vain glory . . . and self-pleasing" (4.3.1099–1100) in preaching,[14] his contemporaries and modern readers stress his own theatricality. According to Walton's description, he often wept and carried his hearers aloft with him in "holy raptures." According to the author of one funeral elegy, parishioners might "take notes, from [his] looke, and hand"; his "carriage" and "gesture" were so eloquent that one "might see / An errour vanquish'd by delivery." But, according to T. S. Eliot, his preaching smacks of an evangelist's camp meeting.[15] In such arresting personal references as those to his own distractions in private prayer (7.10.271–86), to the congregation's comparing his sermon to a better one they heard

13. "Outlandish Proverbs," in *The Works of George Herbert*, ed. F. E. Hutchinson (1941; rpt. Oxford: Clarendon Press, 1978), no. 234.

14. See also 5.1.57–67 and 10.6.246–342.

15. Izaak Walton, *The Life of Dr. John Donne*, in *John Donne: "Devotions upon Emergent Occasions" together with "Death's Duel"* (Ann Arbor: University of Michigan Press, 1959), p. xxi; Jasper Mayne, "On Dr. Donne's death," lines 57–64, in *Donne: Poetical Works*, ed. Herbert J. C. Grierson (London: Oxford University Press, 1929), p. 353; T. S. Eliot, "Lancelot Andrewes," in *Essays Ancient and Modern* (New York: Harcourt, Brace, 1932), pp. 9–10, 20–21.

on the same text (3.3.695–702), and to the hourglass visibly counting off the minutes of his sermon and their sinful lives (7.14.716–25; 8.7.586–93), Donne turns his life and sermons into high drama. Significantly, he viewed those other players across the river at Bankside as his competitors for an audience. He compares spectators "whom lighter affections carry to Shewes, and Masks, and Comedies" to his parishioners, "whom better dispositions bring to these Exercises." Both, he tells them, "conceive some contentment, and some kinde of Joy, in that you are well and commodiously placed, they to see the Shew, you to heare the Sermon" (5.14.972–81). Obviously, Donne was a spellbinder, and, consequently, many readers besides Eliot have questioned his motives as a preacher of the Word.[16]

Yet Donne's goal may not have been so hubristic as leading men all the way to faith. Other, more holy men might do that; by his play he led them only so far as "wonder," which, he says, "stands as in the midst, betweene knowledge and faith, and hath an eye towards both. If I know a thing," he muses, "or beleeve a thing, I do no longer wonder: but when I finde that I have reason to stop upon the consideration of a thing, so, as that I see enough to induce admiration, to make me wonder, I come by that step . . . to a faith" (6.13.106–15).[17] Through the play of allegory, typology, metaphor, paradox (sometimes called the "wonder" by rhetoricians), equivocation, conceit, and high drama, Donne charmed his hearers into wonder that led them out of mere knowledge, but only halfway to faith. Although a preacher, he knew that he was still a player, albeit a redeemed one—that he was still the same man whose lyric play had once dazzled both fictionalized and real readers, leading them only halfway to transcendent intimacy.

Anglican communicants expressed their faith four times a year at the altar, where they were united with each other and God in a holy meal. In between their separate pews and the act of union at the altar, in between reading the first collect and feeding them the sacrament, Donne preached his witty sermons—spatially and temporally mediating his hearers' reception of grace. At play in between, he opened their minds to wonder, preparing them for the grace of faith that only God could give.[18]

16. Hardy, *Donne*, pp. 229, 231. Legouis calls Donne's fanciful expositions of barren texts making something out of nothing and hair-splitting for its own sake (*Donne the Craftsman*, p. 36).

17. See Dennis Quinn, "Donne and the Wane of Wonder," *ELH* 36 (1969), 626–47.

18. Gale H. Carrithers emphasizes the mediational position of the sermon in Anglican liturgy, in *Donne at Sermons: A Christian Existential World* (Albany: State University of New York Press, 1972), pp. 8–17.

13. MEDITATION, TYPOLOGY, AND THE STRUCTURE OF JOHN DONNE'S SERMONS

WALTER R. DAVIS

Proem

The vitality that the Word of God exercised on the imagination of Renaissance English preachers can be observed in the great variety of structures, expressing their individual visions, which the preachers impressed on the standard frameworks presented to them by their rhetorical training. W. Fraser Mitchell has informed us of the three standard textbook structures for a sermon: the older oration model popular among Roman Catholic preachers, the Calvinist method of explication and application, and the "Ramistical" method favored by the Anglicans, consisting of a proem or opening of the text, a division of it into a few parts, amplification of each of its parts, and a sum or application of its doctrines.[1] What is noteworthy are the different uses or significances each individual preacher attached to such structural skeletons in order to form his own style of preaching.

For instance, while Henry Smith employed the explication-application formula to unfold the example of the reformed Nebuchadnezzar and then exhort his audience to follow that example, the satirical preacher Thomas Adams used it to move from illusory doctrine in the explication to reality in the application.[2] For another example, Henry Smith used the "Ramistical" formula in *The Fall of Nabuchadnezzar* to create a narrative structure like that of Scripture.[3] But Lancelot Andrewes used the same formula for quite different purposes in his Easter 1617 sermon on Matthew 12:39–40 to define in three parts the cooperation of judgment and mercy, nature and grace, in the formation of such a liturgical mystery as the Eucharist; he said, "For, one *Mysterie* leads us to another: this in the Text, to the holy *Mysteries* we are providing to partake, which doe work like, and doe work to this: Even to the *raising* of the *soule* with the *first resurrection*."[4]

The models to which preachers looked for suggestions on fleshing out the standard formulas for their own purposes were many, and we have become especially aware of them recently in the work of Barbara Lewalski and Anthony Low.[5] Paramount among such models was, as is natural, Holy Scripture itself, which commentators held to be exemplary in its incorporation of many genres of writing, in its language, and in

---

1. W. Fraser Mitchell, *English Pulpit Oratory from Andrewes to Tillotson: A Study of its Literary Aspects* (1932; rpt. New York: Russell and Russell, 1962), pp. 93–101.

2. Henry Smith, *The Restitution of Nabuchadnezzar* in *The Sermons of Master Henrie Smith, gathered into one volume* (London: for Thomas Man, 1592), pp. 405–28; Thomas Adams, *The Divells Banket* (London: for R. Mab, 1614).

3. Smith, *The Sermons*, pp. 384–404.

4. Lancelot Andrewes, *XCVI Sermons* (London: for Richard Badger, 1629), p. 516.

5. Barbara Kiefer Lewalski, *Protestant Poetics and the Seventeenth-Century Religious Lyric* (Princeton: Princeton University Press, 1979); and Anthony Low, *Love's Architecture: Devotional Modes in Seventeenth-Century English Poetry* (New York: New York University Press, 1978).

its broad view of the life of mankind typologically considered. Many sermons attempted to explicate Scripture along structural lines dictated by Scripture, that is, to imitate Scripture in commenting on it. That could occur in many ways. For one, the simple Calvinist formula of explication and application was often seen as following the method of Scripture; Donne, for instance, considered the first chapter of the Gospel of John to be explication of the Word made Flesh (verses 1–35) and application of it to us (verses 35 to the end).[6] For another, a sermon based on scriptural narrative could also take the form of that narrative: Lancelot Andrewes in his Easter 1620 sermon on the scene at the tomb takes the three "parts" or roles of Mary, the Angels, and the risen Christ as the three "parts" or sections of his sermon.[7] But the most common way in which a sermon might imitate the form of the Scripture it explicates is by incorporating into itself the standard typological or figural interpretation of Scripture, by means of which an event in the Old Testament such as crossing the Jordan prefigured an event in the New Testament such as baptism, which in turn prefigured an event at the end of time, such as crossing from this world to the next.

There were "ancillary genres" to Scripture, too, developed from Church liturgy, from formal meditation, and from mystical contemplation. The sermons of Lancelot Andrewes are perhaps the most striking examples of sermons both conceived of as part of liturgy and modeled on the liturgy that surrounds them. They are more purely vocal than the sermons of other preachers, with dominating rhetorical schemes and complex echo-effects that come forward only when they are read aloud (such as the changes rung on "taking away" in the sermon on Easter 1620).[8] In structure, they tend to imitate the two portions of the Anglican service between which they form a bridge, since they often begin with the Word of God and end with reference to the Word made Flesh in the Eucharist (as in Christmas 1623, Easter 1620, Easter 1617). Therefore, they enact the central matter of liturgy and act as explanation of the mystery to follow: thus T. S. Eliot's view that Andrewes "takes a word and derives the world from it" and Joan Webber's characterization of the sermons as "celebration of word and world."[9] Finally, like Richard Crashaw's great Christmastide hymns, they move through a dialectic that tends to draw together heaven and earth, God and man, in the Incarnation (Christmas 1623, Easter 1617).

As for the meditative model, it is noteworthy that Thomas Gataker subtitled many of his published sermons (1619–1620) "Meditations" and that, as Barbara Lewalski

6. *The Sermons of John Donne*, ed. George R. Potter and Evelyn Simpson, 10 vols. (Berkeley and Los Angeles: University of California Press, 1962), 3.17.14–19. Hereafter, references to Donne's sermons will be parenthetical, and will refer to volume, sermon, and (where appropriate) line number in Potter and Simpson's edition.

7. Andrewes, *XCVI Sermons*, pp. 531–42. See Stanley E. Fish, "Sequence and Meaning in Seventeenth-Century Narrative," in *To Tell a Story: Narrative Theory and Practice* (Los Angeles: University of California Press, 1973), pp. 64, 67.

8. See Joan Webber, "Celebration of Word and World in Lancelot Andrewes' Style," *JEGP* 64 (1965), 255–69; for the changes on "taking away," see Andrewes, *XCVI Sermons*, pp. 536–38 and 541.

9. T. S. Eliot, "Lancelot Andrewes," *Selected Essays, 1917–1932* (New York: Harcourt-Brace, 1932), p. 294; and Webber, "Celebration of Word and World," passim.

has reminded us, John Donne constantly refers to the ideas he is developing as "meditations."[10] Of this, we shall see more later. The sermon modeled on mystical contemplation is difficult to find, given the public nature of the sermon and the intensely private nature of the mystical experience.[11]

The Renaissance sermon was itself designed as an ancilla to Holy Scripture, was embedded in liturgy, and utilized naturally the methods of meditation, among other spiritual techniques. It is my purpose in this essay to demonstrate the structural working of two of these techniques—Scripture considered typologically and meditation—in the sermons of John Donne, both separately and in combination.

Division

In his sermons, John Donne habitually used the "Ramistical" formula favored by the Anglican preachers, but he used it as the foundation for many different structures. Joan Webber has categorized these under six general heads (aside from one anomalous example of explication-application in 8.8): 1, word-by-word interpretation of the sort we have labeled "narrative" in the sermon by Smith discussed above (10.3, 2.11, and 3.10); 2, narrative as handled by Andrewes, taking up each actor in an event (2.13 and 14); 3, exegetical like that of Andrewes on the sign of Jonah, interpreting the text according to several senses (2.18) or taking a word at a time (8.1); 4, imagistic, developing a symbol expressed in the text (2.1) or creating a new symbol to control the whole (9.7); 5, free discussion of points raised by the text (6.6); and, 6, merging text with occasion by developing governing symbols that apply equally to both (3.11 and 6.18).[12] On examination, Webber's types 1 and 3 often approach typological structure in their unfolding of the senses of the text; and her types 4 and 6 are meditative in coloration since they begin with an image and proceed to transcend it. To simplify somewhat, Donne characteristically divides his sermons into three parts, often giving those three parts a typological significance, a meditative significance, or a combination of both. These three are the sermon structures that are peculiar to Donne as to no other preacher.

Part 1

An example of a sermon based structurally on typological reading of Scripture is that preached at the marriage of Mrs. Margaret Washington, at St. Clement Danes, 1621. Donne begins by explicating his text—"And I will marry Thee unto me for ever" (Hosea 2:19)—typologically, as referring to the physical marriage instituted in Genesis in the Old Testament, the spiritual marriage of Christ and the Church instituted

10. Barbara Kiefer Lewalski, *Donne's "Anniversaries" and the Poetry of Praise: The Creation of a Symbolic Mode* (Princeton: Princeton University Press, 1973), pp. 90–91.

11. The only likely candidates are Peter Sterry and George Fox, with their incantatory attempts to invoke a sense of mystery in their auditors.

12. Joan Webber, *Contrary Music: The Prose Style of John Donne* (Madison: University of Wisconsin Press, 1963), p. 165.

in these New Testament times, and the mystical marriage at the end of time. These three senses of the text become the basis of the three parts of the sermon, for, as he says, "Be pleased therefore to give me leave in this exercise to shift the scene thrice . . . first, a secular mariage in Paradise; secondly, a spiritual mariage in the Church; and thirdly, an eternall mariage in heaven" (3.11.20–25). Thus the three senses of the text produce an easy temporal progression from past to present to future, and govern stylistic modulations as well. The first part on the secular marriage is literal, reasonable, and argumentative, using illustrative similitudes drawn from homely matter such as law, medicine, finance, and household affairs; the second part on the spiritual marriage is highly figured and symbolic in style, as well as highly emotive, as in this example:

> And can these persons meet? the Son of God and the son of man? When I consider Christ to be *German Jehovae*, the bud and blossome, the fruit and off-spring of Jehovah, Jehovah himself, and my self before he took me in hand, to be, not a Potters vessell of earth, but that earth of which the Potter might make a vessell if he would, and break it if he would when he had made it . . . can these persons, this Image of God, this God himself, this glorious God, and this vessell of earth, this earth it self, this inglorious worm of the earth, meet without disparagement? (333–57)

And the brief last part on the eternal marriage moves away from argument and analysis to a purely meditative re-creation of a scene at the end of time, full of Apocalyptic images that function literally to signify the end of all imaging. The sermon, by these means, leads from an imperfect apprehension of Providence now to a promise of full apprehension at the end: it exhibits in structure and style the gradual unfolding of Providence that Scripture itself both promotes and exhibits.

Typological exegesis had a strong hold on Donne's mind, as it did on Protestantism in general. The Protestant Reformers gave new life to typology, which they considered part of the literal sense that was the one true sense of Scripture, and also an extension of that sense beyond or beneath its mere words.[13] That was John Donne's position. Dennis Quinn has shown that Donne insists that a strict literal interpretation is always preferable to a figurative one, but that he will often add spiritual or moral senses to the literal in an attempt to intensify the spiritual usefulness of his text.[14] Such senses are usually typological, the meanings of events rather than of words. Thus, he says that Christ gave the Bible its unity by fulfilling in His person the types of the Old Testament, "so when he [a man] comes to the true Scriptures, and compares the new-Testament with the Old, the Gospel with the Law, he finds this to be a performance of those promises, a fulfilling of those Prophecies, a revelation of those Types and Figures, and an accomplishment, and a possession of those hopes and those reversions" (1.8.495–99). Not only does the Old Testament lead to the New by types (6.112), but what it gives in shadows the New presents fully: "The Law was their [the Jews'] *Equinoctiall*, in which, they might see both the Type, and that which was figured in

13. Lewalski, *Protestant Poetics*, p. 117.
14. Dennis Quinn, "John Donne's Principles of Biblical Exegesis," *JEGP* 41 (1962), 320, 322.

the Type: But in the Christian Church the Sun is in a *perpetuall Summer Solstice*; which are high degrees, and yet there is a higher, the Sun is in a perpetuall *Meridian* and *Noon*, in that Summer Solstice" (7.14.16–20). Quinn concludes that it is to typology that Donne turns most often when he wishes to extend the literal meaning in order to make the text a fit tool for meditation, and whenever he wishes to expound the significance of an Old Testament text he does so typologically, as in 9.12.573–635 or 9.2.641–869, in order to show the sun at its full noon (as he put it).[15]

The sermons for which typological interpretation of Scripture forms a structural basis are of many different sorts, the differences stemming from choice of text, from the closeness or looseness with which Donne follows the standard typological procedure, and from the different goals set for that procedure. There are several that simply take an Old Testament text and develop it according to the three traditional times in three parts, as does the sermon on the marriage of Mrs. Washington or the sermon at St. Pauls, 28 January 1627 (7.12), which moves its text in Psalms 65:5 from Nature and law to Gospel. There are several, too, that develop a text into two-part typology, as does the Whitsunday sermon of 1629 on Genesis 1:2, in which the Spirit of God moving on the waters at the Creation (part 1) is moved "*In figura Baptismi*" (9.3.453) to figure forth the second Creation of the New Testament (part 2). On one occasion, Donne finds a text recurring through the parts of Scripture: in the sermon for Christmas 1628 on "Lord, who hath believed our report?" (which occurs in Isaiah 53:1, John 12:38, and Romans 10:16), he takes the opportunity of moving the text, in the three parts of the sermon, from the Old Testament, to the Gospel, to after-times (8.13).

Donne frequently moves a New Testament text back in time, thereby forcing it into a typological treatment, in order to show how Scripture spans all times. An example is the sermon for Easter Day 1622, in which Donne makes the theme of death and resurrection in his text, 1 Thessalonians 4:17, the basis of a three-part structure: part 1 is about death in the past, as punishment for sin; part 2 moves into the death of those present at the Last Day of our time, for which the Church, now, serves as a glass (4.2.375–80); and part 3 moves from death to resurrection, and to the end of all time. In this last part the lying down that had been imaged in dust in part 1 (109–68) becomes reimagined as lying asleep in beds (715–40). Another example is an undated sermon at a Christening in which Galatians 3:27 yields two terms to form the sermon's temporal structure (even though the terms exist simultaneously): part 1 the putting on of Christ, and part 2, baptism. Donne takes the putting on of Christ back to the clothing of Adam and Eve in Genesis, which is treated as prophetic (5.7.31–32). That type is then fulfilled in part 2, wherein baptism is treated as a hinge, opening out toward the future (341–46). It is fitting that the sermon is dominated, hence, by images of dilation (for example, 124–36, 160, 585–605). Similarly, in an

---

15. Ibid., p. 325. On Donne's use of typology, see also William R. Mueller, *John Donne: Preacher* (Princeton: Princeton University Press, 1962), pp. 60–63; and Winfried Schleiner, *The Imagery of John Donne's Sermons* (Providence, R.I.: Brown University Press, 1970), pp. 190–93.

Easter evening sermon of 1624 on Apocalypse 20:6, the resurrection of Christ leads to the final resurrection as does type to fulfillment (6.2).

In the sermons discussed above, unity of action and harmony between the parts of the sermon outlining that action are observed. Such harmony is typical of the typological sermons. It is the kind of harmony that comes out explicitly in a pair of sermons exploring 1 Timothy 1:15 given at Whitehall on 19 April 1618. Donne extracts from his text the phrase "That Christ Jesus came into the world to save sinners" and makes it the basis of a three-part structure. Part 1 takes us back into the Old Testament, into "this first Creation" that is "a shadow, a representation of our second Creation" (1.8.163–64). Here, Donne is concerned to evoke the typological imagination, so that we may see how "All the word of God then conduces to the Gospel; the Old Testament is a preparation and a paedagogie to the New" (230–31; see also 495–500). That is the preparation for the Gospel itself in part 2 (which begins the second sermon of the pair), in which Donne takes the words of the text one by one, always being careful to show how they accomplished fulfillment of prophecy: "All times and all Generations before time was were Christs day" (1.9.194–95). And part 3 is a discourse on humility in general that brings the text up to our times and beyond.

This pair of sermons is characterized by harmonious shifts between its parts, demonstrating in an explicit manner its unity. Separate times and separate situations are said to run together seamlessly, so much so that the past is made to look to the future, the present back to the past (1.8.1–4). The times of the text run together as do root, tree, and fruit, the whole sermon being based on a consideration of growth through time and expressing that concern in its form.

An interesting sermon that spans time in a transcendent motion both temporal and psychological is the Lenten sermon of 1623 on John 11:35, "Jesus wept." Donne uses this singular two-word text as a refrain to punctuate the sections of the sermon as he moves through them (4.13.75, 440–45, 523–31); and these sections correspond to the three times Jesus wept—human tears over Lazarus, prophetic tears over Jerusalem, pontifical tears over mankind on the Cross. Though not linked typologically because they are not three interpretations of a single text, these three episodes both outline the life of Christ and lead one to another, for the tears over Lazarus prophesied the tears over Jerusalem (451–52), and those foretold Christ's own Passion (530–38). This motion is transcendent, for by it the waters of weeping become transformed from a spring to a river and finally to a baptismal sea of salvation. Furthermore, the style changes psychologically from a focus on the details of Lazarus to an understanding of why Christ should weep over Jerusalem, to a final sense of tears as a result of love that we should imitate (666–743).

The sort of psychologically focused typology of "Jesus Wept" enters the late pair of sermons preached at court in April 1629 in a different way. Donne's typological division of his text, Genesis 1:26, is both temporal and spatial. Though his division of the text into four parts by the points of the compass tends to emphasize space in converting the church visible to the congregation into an image of the whole world,

Donne uses that metaphorical conversion to figure temporality by stressing process from life to death in each of the two sermons, from East to West (man's rising and his fall), from North to South (the beginning of God's plan and its completion). His figural interpretation, he insists, will "transport you, by occasion of these words, from this world to the next" (9.1.128–29).

The form of the pair of sermons is circular; part 1 is essentially a disquisition on the Trinity, but part 4 redevelops that concept complexly, both typologically and psychologically. Typologically, the Father's power dominates the Creation, the Son's wisdom Baptism, and the Holy Ghost's goodness the end of time. But since the emphasis is on the union of man with God, the main stress is psychological, and Donne is at pains to develop the image of God in the human soul – the Father in the Understanding, the Son in the Will, the Holy Ghost in Memory (9.2.566–755) – and to then move from this world to final fulfillment in the next (755–65).

Thus, at the end, Donne moves typology inward; in this pair of sermons, as in that on "Jesus Wept," Donne is working toward the incorporation of meditation into typology.

Part 2

Typology makes a sermon into an exploration of Scripture on the part of the preacher and his congregation, a mutual search for the Word's fullest range of meaning, both as a written and transmitted document and as a vital force in the lives of a people. To use meditation in a sermon turns the sermon into something quite different: it becomes dramatic, a display of the preacher affected by the text in a manner that he hopes will speak for and to the congregation and will be imitated by them. So private are the origins of its energy that the public meditative sermon is rare, even in Donne, and is usually found connected to occasions of death. Furthermore, sermons typologically structured focus one's attention on the text and tend to move along a temporal sequence from past to present to future; but meditative sermons focus on the congregation (in the sense that it is the response of the congregation that is the center of interest), and their sequential movement pertains to the psychology of the congregation, involving the faculties of the soul, usually moving from memory to understanding and thence to acts of the will.[16] Therefore the individual parts of a meditative sermon tend to differ considerably, one of them being highly imagistic (as is proper to memory or imagination) for instance, or another of them being urgently exhortative (as directed to arousing the listener's will). There is high contrast between segments, and as a result meditative sermons are highly dramatic in the way their parts go together as well as in their tone.

Such is the case in the funeral sermon for Sir William Cockayne preached on 12 December 1626, on John 11:21, "Lord, if thou hadst been here, my brother had not died." Donne begins the sermon at a distance from his text, creating a large meditative

---

16. Joan Webber comments that the use of the progress of the soul to structure a sermon is unique to Donne, *Contrary Music*, p. 107. See further Webber, *Contrary Music*, pp. 105–14; and Schleiner, *Imagery of John Donne's Sermons*, p. 37, for general suggestions about the use of meditative technique in Donne's sermons.

image that both states and illustrates the conjunction of the diverse that will typify the whole sermon:

> God made the first Marriage, and man made the first Divorce; God married the Body and Soule in the Creation, and man divorced the Body and Soule by death through sinne, in his fall . . . [yet] though they be separated *a Thoro & Mensa*, from Bed and Board, they are not divorced; though the soule be at the *Table of the Lambe*, in Glory, and the body but at the table of *the Serpent*, in dust; Though the soule be *in lecto florido*, in that bed which is always green, in an everlasting spring, in *Abrahams bosome*; And the body in that green-bed, whose covering is but a yard and a halfe of Turfe, and a Rugge of grasse, and the sheet but a winding sheet, yet they are not divorced; they shall returne to one another againe, in an inseparable re-union in the Resurrection. (7.10.1–28)

The result aimed at in this funeral sermon is the assurance of a resurrection and of the reunion of body and soul. The sermon is in three parts: part 1 about imperfection in the spiritual realm, the brief part 2 about impermanence in the physical realm, and part 3 an extended step-by-step demonstration of God's mercy in the life of Sir William Cockayne. The sermon is an exercise in binding together elements of life that exist in tension: in the first part our imperfection and God's mercy in accepting it, in the second our impermanence and God's mercy in granting eventual permanence and perfection, too, and in the third part the binding together of body and soul, life on earth and in heaven as a continuum, man's life and God's response to it.

The method Donne uses to pull together elements in tension is an interesting one, for it is by dramatic reversal, which pulls opposites into paradoxical relation, that the sermon moves. As he proceeds from the second into the third part, Donne avers:

> As we have held you, with Doctrine of Mortification, by extending the Text, from *Martha* to this occasion; so shall we dismisse you with Consolation, by a like occasionall inverting the Text, from passion in *Martha's* mouth, *Lord, if thou hadst been here, my Brother had not dyed*, to joy in ours *Lord, because thou wast here, our Brother is not dead.*
>
> The Lord was with him in all these steps; with him in his life; with him in his death; He is with him in his funerals, and he shall be with him in his Resurrection; and therefore, because the Lord was with him, our Brother is not dead. (597–606)

And the third part is marked by the inverted text used as a refrain. The moment of inversion of the text Donne preceded by an inversion of images, using these examples to specify the impermanence of the body:

> When *Goliah* had armed and fortified this body, And *Jezebel* had painted and perfumed this body, And *Dives* had pampered and larded this body, As God said to *Ezekiel*, when he brought him to the *dry bones, Fili hominis, Sonne of Man, doest thou thinke these bones can live?* they said in their hearts to all the world, Can these bodies die? (552–58)

Then, as the antithetical example of Ezekiel foretold, the reversal:

> And they are dead. *Jezebels* dust is not Ambar, nor *Goliahs* dust *Terra sigillata*, Medicinall; nor does the Serpent whose meat they are both, finde any better relish in *Dives* dust, then in *Lazarus*.

But then a counterreversal, for at the resurrection the meanest of us shall surpass the beauty, strength, and fulness of these three in order to show the power and the mercy of a loving God:

> So the Angels shall know no man from Christ, so as not to desire to looke upon that mans face, because the most deformed wretch that is there, shall have the very beauty of Christ himselfe; So shall *Goliahs* armour, and *Dives* fulnesse, be doubled, and redoubled upon us. (587-91)

The sermon on Sir William Cockayne is much more dramatic than the typological sermons examined above, both because in it Donne attempts to bring home a difficult matter of feeling and because in doing so he is concerned to unite sharply opposed and contrasted matters of doctrine like justice and mercy. As his stress in the Division on hearing and seeing (7.10.63-67) indicates, the opposites to be brought together are less divergent directions in the text itself or the occasion of its use than they are the faculties of the congregation—what they hear or know, and what they see or experience. The sermon, in fact, looks outward toward its audience as it moves through the faculties of the soul in each auditor. Thus the first part starts by intensifying our general understanding of the imperfection of spiritual matters in our life, then moves into our memory of Martha in order to bring that understanding home, and ends by evoking belief in God's mercy in an action of the will. As a whole, the sermon stresses, in its three parts, a full understanding of imperfection, a sharply imaged memory of impermanence, and a willed belief in God's continued presence among us. It is a daring experiment, a public meditation on death; it frequently draws on the private feelings of the congregation and just as frequently turns the intensely private experience of the preacher himself out onto the public stage, as in the celebrated passage on Donne's own difficulty in praying (273-77). And it uses as structural principle the faculties of the soul that figured so large in the meditative tradition.

The importance of formal meditation for Renaissance English spirituality in general, and for Donne in particular, has long been established thanks to the studies of Louis Martz and others deriving from his.[17] In the seventeenth century, meditative thought moved out of the purely private realm. When Edward Dawson in 1614 published *The Practical Methode of Meditation* for the unchurched English Catholics, he sought to blend into it private versions of liturgical form, like the *Gloria Patri* at the beginning and such hymns as *Ave Maris Stella* at the end of an exercise.[18] Gradually, the term *meditation* began to crop up in sermons, such as those of Thomas Adams and Samuel Hieron, and public liturgy and private devotion, which had long been treated as two parallel "tracks," began to merge. Near the end of the century, in fact, Richard Baxter defined meditation as "sermons to the soul"; and the converse, sermon

---

17. Louis L. Martz, *The Poetry of Meditation* (New Haven: Yale University Press, 1954).

18. Edward Dawson, *The Practical Methode of Meditation*, in Louis L. Martz, ed., *The Meditative Poem* (Garden City: Anchor Books, 1963), pp. 10 and 17.

as "meditation to the public," was possible, too.[19] Barbara Lewalski has demonstrated that Donne characteristically uses the terms *meditation, exercise*, and *contemplation* to characterize his sermons. Here are some examples: "We cannot take into our Meditation, a better Rule, then that of the Stoick" (1.2.1–2); "But this is not the object of our speculation, the subject of our meditation" (6.13.584–85); "God poures out the Meditation of the Preacher" (7.13.127–28).[20] And, of course, the *Devotions upon Emergent Occasions* of 1624 shows fully the pressure of this meditative tradition on the mind and art of John Donne.[21]

The meditative tradition, however, enters into the sermons in a different way than does the typological tradition. There are a few sermons, very notable ones, that are constructed as public meditative exercises; but more usually we find sermons either meditative in part or exhibiting a kind of generalized meditative quality. The hallmark of the fully meditative sermon in Donne is the movement, like that of the *Devotions'* three parts of Meditation, Expostulation, and Prayer, from memory to understanding to will. A brilliant example is his famous last sermon, *Deaths Duell*, preached in the beginning of Lent in 1630, on Psalms 67:20, "And unto God the Lord belong the issues of death." Like the sermon on Sir William Cockayne, it is a public meditation on death, thought by Donne's contemporaries to be filled with personal experience.[22] Like the Cockayne sermon, too, it contains considerable tension.[23]

The first part, deliverance from death through the power of the Father, is clotted with images, for in it Donne intends to draw forth from his audience's experience a full sense that life is a long dying from which a powerful God continually saves. This part is notable for its use of grisly conceits that have the effect of pulling the diverse together—with great strain—by sheer intellectual force.[24]

The tension in the first part is not only that between vehicle and tenor: it is an emotional tension that stretches throughout, for, though deliverance is the nominal subject, what comes out to the audience is the ubiquity of the death we are to be delivered from, and each deliverance from death until the last is only to issue into a new form of death. Our memory terrifies us. What is to comfort us is the brief

---

19. Richard Baxter, *The Saints Everlasting Rest*, 9th ed. (London: for Francis Tyton and Jane Underhill, 1663), IV.x.1–2 (p. 744).

20. Lewalski, *Donne's "Anniversaries" and the Poetry of Praise*, pp. 90–91; see also Donne's *Sermons*, 2.1.9 and 7.1.377.

21. See Webber, *Contrary Music*, pp. 183–201, also Thomas F. Van Laan, "John Donne's *Devotions* and the Jesuit Spiritual Exercises," *SP* 60 (1963), 191–202; Janel M. Mueller, "The Exegesis of Experience: Dean Donne's *Devotions upon Emergent Occasions*," *JEGP* 67 (1968), 4; Clara Lander, "A Dangerous Sickness Which Turned to a Spotted Fever," *SEL* 11 (1971), 89–96; and N. J. C. Andreason, "Donne's *Devotions* and the Psychology of Assent," *MP* 62 (1965), 207–16.

22. See the printer's note "To the Reader" in the Quarto of 1632: "This Sermon was, by Sacred Authoritie, stiled the Authors owne funeral Sermon" (Donne, *Sermons*, 10:229).

23. For instance, the structure of the entire sermon is based on so slight a matter as the ambiguity of a Latin genitive: the Latin of "the issues of death" is *exitus mortis*, and Donne builds on three possible interpretations of that phrase his three heavily symbolic parts.

24. See, for example, 10.11.72–76, 79–82, 132–34, 160–63, 308–20.

second part of the sermon, deliverance in death by the comfort of the Holy Ghost, where the understanding enters in to show the limits of our understanding, to show us that any death can be a comfort known to God but not to man. The reasoning here is close, the tone cool—as befits this plateau of comfort.

The third part of the sermon, deliverance by the death of the Son in mercy, falls into the long tradition of meditation on the Passion of Christ—"Our *meditation* of his *death* should be more *visceral*, and affect us more because it is of a thing already done," he says explicitly (10.11.553–54)—and its motive is to activate our wills, in fact to make us weep. "Inlarge your devotion," Donne cries, "*Christ* bled not a droppe the lesse at the last, for having bled at his *Circumcision* before, nor will you shed a tear the less then, if you shed some now" (479–83). He faces the congregation directly here, activating the will by making demands on it and acting like a spiritual director ("let me be thy *Cock*," 621). He starts with composition of place, inviting the congregation to make its time and place Christ's time and place (576–82). He proceeds to a consideration of each of the acts of Christ, then to the presumed acts of the members of the congregation, and then moves to an emotional response. By the end of these "*steps*," he suggests colloquy: "There wee leave you in that *blessed dependancy*, to *hang* upon *him* that *hangs* upon the *Crosse*, there bath in his teares, there *suck* at his *woundes*, and *lye downe in peace* in his *grave*" (668–70). Resolution of tension has been reached by meditation, that consistent manner of uniting the human and the divine in daily life. And the sermon that has developed by meditative procedure, through image to understanding to colloquy and prayer, ends in an actual formal meditation that lays forth openly the source of its power.

Another explicitly meditative sermon is that for Whitsunday 1625 on John 16:8–11, which is divided according to the faculties of the soul, moving as it does from an evocation of the person of the Holy Ghost in a crowd of images and references to recorded events in part 1, through memory to true understanding (by making progressive distinctions among opinion, understanding, and faith) in part 2, to the exhortation to self-reproval in the will, which is defined as "the last act of the Understanding" (6.16.370–71), in part 3. The sermon that proceeds thus Donne defines, in his opening composition of place, as a public devotional exercise: "Our *Panis quotidianis*, Our daily bread, is that *Iuge sacrificium*, That daily sacrifice of meditating upon God; Our *Panis hodiernus*, This dayes bread, is to meditate upon the holy Ghost. To day if ye will heare his voice, to day ye are with him in Paradise" (6.16.1–5).

It is among the early sermons that we occasionally find Donne using one portion of the meditative process to the exclusion of others. For example, the sermon of valediction at Lincoln's Inn of 18 April 1619 begins, "Here then the holy-Ghost takes the neerest way to bring a man to God, by awakening his memory; for, for the understanding, that requires long and cleer instruction; and the will requires an instructed understanding before, and is in it self the blindest and boldest faculty; but if the memory doe but fasten upon any of those things which God hath done for us, it is the neerest way to him" (2.11.13–19); Donne then proceeds to show the memory subsuming the other faculties in a long nine-part meditation on his text, "Remember now thy creator in the dayes of thy youth." Likewise, a Lenten sermon at Whitehall for 12 February 1618 on Ezekiel 33:32 emphasizes the will and dwells on the relation between hearing and doing (2.7.131–32). The sermon for Trinity Sunday 1620 moves from its first part to its second by taking the Trinity inward into the three functions of the human soul (3.5.390–409) and ends with an exhortation to the will to "accustome thy selfe to meditations upon the Trinity, in all occasions, and finde impressions of the Trinity, in the three faculties of thine owne soule, Thy Reason, thy Will, and thy Memory" (3.5.750–53).

The sermons of Donne's later years of preaching are sometimes meditative in part, usually toward the end, like the Court sermon of April 1629 (9.2.354–55) or the sermon at Whitehall in February 1625 (8.7.585–656). But, more frequently, meditation tended to diffuse its influence in creating an ambience around a sermon; that is what Joan Webber noticed in Donne's middle and later years:

> The use of proem and sermon divisions to give the text a status as time leading to eternity and as space in which the listener can move around encourages the kind of concentration of all the senses upon the meditation that was advocated for individual practice in spiritual exercises. The environment of the congregation during the course of the sermon is to be the space and time that it represents, not the physical surrounding of church and fellow-worshippers.[25]

Meditation, as an "ancillary genre" to Scripture rather than a feature of Scripture itself, diffused its influence, and often entered into combination with other models, as we shall now see in examining "meditative typology."

Part 3

Sermons structured on the typological model crop up throughout Donne's career, from the earliest in 1618 to the latest in 1629, and for a variety of occasions and audiences, applied to a variety of texts both Old and New Testament. The meditative sermons appear in their pure and full form in 1625, but soon diffuse their influence. Neither of these forms presents a clear history in the body of the sermons; both models had, after all, been important elements in Donne's intellectual make-up since before his ordination, in *An Anatomy of the World* of 1611, for example, or the *Essays in Divinity* of 1614. But of the sermons that blend the two models in "meditative typology," we can say that their origin is clearly determinable and their development clearly traceable: they grew out of Donne's study of the Psalms.

Whenever Donne speaks explicitly of using Scripture as a model for the form of a sermon, it is usually the Psalms he has in mind. God, he says, "gives us our instruction in cheerful forms. . . . in Psalms, which is also a limited, and a restrained form. . . . God speaks to us *in oratione stricta*, in a limited, in a diligent form; Let us [not]

---

25. Webber, *Contrary Music*, p. 159.

speak to him *in oratione soluta*; not *pray*, not *preach*, not *hear*, slackly . . . let us be content to preach, and to heare within the compasse of our Articles . . . in those *formes* which the Church hath meditated for us, and recommended to us" (2.1.25–42). So, he says of Psalm 63:7, "we have here the whole compasse of Time, Past, Present, and Future; and these three parts of Time, shall be at this time, the three parts of this Exercise" (7.1.35–37). The Psalms had long been subject to typological reading, especially because they were often considered to form a bridge between the Old and the New testaments. They had also been a primary conduit of the meditative tradition. Louis Martz notes, "In the Psalms lay the prime models for the soul in meditation; here, above all places, lay a precedent for what I have called the poetry of meditation."[26] Thus William Temple in his dedication of *A Logical Analysis of Twentie Select Psalmes* to Prince Henry, remarks, "The subject analysed is a meditation performed by a great Prince."[27] In basing a sermon on a form both typologically determined and meditatively exfoliated, such as the Psalms, Donne could make that sermon a faithful model of Scripture, spanning time, and he could also offer to take his text into the devotional or psychological lives of his congregation: past time awakens memory, the present makes demands on the understanding, and the will is kindled toward the future.

We can observe this combination of scriptural and meditative models developing together in Donne's first distinguished sermons, the series of five sermons on Psalm 38 he delivered at Lincolns Inn in the spring or summer of 1618.[28] Donne's editors characterize his first years in the pulpit, 1615–1618, as devoted to rather dry reasoning; the sermons of those years, solemn in their almost exclusive concern with sin, are logical in their attempt to deal with it and show little of his later emotional appeal.[29] That is not true of the Lincolns Inn sermons: their emotional fervor rises as they treat the entire salvational cycle of sin and redemption, with its attendant topics of justice and mercy (which must have struck deep in his audience of lawyers);[30] and both the nature of this cycle and the pressure it exercised on the form of the sermon arose from the Psalms.

In the first, on Psalm 38:2, Donne sees fit to share, for the first time, his concern for the form of a sermon with his congregation. God, he says, "gives us our instruction . . . in Psalms, which is also a limited, and restrained form," so strict as to be organic in that it "can have nothing, no syllable taken from it, nor added to it" (2.1.25–31). And this strict form ought to be the model of our preaching, the *oratio stricta*

26. Martz, *The Poetry of Meditation*, p. 279.

27. William Temple, *A Logical Analysis of Twentie Select Psalmes* (London: for Thomas Man, 1605), sig. A4v.

28. There are actually six of these contained in vol. 2 of Donne's *Sermons*; only five of them, however, were published in the seventeenth century, the sixth being printed by Potter and Simpson from manuscript.

29. See Donne's *Sermons*, 1:121.

30. On these sermons as an extensive analysis of the phenomenology of sin, see Gale H. Carrithers, Jr., *Donne at Sermons: A Christian Existential World* (Albany: State University of New York Press, 1972), p. 46; see also p. 298 n. 50 on the effect of the legal congregation on these sermons.

outlined in the passage quoted before. This strict form, in the Psalm and in the sermon imitating the Psalm, he relates to his personal devotional life, explicitly in the form of meditation: "For, as a hearty entertainer offers to others, the meat which he loves best himself, so doe I oftnest present to Gods people, in these Congregations, the meditations which I feed upon at home." "These *publike* exercises to Gods Church," he avers, grow out of his own "meditations," based on "Scriptures, written in such forms, as I have been most accustomed to; Saint *Pauls* being letters, and *Davids* being Poems" (10–22). Here in this sermon lie the foundations of Donne's characteristic art: the sermon founded on Scripture, arising explicitly from his meditation on this form, presented implicitly as a form to awaken meditation in his audience. Samuel Hieron had exhorted his audience, "When you are departed from this sermon . . . commune with your own heart. . . . This is that which wee call meditation."[31] Donne here at Lincolns Inn is engaged in creating a form that will exemplify for his audience such a private use of the public exercise, by combining the exfoliation of the text with the opening of the faculties of the soul turned in concentration upon it.

The first sermon issues a call for such a form, and it starts Donne's exploration of that form. "This whole Psalm is a *Prayer*," he says, "And a Prayer grounded upon *Reason*" (2.1.44–45). It is reason or understanding that forms the basis of the first two parts of the sermon. With the third part, which operates much like an "application" section, the comparisons between David and the congregation in the first two parts are made explicit and are related to typology:

> To end all, and to dismisse you with such a re-collection, as you may carry away with you; literally, primarily, this text concerns *David* [in the present of the text]. . . . The Psalm hath a *retrospect* too, it looks back to *Adam*, and to every particular man in his loines, and so, *Davids* case is our case, and all these arrowes stick in all of us. But the Psalm and the text hath also a *prospect*, and hath a *propheticall* relation from *David* to our Saviour Christ Jesus. (747–56)

The third part of the sermon, which this passage introduces, dwells on the third element in the typological pattern, Christ; it is addressed to Christ and ends in prayer. Thus it acts as colloquy, turning from the understanding to the kindling of the will; and it is offered to the congregation as a goad to their private meditations: "Turne we therefore to *him*, before we goe, and he shall return home with us" (759–60). The parts of both the meditative and the typological structures are present in this sermon, but they have not been connected together to form a whole; the sermon does move from understanding to will, and its third part moves toward the third term typologically. But it leaves out memory and the second typological term, and these structural possibilities have neither been utilized to organize the whole nor been blended meaningfully. In the first sermon, the call for a form of "meditative typology" had been sounded, but the form has not yet been developed.

31. Samuel Hieron, *All the Sermons* (London: J. Legatt, 1614), p. 550; cited by Lewalski, *Donne's "Anniversaries" and the Poetry of Praise*, p. 87.

It is in the second sermon that we find such a form clearly emerging. Donne divides his text, Psalm 38:3, into the three portions of his sermon, historical, universal, and prophetic, now using the same scheme he has noticed in passing in the previous sermon as a structural principle (2.1.113–20). In the opening of his text, stressing the fact that this was a Psalm of remembrance, Donne saw fit to draw on the analogy of the three faculties of the soul to the Holy Trinity: "As the three Persons of the *Trinity* created us, so we have, in our soul, *A threefold impression* of that image, and, as Saint *Bernard* calls it, *A trinity from the Trinity*, in those three *faculties* of the soul, the *Understanding*, the *Will*, and the *Memory*" (2.2.21–24).[32] He goes on to relate the three faculties to the individual's process of salvation, basing it on the memory (48–52).

That the body of the sermon is to blend the typology of the division with the proem's discussion of the three faculties of the soul is implied by Donne's words just before the Division: "So have I let you in, into the whole Psalm, by this key, by awaking your memory" (105–10). The awakening of memory leads to the understanding that calamities come from God, and that realization leads us both to a feeling awareness of our own sinfulness and to a will to trust God's mercy. On this complex basis the three parts of the sermon proceed.

The first part, the present of the text (but the past of the congregation), dwells on David and on remembering our stake in his afflictions: "*Remember David and all his afflictions*, says our translation [of Psalm 132:1]" (187–88). The second part, the past of the text (but the present of the congregation, as they are figured in the continuity of the race of Adam) considers the state of mankind: "in this second part, . . . we contemplate *man*, as the Recepticle, the Ocean of all misery" (229–30). In this part, much longer than the first, Donne works from memory and images to understanding. He dwells on the names of our misery, our lack of health, of soundness in the flesh, and of peace in our bones; and in each case he awakens the understanding in order to winnow appearance from reality (400–411). Toward the end of this section, he assumes that much of this work has been accomplished and that his congregation can move on to full understanding of causes and hence of necessary effort. This perception of the cause of God's anger in our own sin prepares us for the third part, the future of the text and of our time too, in Christ, whose participation in our afflictions cleansed us from affliction.

Part 3 turns from justice to mercy in terms of death and rebirth; Donne has, he says, "laid man thus low" by displaying his misery; but from that metaphorical burial he will raise us "with that *Consolation*, which was first in our intention" (714), the atonement of Christ. And that atonement and raising he links to the passing from David to Adam to the second Adam who saves all. He sums up the miseries of mankind in that man-god simply by pointing to him, "*Ecce homo*, behold man, in *that* man" (727); in so involving our miseries in his, he activates our will to accept mercy. He

32. Though Donne cites St. Bernard, the origin of the analogy is probably St. Augustine, *De Trinitate*, 10.18.

is awakening our consciences to desire reformation: "Our physick is not eloquence, not directed upon your *affections*, but upon your *consciences*" (799–800). Thus the sermon ends in exhortation, activating the will to penitence in an eschatological milieu established in the mind.

The other three sermons follow this lead. The third, on Psalms 38:4, first recalls the sins of David, then leads us to understand our own sins, and finally exhorts us, by the method often recommended in devotional manuals of "application of the senses" in order to activate the will,[33] to embrace Christ. The fourth, which turns out to be the second of a series of three on Psalm 38:4, moves over the heaviness of sins (their multiplicity having been treated in the previous sermon), from memory of David to consideration of ourselves and then to trust in Christ; its stress is less on David than on us. And the fifth (the last in the series) is affective in mode, proceeding surely from memory to understanding to will in order to arouse our love and trust of Christ. It is in this sermon that Donne pauses to comment on the structure of his suit of three as a whole:

> when the Congregation is dissolv'd, and every man restored to his own house, God, in his Spirit, is within the doores, within the bosomes of every man that receiv'd him here. Therefore we have reserved for the conclusion of all, the application of this Text to our *blessed Saviour* . . . *Christ Jesus* himself; and that remains for our conclusion and consolation. (2.5.212–21)

The three sermons on Psalm 38:4, each moving from David to us and to Christ through the faculties of memory, understanding, and will, also form a sequence in which the first stresses David and us in memory, the second us in understanding, the third us and Christ in "astonishment" and love. Thus in them we can see on a large scale what we have seen in small in each of the Lincolns Inn sermons—a quiet yet complex blending of two different bases for sermon structure. The sermons of "meditative typology" do not feature the stylistic and modal contrasts between parts that we observed in the meditative sermons, because the serene connections supplied by typology tend more to unify than to contrast. These sermons, also, combine the strict attention to scriptural meaning of the typological with the personal application of the meditative and individual psychology. It is in this combination of the objective and historical with the personal, and with the overlay of psychological force and interpretive flow, that the strength of these sermons resides.

In the Lincolns Inn sermons Donne first sought and then found a sermon structure that would combine the objective and the deeply psychological. A year or so later, he had so far mastered this new form he had created as to make it a full scaffolding for a brilliant psychological movement. The sermon for Easter day 1619, "The King being then dangerously sick," was preached on another Psalm text, Psalm 89:48, "What man is he that liveth, and shall not see death?" By the time of this sermon, Donne

---

33. See, for example, Dawson in Martz, ed., *The Meditative Poem*, p. 20.

had developed a practice in his *Divisio* section that became characteristic; he goes over his division many times from many different angles. In so doing (in contrast to Andrewes, who tended, in keeping with oral forms, to give the whole sermon in small at the start in the division, and then develop it),[34] he focuses his audience's attention on the significance of the division, so that he achieves what is in effect a meditation on the division that keys us in to the whole sermon. In the case of the Easter 1619 sermon, he lays out his division according to three possible answers to the question posed by his text:

> In these words, we shall first, for our generall humiliation, consider the unanswerableness of this question, There is no man that lives, and shall not see death. Secondly, we shall see, how that modification of Eve may stand, *forte moriemur*, how there may be a probable answer made to this question, that it is like enough, that there are some men that live, and shall not see death: And thirdly, we shall finde that truly spoken, which the Devill spake deceitfully then, we shall finde the *Nequaquam* verified, we shall finde a direct, and full answer to this question; we shall finde a man that lives, and shall not see death, our Lord, and Saviour Christ Jesus, of whom both S. *Augustine*, and S. *Hierome*, doe take this question to be principally asked, and this Text to be principally intended. Aske me this question then, of all the sons of men, generally guilty of original sin, *Quis homo*, and I am speechlesse, I can make no answer; Aske me this question of those men, which shall be alive upon earth at the last day, when Christ comes to judgement, *Quis homo*, and I can make a probable answer; *forte moriemur*, perchance they shall die; It is a problematicall matter, and we say nothing too peremptorily. Aske me this question without relation to originall sin, *Quis homo*, and then I will answer directly, fully, confidently, *Ecce homo*, there was a man that lived, and was not subject to death by the law, neither did he actually die so, but that he fulfilled the rest of this verse; *Eruit animam de inferno*, by his owne power, he delivered his soule from the hand of the grave. From the first, this lesson rises, Generall doctrines must be generally delivered, All men must die: From the second, this lesson, Collateral and unrevealed doctrines must be soberly delivered, How we shall be changed at the last day, we know not so clearly; From the third, this lesson rises, Conditionall Doctrines must be conditionally delivered, If we be dead with him, we shall be raised with him. (2.9.27–56)

First of all, this division spans time typologically, since the three answers correspond to three strata of time, this life after the Fall, life in the last days of the earth, and life in Christ after the end of the world. It also involves three modes of statement, the unanswerable and fearful, the questioning and probable, and the full and confident; these three modes, as we shall see in the body of the sermon, evoke the sensory, the intellectual, and the faithful. They also suggest different styles and different tones.

The first part of the sermon is conducted in a strongly imagistic manner, playing on our senses in order to keep it in our memory that we are of the race of Adam devoted to death:

---

34. See, for example, Andrewes's sermon for Easter 1617, *XCVI Sermons*, pp. 505–16.

> *Mi Gheber*, sayes the Originall; It is not *Ishe*, which . . . signifies nothing but a *sound*, a voyce, a word; a Musicall ayre dies, and evaporates, what wonder if man, that is but *Ishe*, a sound, dye too? It is not *Adam*, which signifies . . . nothing but *red earth*; Let it be earth red with blood, (with the murder that we have done upon our selves), let it be earth red with blushing. (114–21)

Donne images life as a circle of earth, born from dust and returning to dust (31–32), and this image of enclosure is the foundation of the sensory prison with which he environs his congregation. All the senses—seeing, touching, tasting—are evoked, and they circle us around in time. The imagistic style speaks to our memory, to our sense of being embedded in Adam's earth, and the tone is one of dismay, of still and wordless conviction of the very fact of death.

The second part is addressed to our understanding. It begins with a subtlety and a distinction between the generality of men in our age and mankind in the last days. By defining the matter in question as a matter of opinion rather than one of fact, Donne lays out all the various opinions drawn from Scripture and the authorities (citation here is as thick as in the "Expostulation" segments of the *Devotions*). The mode is open questioning, and it introduces a sense of intellectual freedom that is refreshing after the grim sensory prison that the first part evoked.

The answers of the third part are given not "peremptorily" or "problematically" but positively: "We answer directly, here is the man that shall not see death" (367–93). Donne here moves into the future confidently, in a style—forceful declarative sentences, reiteration—that enacts the attitude he recommends. This is the style of faith, and it is meant to kindle our wills to desire participation in that faith. After proving that Christ did not die and will not ever die, he asks us to depend on that fact, and in his own voice enacts that movement of the will:

> God . . . shall bring that scourge, that is, some medicinall correction upon me, and so give me a participation of all the stripes of his son; he shall give me a sweat, that is, some horrour, and religious feare, and so give me a participation of his Agony . . . and if he draw blood, if he kill me, all this shall be but *Mors raptus*, a death of rapture towards him, into a heavenly, and assured Contemplation, that I have a part in all his passion. (519–27)

Here is the meditative moment of oneness between the exercitant and the object of his meditation; and, in alluding to that, Donne's tone becomes one of deliberate and careless joy: "I know I must die that death, what care I? . . . why despaire I? but I will finde another death, *mortem raptus*, a death of rapture, and of extasie" (497–500). In adopting this tone, he says, "If I come to a true meditation upon Christ, I come to a conformity with Christ" (548–49). This is the colloquy. Through the meditative process of this sermon, man comes into conformity with Christ, what began with death ends with life, and the very nature of mankind is transformed in the action of the mind, from the old Adam to the new Adam. For, near the end of the sermon, Donne picks up the earlier image of man in Adam as red earth and transforms it thus:

The contemplation of God, and heaven, is a kinde of buriall, and Sepulchre, and rest of the soule; and in this death of rapture, and extasie, in this death of the Contemplation of my interest in my Saviour, I shall finde my self, and all my sins enterred, and entombed in his wounds, and like a Lily in Paradise, out of red earth, I shall see my soule rise out of his blade, in a candor, and in an innocence, contracted there, acceptable in the sight of his Father. (503–9)

In this sermon, meditative typology, spanning past, present, and future as they are presented serially to the memory, the understanding, and the will, acts as a basis for a psychological process—induced by changes in style and tone—in the audience from despair to uncertainty to joy. It is a process of meditation on Scripture typologically unfolded that transforms the vision of humanity. The center of interest here is tone, the modulation of the congregation's emotions.

The mastery of the meditative typological form that Donne exhibits here surfaced later throughout his sermons, almost year by year. For example, the sermon for Easter Monday 1622 on "lights" derived from 2 Corinthians 4:6 spans all times. On these three times—our making, our mending, our perfection (4.3.126–61)—Donne builds his sermon and thus makes the text "carry us . . . from the Cradle of the world . . . to the Grave; and beyond the Grave of the world, to the last Dissolution" (66–69). The temporal structure expands to a psychological structure, for at the end of all the knowledge that these shining lights give is love, an act of will (1404–8). In the next year's sermon in the spring of 1623 on the penitential Psalm 6, Donne conceives the spanning of time in a purely personal way instead of superimposing the personal and meditative on the temporal: it begins with David's present thankfulness (the building), then proceeds into God's past help as cause of his trust in the future (its foundation), and ends with his present assurance (its prospect). In this personal and psychological spanning of time, the temporal is the element that integrates the personality in meditation, leading the congregation at the end to realize that "a precedent meditation, and a subsequent rumination, make the prayer a prayer" (6.1.489–90).

Most notably, we find meditative typology in Donne's fine series of Prebend Sermons on the Psalms. Of them, the Second Prebend Sermon, preached 29 January 1626, is especially noteworthy because it varies the usual pattern by associating the present with memory and the past with understanding (and, as usual, the future with will). As in the Easter 1619 sermon, Donne meditates on his division of the text, Psalm 63:7, by reiterating it and varying it:

The key of the psalme, (as S. *Hierome* calls the Title of the psalmes) tells us, that *David* uttered this psalme, *when he was in the wildernesse of Judah*; There we see the present occasion that moved him; And we see what was passed between God and him before, in the first clause of our Text; (*Because thou hast been my helpe*) And then we see what was to come, by the rest, (*Therefore in the shadow of thy wings will I rejoyce*). So that we have here the whole compasse of Time, Past, Present, and Future; and these three parts of Time, shall be at this time, the three parts of this Exercise; first, what *Davids* distresse put upon him for the present; and that lyes in the Context; secondly, how *David* built his assurance upon that which was past; (*Because thou hast been my help.*) And thirdly, what he established to himselfe for the future, (*Therefore in the shadow of thy wings will I rejoyce.*) First, His distresse in the Wildernesse, his present estate carried him upon the memory of that which God had done for him before, And the Remembrance of that carried him upon that, of which he assured himselfe after. Fixe upon God any where, and you shall finde him a Circle; He is with you now, when you fix upon him; He was with you before, for he brought you to this fixation; and he will be with you hereafter, for *He is yesterday, and to day, and the same for ever.* (7.1.29–49)

In his first announcement of the division, Donne notes that the text spans the time of David's life. The second time he goes over it, he generalizes it typologically into the whole compass of time and then relates the structure of the sermon to the structure of the text. With the third reiteration, he moves into David's mind, and as he does so the three terms of time become not merely divisions but integrally connected, personally and psychologically, to memory, understanding, and will. Finally, the three divisions of time are presented as parts of a whole in the mind of God and in his operations; in the image of the circle the idea of separate times dissolves, and that sense of Providence is brought into the lives of the congregation by direct address to them. Thus, by the end of the division, present affliction has been inundated by a sense of the benevolent care of God in spite of all pain.

William J. J. Rooney has attacked this sermon as professing by its structure to arouse a feeling of confidence in God but belying that in its details, which stress the affliction itself rather than release from it.[35] The division suggests an answer to Rooney's argument—that affliction is not to be played down but rather to be, at one and the same time, both directly faced and placed in a Providential context that forces us to see that it is not final. The sermon is to arouse us to trust God *in spite of* a feeling sense of the pain of the mortal moment: to that end, time becomes part of a cycle, and phrases suggesting dilation abound ("Psalms . . . spread themselves over all occasions," 10–11, for example).

The first part of this sermon, on present afflictions, dwells on memory, the sensory; it proceeds through the weight of afflictions in the flesh and then in the spirit, to end concretely with David's case. It is insistent in presenting life, as we experience it, as full of ironic reversals like the just Job suffering, and as repressive (113–14). The sensory experiences here evoked fill this part with images, usually those of touch in keeping with the concept of affliction as burden (82–85).

The second part, in remembrance of God's past benefits, focuses on us more than on David, and in it time starts to flatten out, as the pain of the present in sharp images leads into the eternal Idea of time with past, present, and future as its divisions instead of its conditions. The past becomes linked with the present in the economy of God's ways; to dip into the past is to touch the eternal. This second part, Donne

35. William J. J. Rooney, "John Donne's 'Second Prebend Sermon'—A Stylistic Analysis," *Texas Studies in Literature and Language* 4 (1962), 24–34.

says, moves through logical steps, instead of the reiterative, circling movement of the first part (320–30).

Now that Donne has pulled together man and God, past and present, memory and understanding in this text, he is ready to lead his congregation into the future with an act of the will. The third part moves by two steps. The first is the demonstration that what God promises is not avoidance of affliction but rather salvation and refreshment from it under the shadow of his wings. It is "this Metaphor of Wings" (583), with its associations of flying, rising, and freedom, that he makes a pivot to the second step, the last in the sermon:

> if hee refresh us in the shadow of his Wings, . . . this should not only establish our patience, (for that is but halfe the worke) but it should also produce a joy, and rise to an exaltation, which is our last circumstance, *Therefore in the shadow of thy wings, I will rejoice.* I would always raise your hearts, and dilate your hearts, to a holy joy, to a joy in the Holy Ghost. (628–35)

The arousing of the affections and the will here is deliberately hortatory: imperative verb forms, images, and metaphorical terms abound, and it is governed by the idea of "dilating" or "spreading" in many senses—the opening of the heart to joy, the opening up of this life to the next so that "true joy in this world shall flow into the joy of Heaven, as a River flowes into the Sea" (721–22), the opening up of death to rebirth. As this emotionally infused part began with exhortation, so it ends with incantation: "I shall have a joy, which shall no more evaporte, then my soule shall evaporte, A joy that shall passe up, and put on a more glorious garment above, and be a joy super-invested in glory. Amen" (746–49). It is by this means, with the faculties of the soul fusing together in each part, that this sermon becomes, in the words of Joan Webber, "a temporal symbol of the eternal joy that is its chief theme."[36] That is, meditative typology has created an emotionally compelling sense of Providential order in the midst of felt adversity.

One final example of this model is worth noting, and it comes at Easter 1628, ten years after Lincolns Inn, toward the end of Donne's career. It is unusual in two respects: it divides its text into two parts instead of the usual three, and it envisions time in terms of mental process or ways of knowing. Donne asserts that his text, 1 Corinthians 13:12, spans all time, as is proper to the occasion of the Resurrection that linked this life with the next (8.9.1–22). The sermon takes us through the time of this text as personal and racial time by its division into *Nunc*, our conditions in this life, and *Tunc*, our conditions after this life. And these two times are made psychological, made our time, by being envisioned in terms of knowing in the subdivisions.

The typological structure of this sermon is clear and brilliant, since it takes us from Creation to Resurrection, from this sermon to what it tells us of, and from each person's life on earth to his life after death. As that personal reach of theology indicates, moreover, it operates psychologically by a meditative process. The general division

---

36. Webber, *Contrary Music*, p. 152.

is in two stages, seeing and knowing now and seeing and knowing then. But in the actual working-out of this division in the sermon, the process moves from a short section on seeing now, or memory, to an extended section on knowing now and seeing then, or understanding, and ends in a movement of the will in love. For, as Donne said early in the sermon, "It is impossible to love anything till we know it; First our Understanding must present it as *Verum*, as a Knowne truth, and then our Will imbraces it as *Bonum*, as Good, and worthy to be loved. Therefore . . . naturally all men desire to know, that they may love" (101–6).

As Donne moves through these four sections, his style—and style here clearly is an emblem of ways of knowing—changes in accord with the mental stages of time that the sermon outlines. Thus the first section, on seeing God by the light of natural reason, has a style repetitive and imagistic, as is proper to meditation on the creatures:

> There is not so poore a creature but may be the glasse to see God in. . . . If every gnat that flies were an Arch-angell, all that could but tell me, that there is a God; and the poorest worme that creeps, tells me that. If I should ask the Basilisk, how camest thou by those killing eyes, he would tell me, Thy God made me so; And if I should ask the Slow-worme, how camest thou to be without eyes, he would tell me, Thy God made me so. The Cedar is no better a glasse to see God in, then the Hyssope upon the wall. (185–93)

The second half of part 1, on knowing now, moves with the understanding into doctrine, arguing out what we have been told in Scripture and by the Church in order to confirm our faith. Fittingly, its style is auditory rather than visual, for "the eare is the Holy Ghosts first door" (332–33).

Part 2 begins with images again, but it evokes the images of part 1 only to indicate their transcendence of the sensory:

> To this light of glory, the light of honour is but a glow-worm; and majesty it self but a twilight; The Cherubims and Seraphims are but Candles; and that Gospel it self, which the Apostle calls the glorious Gospel, but a Star of the least magnitude. . . . I shall not only *see God face to face*, but I shall *know* him (which, as you have seen all the way, is above sight) and *know him, even as I am knowne*. (499–508)

The crucible of the understanding has transformed images into emblems of ideas and used them thus to indicate transcendence. This process of the understanding is completed in the final section of the sermon, wherein the terms of sphere, medium, and light, all from God, are merged together (in earnest of transcendence once more) and the distinction between knowing and loving is obliterated by an act of the will. As the last section proceeds, it creates distinctions and equations whereby to know becomes to change, to change to be like God, and to be such to love God. The boundaries are thrown down, as we will resemble God:

> And so it shall be a knowledge so like his knowledge, as it shall produce a love, like his love, and we shall love him, as he loves us. For as S. *Chrysostome*, and the rest of the Fathers, whom *Oecumenius* hath compacted, interpret it, *Cognoscam practice, id est, accurrendo*, I shall know him, that is, imbrace him, adhere to him. *Qualis sine fine festivitas*! what a Holy-day

shall this be, which no working day shall ever follow! By knowing, and loving the unchange-able, the immutable God, *Mutabimur in immutabilitatem* we shall be changed into an un-changeablenesse. (600–608)

The understanding's final act is to transform itself into love.

In this Easter sermon, the typological and the meditative blend more completely than in any other. By conceiving of time epistemologically, Donne creates an identity between time, the basis of typology, and the human soul, the basis of meditation. And the seamless progress from this world to the next is conducted in a transformation of styles by means of which one realizes that to see becomes to know, and to know becomes to love.

The special form of sermon modeled on "meditative typology," unique to Donne, operated to involve the congregation fully in the unfolding of the text laid before it. A preacher like Lancelot Andrewes may be said to bring his congregation to his text. John Donne brings his text to his congregation, the text both fully interpreted and fitted to its meditations. These sermons span all time, thus bringing the congregation imaginatively from this world to the next. And they so involve the faculties of each person's soul in such a progress that they "bring the whole soul of man into activity,"[37] tracing response, guiding response in such a way that each person can feel how the soul reflects the Trinity, the mind the Word of God. Thus they bring to light most clearly those qualities that have led many readers to label Donne's sermons especially "poetic." Donne was to utilize this model for emotional effects throughout his career,[38] as he used the typological model to elucidate and apply Scripture fully and the purely meditative model to lead his congregation to search their consciences.

Sum

Several years ago, M. M. Mahood characterized Donne as "The Baroque Preacher" and suggested that his style was marked by strict structure and molten fluidity.[39] We can observe an example of this trait in a passage on the meeting of the human and the divine quoted near the beginning of this paper from the wedding sermon for Mrs. Washington, in which schemes like anaphora keep the structure firm, and lists, or what Joan Webber calls "runs," supply the fluidity or emotive pulsation.[40] In terms of overall structure, the typological organization supplies a sermon with a logical and seamless structure as one moves through prophecy to fulfillment, while the meditative structure leads to emotive flow, especially as it begins with the sensations and ends by trying to move the wills of the members of the congregation. The two meet, of course, in meditative typology, wherein logical structure and emotive development come to-gether, as do the objective and the subjective, the doctrinal and the personal.

37. Coleridge, *Biographia Literaria* (London: Everyman's Library, 1906), chap. 14, p. 151.

38. For instance, in the Lenten sermon of 1623 on John 11:35 (4.7) or in the pair of sermons of 1629 on Genesis 1:26 (9.1 and 2).

39. M. M. Mahood, *Poetry and Humanism* (London: Jonathan Cape, 1950), pp. 88–89, 113.

40. Webber, *Contrary Music*, pp. 31, 42–49; the whole of her chap. 2, pp. 29–70, is apposite to this matter.

AND HOW POSTERITY SHALL KNOW IT TOO

14. DIAMOND'S DUST
Carew, King, and the Legacy of Donne

MICHAEL P. PARKER

What to do with Donne was a problem that perplexed the poet's seventeenth-century successors as much as, if not more than, his twentieth-century critics. In addition to the purely aesthetic questions raised by Donne's innovative, idiosyncratic style, poets of the 1630s had to grapple with the prickly personal issues raised by the apparent disparity between "Jack Donne," the young scribbler of amatory verse, and "Doctor Donne," the dignified Dean of St. Paul's.[1] The twelve men who contributed elegies to the 1633 *Poems* responded to the problem in various ways: some, like Izaak Walton, suppressed any reference to the amatory poems altogether; others, like Jasper Mayne, squeezed Donne's life into an Augustinian model and dismissed the secular lyrics as youthful follies.[2] The two best elegies, those composed by Thomas Carew and Henry King, seemingly leap over the obstacle that proved such a stumbling block to lesser talents. The failure to address the biographical problem directly, however, does not preclude its pertinence; in their very different interpretations, both Carew and King necessarily touch on the issue. Although Carew proclaims the death of English poetry with Donne, his execution belies the elegiac commonplace: Donne's legacy is indeed a living one, and future poets can profit from the lessons he teaches and make his discoveries their own.[3] In the epitaph that closes his elegy, Carew tactfully offers a solution to the biographical controversy that attempts to do justice to both aspects of Donne's career. King's elegy appears to be both a response to Carew's poem and a refutation of it. King, a fellow churchman and the executor of Donne's will, also argues Donne's inimitability; unlike Carew, he proffers no hope that Donne's poetic influence will live on. Although King's motives are complex, the language of his poem suggests an attempt to shield Donne's memory from other, unauthorized elegists and to avert the discussion of the Dean's unedifying early career that such elegies would surely entail. King's efforts were ultimately (and fortunately) unsuccessful, but the contrasting interpretations of Donne that he and Carew propound—inimitable genius or master in a tradition—demarcate the battle lines in the skirmish over his memory in the early 1630s.

The first elegies on Donne to see print were those by King and Edward Hyde, perhaps the future Lord Chancellor but more probably a clerical cousin of the same

---

1. The distinction is one made by Donne himself in a 1619 letter to Sir Robert Ker, cited in R. C. Bald, *John Donne: A Life*, ed. Wesley Milgate (New York: Oxford University Press, 1970), p. 342.

2. The 1633 elegies on Donne are reprinted in *The Poems of John Donne*, ed. Herbert J. C. Grierson, 2 vols. (Oxford: Clarendon Press, 1912), 1:371–95. With two exceptions, I follow Grierson's texts: for Carew's elegy, I use the text in *The Poems of Thomas Carew with His Masque "Coelum Britannicum,"* ed. Rhodes Dunlap (1949; rpt. Oxford: Clarendon Press, 1970); for King's elegy, I use the text in *The Poems of Henry King*, ed. Margaret Crum (Oxford: Clarendon Press, 1965).

3. For a discussion of this topos and other elegiac conventions, see O. B. Hardison, Jr., *The Enduring Monument: A Study of the Idea of Praise in Renaissance Literary Theory and Practice* (Chapel Hill: University of North Carolina Press, 1962), pp. 113–18.

name. Both poems appeared unsigned at the end of the 1632 *Deaths Duell*, Donne's last sermon, which was probably published at the instigation of King.[4] These two elegies were reprinted along with ten others, including Carew's, in the 1633 *Poems*, published by John Marriot with the connivance of some still unidentified member of Donne's inner circle.[5] Priority of publication, however, does not necessarily establish priority of composition; external and internal evidence suggests, in fact, that Carew may have been the first to pen an elegy on Donne. "An Elegie upon the death of the Deane of Pauls, Dr. John Donne" undoubtedly circulated in manuscript for some time previous to publication. Lord Herbert of Cherbury mentions only Carew's piece in his own elegy of Donne; Aurelian Townshend, in a poem on the death of Gustavus Adolphus that dates from December 1632/January 1633, praises the "Ambrosian teares" that Carew shed "like manna on the Herse / of devine Donne" (13–16).[6] The initial lines of Carew's elegy, moreover, read in conjunction with his apology for breaking "the reverend silence" attending Donne's death, imply that Carew had the start on the swarm of elegists who tried their hand at penning Donne's praises.

Carew's elegy opens with a series of four questions whose answers provide the framework for his argument:

> Can we not force from widdowed Poetry,
> Now thou art dead (Great DONNE) one Elegie
> To crowne thy Hearse? Why yet dare we not trust
> Though with unkneaded dowe-bak't prose thy dust,
> Such as the uncisor'd Churchman from the flower
> Of fading Rhetorique, short liv'd as his houre,
> Dry as the sand that measures it, should lay
> Upon thy Ashes, on the funerall day?
> Have we no voice, no tune? Did'st thou dispense
> Through all our language, both the words and sense? (1–10)

Beginning with the second question, Carew responds to each affirmatively; in the final lines of the elegy, he returns to the initial, immediate question with the answer that all the present age can compose for Donne is an epitaph. Surveying this structure, Ada Long and Hugh MacLean argue that it violates the usual form of the Renaissance funeral elegy, defined by O. B. Hardison as consisting of "praise, lament, and consolation": "From this established pattern the structure of Carew's elegy on Donne significantly diverges. In effect, the poem consists almost entirely of praise and lament. . . . there is no hint of *consolatio* or of an 'exhortation that the audience imitate the virtues

4. *The Sermons of John Donne*, ed. Evelyn M. Simpson and George R. Potter, 10 vols. (Berkeley: University of California Press, 1962), 10:273–74.

5. See *John Donne: The Elegies and The Songs and Sonnets*, ed. Helen Gardner (Oxford: Clarendon Press, 1965), pp. lxxxiii–lxxxviii; and *The Poems of John Donne*, ed. Grierson, 2:255. Although Grierson postulated that King may have been the editor of the 1633 *Poems*, Margaret Crum discounts this hypothesis in *The Poems of Henry King*, pp. 14–15.

6. Townshend's poem is reprinted in *The Poems of Thomas Carew*, ed. Dunlap, pp. 207–8.

of the subject of the poem.'"[7] The key word is "imitate"; although Carew does not explicitly exhort his audience to imitate Donne's poetic virtues, the assertion that such imitation is not only possible but inevitable is implicit in the style and diction of the poem. As a number of critics have remarked, "An Elegie upon . . . Dr. John Donne" constitutes a remarkable pastiche of the elder poet's entire poetic corpus.[8] The initial rhetorical questions, sweeping enjambment, metrical substitutions, and complex syntax of the elegy, while characteristic of Donne's style, are not at all typical of Carew's previous works, the lyrics of the 1620s. A thread of verbal and imagistic allusions to Donne's works, moreover, runs through the fabric of Carew's poem.[9] Invoking the same conventions that compelled Donne to anatomize the death of the world in the *Anniversaries*, Carew insists that the genius of English poetry lies a-moldering in the urn with Donne, yet the execution of his poem belies the thesis.

The solution to this paradox rests in the easily overlooked fact that Carew's elegy contains more Carew than it does Donne; the younger poet gives his audience only a pastiche of Donne's style, not a facsimile. In his subtle but frequent soterial allusions — Donne has purged the fallen garden of the Muses; he has "redeem'd" the sins of English poetasters; he has "dispens'd" both "words and sense" throughout the language — Carew suggests that Donne, like Christ, embodies an ideal that can be approached but not perfectly attained. Like the *imitatio Christi*, the imitation of Donne must necessarily be partial. And in good Pauline fashion, Carew and his fellow Carolines are imperfect disciples, able to recognize the genius of Donne but unable to match it: "The good that I would do, I do not; but the evil which I would not, that I do" (Romans 7:19). Thus, with Donne's death "Libertines in Poetrie" (62), including Carew himself, will relapse into apostasy. Already in 1631 the abuses of which Carew complains were clearly in evidence. Sandys's translation of the *Metamorphoses* and Waller's new-model classicism would combine to restore the "gods and goddesses" that Donne had "banish'd nobler Poems" (64–65); Suckling was dashing off the pieces in "ballad rime" that would so influence Civil War and Restoration verse (69); even Jonson, who had announced his intention to return to the company of Anacreon and Pindar in the petulant 1629 "Ode. To Himselfe," was ripe to succumb to "a Mimique fury" not his own (30–33).

These backslidings notwithstanding, the "fresh invention" (28) planted by Donne will continue to bear fruit. Carew's depiction of poetry as "the Muses garden" (25) and the agricultural conceit of lines 53–60 place Donne's genius within an organic, living tradition; images of rebirth are a commonplace of *consolatio* in other, more conventional elegies. New seeds will undoubtedly sprout from the sheaves Donne has

---

7. Ada Long and Hugh Maclean, "'Deare *Ben*,' 'Great DONNE,' and 'my *Celia*': The Wit of Carew's Poetry," *SEL* 18 (1978), 85.

8. See especially Louis L. Martz, *The Wit of Love* (Notre Dame: University of Notre Dame Press, 1969), p. 98; and Joseph H. Summers, *The Heirs of Donne and Jonson* (London: Chatto and Windus, 1970), p. 65.

9. Specific echoes of Donne in Carew's elegy include "dowe-bak't" (4) from "A Letter to the Lady Carey, and Mrs. Essex Riche, from Amyens" (20); the figure of "the Muses garden" (25ff.) from "To Mr. Rowland Woodward: Like one who'in her third widdowhood" (3–6); and the conceit of the turning wheel (79–82) from "The First Anniversarie" (67–73) and "The Second Anniversary" (7–22).

"gleaned." Carew's other major pattern of imagery in the poem, that of gold and currency, reinforces the suggestions of fecundity and growth. Donne, claims Carew, has

> open'd Us a Mine
> Of rich and pregnant phansie, drawne a line
> Of masculine expression, which had good
> Old Orpheus seene, Or all the ancient Brood
> Our superstitious fooles admire, and hold
> Their lead more precious, then thy burnish't Gold,
> Thou hadst beene their Exchequer, and no more
> They each in others dust, had rak'd for Ore. (37–44)

Aristotle notwithstanding, Donne's gold is no barren metal—it will pass current and multiply its benefits among poets in any period or clime. The treatment of Donne's "phansie" recalls the image Carew employs in "A Rapture" to describe Celia's "virgin-treasure": "the rich Mine, to the enquiring eye / Expos'd, shall ready still for mintage lye, / And we will coyne young *Cupids*" (33–35). Donne's decease, to employ a doublet the doctor himself favored, proves not the tomb of English poesy but its womb; the figure of Donne himself now presides in place of the pagan muses he has exiled. And, despite the maladversions he had cast on his poetic productions during his lifetime, Donne himself would probably not resent the often extensive quarrying of his works by successors like Carew. The obsession with use and with the moral economy that John Carey notes throughout Donne's career might well extend to the posthumous fate of his poems.[10] When considering the "Mine / Of rich and pregnant phansie," we could do worse than remember Donne's meditation in a sermon preached to the King on 1 April 1627: "If gold could speake, if gold could wish, gold would not be content to lie in the darke, in the mine, but would desire to come abroad. . . . He that desires to *Print* a book, should much more desire, *to be* a book; to do some such exemplar things, as men might read, and relate, and profit by."[11]

The achievement of "An Elegie upon . . . Dr. John Donne" lies in Carew's ability to distance himself from the dean in order to survey the man as a whole. He displays a remarkable ability to avoid the personal and moral quagmires that claimed so many of the other elegists; his appreciation of Donne's poetry, paramount in the elegy from the first line, is primarily aesthetic rather than biographical. Carew is not, however, utterly oblivious to the scandal attached to the poetry. The epitaph that concludes his elegy evinces both an awareness of that problem and an ability to place it in perspective:

> Here lies a King, that rul'd as hee thought fit
> The universall Monarchy of wit;
> Here lie two Flamens, and both those, the best,
> Apollo's first, at last, the true Gods Priest. (95–98)

---

10. John Carey, *John Donne: Life, Mind and Art* (New York: Oxford University Press, 1981), p. 209.
11. Donne, *Sermons*, 7:410.

The formulation nicely reconciles the claims of balance and of priority. While Donne's religious vocation is "at last" given its due, the early devotion to poetry earns equal praise. The phrase "two Flamens" suggests a continuity between the poet and the priest that the other elegies in the 1633 *Poems* either deny or distort, and the reference to Apollo invests the secular poetry with dignity and grandeur. In its successful integration of the two facets of Donne's life, Carew's conceit recalls Donne's own assessment of his career in a 1623 letter to the Duke of Buckingham in which he refers to "the Mistresse of my youth, Poetry" and "the wyfe of mine age, Divinity."[12] Poetry and divinity are here complementary, objects of the same basic impulse. It is this recognition of the wholeness of the doctor's life—what we might call "the compleat Donne"—that renders Carew's elegy worthy of Martz's tribute, "If we grasp the poem we grasp Donne."[13]

The greatness of Carew's elegy, however, was not universally recognized in its own time. The elegy written by Henry King, in fact, appears to be a testy refutation of Carew's assessment and an attempt to secure Donne's memory from injury by non-ecclesiastical interlopers. The elegies by King and Edward Hyde, as I have mentioned, were the first to be published, appearing in the 1632 *Deaths Duell*. That these two elegies were not the first to be composed, however, is implied by the early references to Carew's poem and by allusions on the part of both King and Hyde to some un-authorized tribute to Donne already in circulation. Hyde, in declaring that Donne is above all praise, grumbles,

> There may perchance some busie gathering friend
> Steale from thy owne workes, and that, varied, lend,
> Which thou bestow'st on others, to thy Hearse,
> And so thou shalt live still in thine owne verse. (9–12)

This sounds very much like a criticism of Carew's elegy, which borrows from a number of Donne's works, especially the *Anniversaries*, to demonstrate how the doctor's influence lives on. As we shall see, the more explicit verbal echoes of "An Elegie upon . . . Dr. John Donne" in King's piece testify that Carew, indeed, is the unnamed target.

Like Carew's poem, King's "Upon the Death of my ever Desired Freind Dr. Donne Deane of Paules" argues that English poetic fires are quite put out with Donne's de-mise. But whereas Carew's witty imitation suggests how Donne's poetic influence will continue to shape the works of his successors, King admits no such consolation. In the climax of his poem, a description of the delivery of *Deaths Duell* on 25 February 1630/31, King stresses Donne's self-sufficiency:

> Thou, like the dying Swann, didst lately sing
> Thy mournfull Dirge in audience of the King;

---

12. Cited in Bald, *A Life*, p. 446.
13. Martz, *The Wit of Love*, p. 97.

When pale Lookes, and faint accents of thy breath
Presented so to Life, that Peece of Death,
That it was fear'd and prophesy'd by all,
Thou thither camst to preach Thy Funerall.
O! hadst thou in an Elegiack Knell
Rung out unto the world thine owne Farwell,
And in thy high victorious Numbers beat
The solemne measure of thy griev'd Retreat;
Thou mightst the Poet's service now have mist
As well, as then Thou didst prevent the Priest,
And never to the World beholden bee
So much as for an Epitaph for Thee. (29–42)

For King, Donne's genius is solipsistic. Since only Donne can do justice to Donne, the rest is—or at least should be—silence. King's admiration for Donne is undoubtedly sincere and his protestations of insufficiency justified; yet the insistence that *nothing* can be said of Donne goes beyond the usual commponplaces. As Hardison observes, when the poet remarks that the greatness of his theme far surpasses his capabilities, he usually adds that "he only continues with divine aid or because of an overpowering emotion or because of the insistence of others."[14] In "The Second Anniversary," for instance, Donne takes recourse to an extended meditation on the verse "There is motion in corruption" to explain how he came to write a sequel after consigning the entire world to the grave just a year before. Carew, for his part, employs the simile of the turning wheel to account for the energy he musters to praise Donne. King, however, offers no such elucidation of his tribute to Donne: he is dead, and the poet seemingly cannot explain the excellence of his own tribute. Closely related to the inadequacy topos is the element of consolation. Donne resorts to Christianity to solace the world for the loss of Elizabeth Drury; Carew, as we have seen, transmutes *imitatio* into *consolatio* to assure the reader that Donne lives on. Of the thirteen varieties of consolation enumerated by Hardison, however, King extends not one.[15] For a poet of the temper of King, such straying from convention is significant, and it is necessary to postulate some motivation.

Some twenty years younger than Donne, King seems to have regarded himself as the Dean's disciple. His awe of Donne was real, and his failure to offer the reader any consolation in the elegy rings sincere. King, moreover, seems to have been unusually given to self-deprecation. Margaret Crum, for example, cites a sermon King delivered to defend his father, Bishop John King, against posthumous charges of papism. Henry launches into his vindication with startling modesty: "I have at last adventured to speake: Not that I hold my selfe fit or able for this taske at any time, much lesse now; but onely for that I hoped what I should say might win more beliefe, as having been an

14. Hardison, *The Enduring Monument*, p. 116.
15. Ibid., p. 118.

eare-witnesse."[16] In retrospect, the diffident King might seem an odd choice to act as executor for the dynamic and histrionic Donne; given the charge, however, he shouldered it with determination, assuming responsibility for disseminating the story of the Dean's edifying end. He seems, however, to have taken the duty of protecting Donne's memory more seriously than even Donne himself might have wished. In *Deaths Duell* and in his friend Walton's *Life of Donne*, a clear hagiographic impulse is discernible.[17] King's elegy, I believe, is motivated in part by the perceived necessity to safeguard the Donne legend and to protect his memory from unauthorized incursions. Only by asserting that nothing can be said of Donne, and thus ensuring that he himself has the last word, can King rest certain that the heavenly crown he hastened to accord the Dean would remain untarnished.

As does Hyde, King lashes out at the presumption of those who would eulogize Donne:

> Indeed a Silence does that Tombe befitt,
> Where is no Herald left to blazon it.
> Widdow'd Invention justly doth forbeare
> To come abroad, Knowing Thou are not here. (11–14)

These lines may well echo Carew's apology, "Oh, pardon mee, that breake with untun'd verse / The reverend silence that attends thy herse" (71–72). Likewise, "Widdow'd Invention" recalls the "widdowed Poetry" of the opening line of Carew's poem. Given the proper inflection on "Indeed" and "justly," the passage can be read as an ironic rejoinder to Carew's professed inability to pen an elegy—a profession, as we have seen, that is not altogether ingenuous. King continues his castigation in terms that veer alarmingly close to a curse:

> Who ever writes of Thee, and in a Stile
> Unworthy such a Theame, does but revile
> Thy pretious Dust, and wake a Learned Spiritt
> Which may revenge his rapes upon thy meritt.
> For all a lowe-pitch't Phant'sie can devise
> Will prove, at best, but hallow'd injuryes. (23–28)

The warning brings to mind Carew's description of Donne's "brave Soule," that from the pulpit

> shot such heat and light,
> As burnt our earth, and made our darknesse bright,
> Committed holy Rapes upon our Will,
> Did through the eye the melting heart distill;

16. Cited in *The Poems of Henry King*, ed. Crum, p. 9. Although the protestation of inadequacy is a rhetorical commonplace, King's predilection for the topos is certainly indicative of traits in his own character.

17. For a discussion of Walton's technique and motives in compiling and revising the *Life of Donne*, see David Novarr, *The Making of Walton's "Lives"* (Ithaca: Cornell University Press, 1958), pp. 19–126.

And the deepe knowledge of darke truths so teach,
As sense might judge, what phansie could not reach. (15–20)

King preserves the key words, "Rapes" and "phansie," but reshapes them into an attack on the impiety of his source.

The most convincing link between the two poems, however, is King's recision of Carew's extended financial image:

Nor is't fitt
Thou, who didst lend our Age such summes of witt,
Shouldst now re-borrow from her bankrupt Mine
That Ore to bury Thee, which once was Thine.
Rather still leave us in thy debt; And Know
(Exalted Soule!) more glory tis to owe
Unto thy Hearse, what wee can never pay,
Then with embased Coine those Rites defray. (43–50)

Carew, it should be remembered, describes how Donne did "pay / The debts of our penurious bankrupt age" (28–29) and "open'd Us a Mine / Of rich and pregnant phansie" (37–38); had the ancients known this "Exchequer" of wit, they would never have "rak'd for Ore" in each other's dust (40–44). The similarities between the diction of the two passages seem too strong to be coincidental. King echoes Carew, of course, to ensure that his readers (or one reader, at any rate) recognize the identity of his target, thus discrediting Carew's poem and discouraging other would-be elegists from following suit. Yet, the strategy is inherently paradoxical. In asserting Donne's inimitability, King is forced to fall back on Carew's imitation of Donne to make the assertion. In capturing his opponent's guns in order to turn them against him, King implicitly admits the excellence of Carew's artillery; blame becomes an indirect form of praise. Under the combined weight of these *paradoxia epidemica*, the poem begins to totter.

In his penultimate stanza, King shoots off his final barrage at the unauthorized elegy:

Committ wee then Thee to Thyself: Nor blame
Our drooping Loves, which thus to Thy owne fame
Leave Thee Executor. Since, but Thy owne,
No Pen could doe Thee Justice, nor Bayes crowne
Thy vast desert; save That, wee nothing can
Depute to be thy Ashes' Guardian. (51–56)

Carew, it will be remembered, had not only presumed to write an epitaph for Donne but had also characterized his well-wrought poem as a "crowne of Bayes" hurled on Donne's "funerall pile" (83–86). In launching this final salvo, King divulges the pent-up anxieties he suffers as custodian of Donne's memory. The earlier admission, "I doe not like the Office" (43), undoubtedly refers to more than the "office" of penning an epitaph; King's insistence that Donne is his own "Executor" and that no one or no thing can be his "Ashes' Guardian" betrays an unmistakable uneasiness about the role Donne has thrust upon him. His anxieties, perhaps, were not ill-founded. Although King seems to have been a conscientious and thorough executor, he was perhaps too scrupulous and too naive in the ways of the world to carry out his duties imaginatively. His major contributions to Donne's memory—seeing to the carving of the famous effigy and publishing the last funeral sermon, *Deaths Duell*—are acts of preservation rather than propagation. The still mysterious loss of the papers with which King was entrusted to the scapegrace John Donne Junior was undoubtedly a boon in all respects: to Donne, who made a tidy profit publishing the sermons; to posterity, which might never have read the sermons had not Donne filched them; and to King, who was probably thankful to be relieved of the burden.[18]

The epigram that closes "Upon the death of my ever Desired Freind Dr. Donne Deane of Paules" is the best thing in King's elegy: "So Jewellers no Art, or Mettall trust / To forme the Diamond, but the Diamond's Dust" (57–58). The conceit sums the difference between King's and Carew's attitudes toward Donne. King views Donne as some rich jewel, a work of art finished and complete unto itself. Carew's view of Donne as a "Mine" and an "Exchequer," though superficially similar to King's jeweler's image, stresses use as much as display. King gives us the lapidary Donne; Carew, had he employed the conceit, would undoubtedly have emphasized the diamond's industrial applications.

In his study of Henry King, Ronald Berman suggests that "Upon the Death of my ever Desired Freind" transcends the paradox of its own insufficiency in a fashion that resembles Carew's procedure in his elegy.[19] The strength of the concluding epigram demonstrates that King is, after all, "Diamond's Dust," as able to shape Donne after death as Donne had shaped him before. But it is questionable that King had any such intention. King seems so overwhelmed by the personality of Donne that his muse is stifled; even Berman admits that the tone of the elegy is strangely "impersonal." Carew, fettered by no obligations and, as far as we know, by no personal ties, transforms his distance from his subject into an advantage. As Jonson observes in his *Discoveries*, "*Greatnesse* of name, in the Father, oft-times helpes not forth, but o'erwhelmes the Sonne: they stand too neere one another. The shadow kils the growth."[20] Proximity to Donne certainly stunted King's elegy; for Carew, Donne's shadow perhaps provided a cool and revitalizing resort from the "red and blushing evening" of his true poetic father, Ben Jonson.[21]

The relationship between the early elegies on John Donne is a complicated one, but I believe it is clear that King's 1632 poem responds to a manuscript version of

18. For the details of Donne's will and Donne Junior's acquisition of his father's papers, see Bald, *A Life*, pp. 530–33.

19. Ronald Berman, *Henry King and the Seventeenth Century* (London: Chatto and Windus, 1964), pp. 112–14.

20. *Ben Jonson*, ed. C. H. Herford and Percy and Evelyn Simpson, 11 vols. (Oxford: Clarendon Press, 1925–1952), 8:576.

21. "To Ben. Johnson. Upon occasion of his Ode of defiance annext to his Play of the new Inne" (7–8).

Carew's elegy; it is apparently only by an ironic chance that we now know the poems primarily from their side-by-side appearance in the 1633 *Poems*. Carew's fascination with Donne's achievement led him to explore the ways in which his poetry had transfigured and continues to transfigure English verse. King, charged with the duty of protecting Donne's memory, was concerned more with the man than with his works. A primary threat posed by unauthorized elegies was the very real possibility that analysis of the poetry would unearth the scandal of the amatory poems, thus undermining the edifying monument to the saintly Donne that King and Walton labored to erect. The publication of Donne's *Poems* in 1633 obviated the danger but not the general embarrassment: the dozen elegists represented in the volume were still hard-put, or hesitant, or both, to integrate the elegies and Songs and Sonets into the popular version of the holy dean. Only Thomas Carew rose to the challenge successfully, testifying that he, indeed, was of the stuff that Donne was made of—Diamond's Dust.

15. BRITTEN'S DONNE AND THE PROMISE OF TWENTIETH-CENTURY SETTINGS

PAUL L. GASTON

Although there is little biographical information that refers directly to Donne's interest in music, we know he found there a source of just metaphor. The dying penitent in "Hymne to God my God, in my sicknesse" looks forward to joining the "Quire of Saints" (2) and to becoming God's "Musique" (3). First, though, he must stand "at the dore" (4) of the stage or rehearsal hall to tune his instrument and rehearse the part he will assume. Similarly, "Of the Progres of the Soule: The Second Anniversary" urges the devout to anticipate their "laboring now with broken breath," just before life ebbs away, "And thinke those broken and soft Notes to bee / Division, and thy happiest Harmonee" (90–92).[1]

We know as well that Donne wrote several of his "songs" as parodies (fresh lyrics for well-known melodies) and that he expected his poems, whether "songs" or not, would become fair game for composers. Indeed, the first appearance of a Donne poem in print ("The Expiration") is in a collection of songs published in 1609: Alfonso Ferrabosco's *Ayres*.[2] Moreover, in "The triple Foole" Donne pays music a wry tribute by complaining that a song setting can revive feelings once neatly fettered in verse:

> Some man, his art and voice to show,
> Doth Set and sing my paine,
> And, by delighting many, frees againe
> Griefe, which verse did restraine. (13–16)

A similar idea, but one expressed in more positive terms, appears in remarks attributed to Donne by Walton. Having heard "A Hymne to God the Father," set for organ and choir and performed at St. Paul's, Donne "did occasionally say to a friend, The words of this Hymn have restored to me the same thoughts of joy that possest my Soul in my sickness when I composed it. And, O the power of Church-musick! that

---

1. "Not much is known about Donne's interest in music," R. C. Bald observes in *John Donne: A Life* (Oxford: Oxford University Press, 1970), p. 442. I would not go so far as Brian Morris, who finds negative evidence in the spare biographical record and in the quantity and quality of Donne's allusions to music. He infers "that Donne was not interested in music . . . and that it moves his imagination only in the most obvious ways" ("Not, Siren-like, to tempt: Donne and the Composers," in *John Donne: Essays in Celebration*, ed. A. J. Smith [London: Methuen, 1972], p. 233). Such a view must rest largely on this kind of negative evidence and must discount the striking references to music that do appear in Donne's poetry. One *OED* definition for division reads: "a florid phrase or piece of melody, a run."

2. See Helen Gardner, "Musical Settings of Donne's Poems," in *John Donne: The Elegies and the Songs and Sonnets* (Oxford: Clarendon Press, 1965), p. 238. See also *Ayres: By Alfonso Ferrabosco* (London: for John Browne, 1609). An accessible edition is that of E. H. Fellowes, *The English School of Lutenist Song Writers*, vol. 16 (London: Stainer & Bell, 1927), 13–14.

Harmony added to this Hymn has raised the Affections of my heart, and quickned my graces of zeal and gratitude."[3] Though not entirely reliable, the anecdote seems consistent with the few other indications we have of Donne's musical concerns. Donne may not have participated in musical activities as fully as did his young friend George Herbert, but it seems safe to conclude that he enjoyed, respected, and understood music.

This understanding did not influence Donne to adopt a poetic style readily amenable to musical settings, however. Unlike the lyrics of Herrick, Carew, or Jonson, the poems of Donne seem to have deterred most composers of the period. According to a survey by Vincent Duckles, only eight of Donne's authenticated lyrics were set to music by seventeenth-century English composers.[4] Composers of this time sought instead lyrics with clear images, simple syntactical patterns, and a regular metrical pulse. Above all, they wanted to convey feelings. "Music is a language of the emotions not of verbal ideas," says one modern historian of English song.[5] But in Donne, the composers of his time found verbal ideas aplenty. What is more, Donne's images are often recondite, his structures complex, his rhythmic patterns irregular.[6] We need not be historians of music to perceive that composers of Donne's time must have been hard-pressed to cope with the challenges Donne's poetry offers. Or, as Professor Duckles puts it, "What is most distinctive and personal in his expression moves into a realm beyond the reach of the composers of his time."[7]

The seventeenth-century settings we do have possess considerable charm. But even as they exploit the appeals of the early seventeenth-century song idiom, they illustrate its limitations in accommodating even the simpler lyrics of Donne. Two of these settings, that of "The Expiration" by Ferrabosco and that of "A Hymne to God the Father" by John Hilton, may serve as examples.

---

3. Isaak Walton, *The Lives of John Donne, Sir Henry Wotton, Richard Hooker, George Herbert, and Robert Sanderson* (Oxford: Oxford University Press, 1927), p. 62. If Donne here refers to the setting he commissioned, he may well be referring to the one by John Hilton, which I discuss. See Peter Le Huray, "John Hilton," *The New Grove Dictionary of Music and Musicians* (London: Macmillan, 1980), 8:569.

4. Duckles lists "The Baite," "Song: Dearest love, I do not go," "The Message. Send home my long stray'd eyes," "Song: Go and catch a falling star," "The Expiration," "Breake of Day," "A Hymn to God the Father," and "How sits this city, late most populous" from "The Lamentations of Jeremy" ("The Lyrics of John Donne as set by his Contemporaries," in *Bericht über den siebenten Internationalen Musikwissenschaftlichen Kongress Köln 1958* [Kassel, 1959], 91–93). Compare Jean Jacquot, "Introduction," *Poèmes de Donne, Herbert et Crashaw mis en musique par leurs contemporains,* comp. and arr. André Souris (Paris: Editions du Centre National de la Recherche Scientifique, 1961), pp. 1–19. Gardner's account is based on the Duckles and Jacquot lists ("Musical Settings," *Elegies and Songs and Sonnets,* p. 238).

5. Ian Spink, *English Song: Dowland to Purcell* (London: B. T. Batsford, 1974), p. 78.

6. John Hollander provides a thorough analysis of the rhythmic difficulties encountered by Donne's contemporaries in their musical settings of Donne texts, but he finds an even greater difficulty for songwriters in "a matter of modality that marks the metaphysical lyric from a musical point of view, a mixture of basic tonalities within a particular song." As Donne's lyrics often provide "a constant process of dialectic between modalities," they embody a complex musical challenge beyond the resources of seventeenth-century art song ("Donne and the Limits of Lyric," in *Essays in Celebration,* ed. Smith, pp. 259–72).

7. Duckles, "The Lyrics of John Donne," p. 92.

So, so,   leave off   this last la-

Illus. 1.

Ferrabosco's setting reaches toward the later declamatory style in English song as it responds with some sensitivity to the meaning and syntax of "The Expiration." The first measure, with its rising thirds conveying the imperative movement of "So, so, leave off . . . ," promises close attention to the verbal stresses of Donne's stanza (Illus. 1). In a more general sense, "turnings" (such as *circulatio*) in the melody represent those of the characters in the poem, sudden modal shifts reflect shifts in argumentative strategies, and repetition of the stanza's concluding couplet emphasizes its effectiveness as both poetic and musical resolution. The lovers' harmony parallels that of the music, just as the lovers form their resolution in tune with an easily recognized closing cadence[8] (Illus. 2).

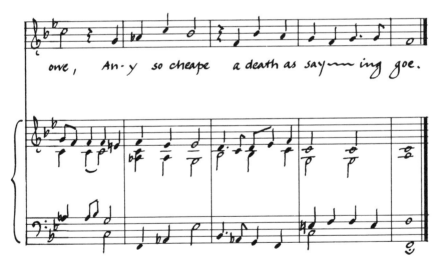

owe,   An·y   so cheape   a death as say ___ ing goe.

Illus. 2.

8. Cf. Brian Morris, who finds Ferrabosco's treatment "foursquare." I find considerable pathos expressed in a shift of keys and drop in pitch at the words "that way," but Morris concludes, "Ferrabosco responded only to the cavalier note of the lovers' defiance" ("Not, Siren-like," in *Essays in Celebration*, ed. Smith, p. 233).

For all its charm, however, Ferrabosco's setting proves no match for its text. Lute-song conventions still at work in this transitional air restrict its vocal range, rule out extensive illustrative phrases, and discourage dramatic melodic intervals. Means that Ferrabosco might have found useful in the setting of Donne's poem were not yet generally available, and means that were available to him, such as those for scene painting, were of little use in the setting of a poem almost wholly devoid of visual images. These limitations appear even more clearly in the setting as it applies to Donne's second stanza. The strophic nature of lutesong prevents Ferrabosco from responding to the stanza's rhythmic values and verbal structures, with the result that melodic lines barely adequate to the first stanza fail entirely to reflect the wit and force of the poem's conclusion (Illus. 3).

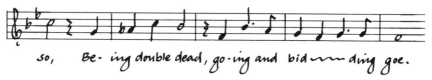

Illus. 3.

John Hilton's setting of "A Hymn to God the Father" might be that "most grave and solemn tune" that Donne (according to Walton) praised so highly.[9] Such matters are not beyond all conjecture, as Sir Thomas Browne might have said. Certainly, Hilton's setting is grave and solemn. Though more conservative in its musical idiom than the Ferrabosco setting of "The Expiration," it does show some sensitivity to the prevailing tone of Donne's poem. Unlike "The Expiration," a poem of constantly shifting premises and reinvented strategies, "A Hymn to God the Father" sustains a firm, though difficult, devotional posture as it undergoes a subtle shift of emphasis from contrition to supplication. Hilton creates a responsive setting by subtle means. Within the key of G minor, traditionally considered a "dark" key, Hilton provides suggestions of the relative major (B-flat) to convey limited but important variations in the emotional reference of Donne's text. That is, Hilton interprets Donne's anxiety about original sin — "Which is my sin, though it were done before?" (2) — as marginally less compelling than his concern with his present sins, and he registers this interpretation by a carefully limited hint of modulation from minor to the relative major and back again. We may not agree with Hilton's reading, but, in listening to his setting, we consider his interpretation, his critical reading of Donne's line. Another of Hilton's subtle means lies in his setting of the stanza's final two lines, as the wordplay on "done" occupies a tonal

9. Spink, *English Song*, p. 69. Le Huray ("John Hilton," *New Grove Dictionary*, 8:569) agrees with Spink. Morris ("Not, Siren-like," in *Essays in Celebration*, ed. Smith, p. 238) thinks it "unlikely" that Donne's reference as quoted by Walton is to the Hilton setting.

sequence (the repetition of the four-note phrase "When thou hast done," a third lower for "thou hast not done") that anticipates the conclusive grave cadence[10] (Illus. 4).

When thou hast done,   thou hast not done for

Illus. 4.

Yet even this most pleasing figure in Hilton's setting points to its thorough conventionality. As Diana Poulton points out in a recent note on John Dowland, similar four-note descending phrases appear in compositions "too numerous to mention," probably because the phrase had become a formula, "even . . . a symbol for tears."[11] Hilton re-employs the figure to good effect, certainly, but it seems telling that his most striking effect arises from his least original musical phrase.

As with the Ferrabosco setting, the setting by Hilton fails to operate effectively beyond the first stanza of the poem. Hilton thus cannot track the poem's modest shifts from penitence to supplication. Even as applied to the first stanza alone, Hilton's suggestions of the major in the second and fourth lines may afford a premature sense of resolution. In short, Hilton's pleasant lutesong finally does little justice to Donne's poem.

Although the Ferrabosco and Hilton settings can charm, they also reveal effectively the limitations with which a lutesong composer must contend in the setting of a complex text. With such limitations in mind, we can appreciate what they and their peers did accomplish with Donne's poems. But we also can understand more fully why Donne's texts consistently dominate their settings and why these settings fail to develop satisfying interpretations. We may well enjoy the seventeenth-century settings of Donne's poetry, but we must admit how far they fall short in accommodating the intellectual depth and agility of Donne's work.

Fortunately, however, this is not the whole story. If seventeenth-century settings of Donne's poetry establish a brief interpretive tradition of some interest, twentieth-century settings represent a continuing interpretive opportunity. (A very few settings may derive from the eighteenth and nineteenth centuries, but no definitive identifications exist.) In some ways similar to those of their colleagues in literary studies, modern composers have rediscovered the achievements of the early seventeenth century

10. Hollander observes that Hilton's setting "has not reduced the paradox [represented by the pun] to the more trivial one by implying with musical ictus a speech rhythm of 'When thóu hást dóne, thóu hást nót dóne'" ("Donne and the Limits of Lyric," in *Essays in Celebration*, ed. Smith, p. 270).

11. Diana Poulton, "Dowland Rehabilitated," *The Musical Times* 118 (January 1977), 25.

in England, and Donne has become one of the beneficiaries of their attention. Not all modern interpretations will please Donne's readers, of course. But, taken together, they will persuade many that twentieth-century composers may have begun to develop an idiom sufficiently flexible and responsive to accommodate Donne's poetry. For we now have settings that interpret Donne's poetry without reducing it, settings that convey both fresh musical ideas and faithful attention to the intellectual and syntactic integrity of Donne's text. For instance, we have settings of the Holy Sonnets by John Eaton and by Douglas Moore, settings of "A Valediction forbidding mourning" and "Loves growth" by Ross Lee Finney, a setting of "Song: Goe, and catche a falling starre" by Lee Hoiby, and settings of various Donne songs by Mary Howe.

All these settings reflect and benefit from a number of developments in musical style and performance capabilities, which together describe a historical context for modern musical idioms. Relaxed standards for musical decorum and a respect for serious experiments have encouraged composers to employ dialects in which harmonic instability and rhythmic irregularity are but the most obvious characteristics. Improvements in musical instruments (the piano, especially) and in vocal and instrumental performance technique have greatly extended the range of possibilities for composers. Modern poetry itself has helped to create an atmosphere in which experiments find audiences and win support. Those who listen to twentieth-century song, together with those who read contemporary poetry, no longer place a high value on ease of access. Those who write benefit from such tolerance for the complex, as does Donne.

One contemporary work in particular, Benjamin Britten's setting of nine of the Holy Sonnets, illustrates the success a modern composer can enjoy in the setting of Donne's poetry. Published in 1946 (London: Boosey & Hawkes), this work for high voice and piano stands as an elegant bridge between the twentieth and seventeenth centuries. Without compromising the freshness of his idiosyncratic idiom, Britten in this cycle draws on musical ideas developed by Henry Purcell in the *Harmonia Sacra* (1691) as he provides an attentive and provocative reading of his chosen poems.

In many ways, Britten's cycle demonstrates not just the genius of a single composer but also the opportunities available for the first time to an entire generation of composers. His interpretations are selective, as all interpretations must be. But his settings respect the complexity of the Donne poems as they convey an impressive measure of their power.

"Oh my blacke Soule," with which Britten begins his cycle, announces in its first two measures the familiar iambic pulse that defines the poem's issue as a matter of life and death. When the voice enters fortissimo in the third measure, it can then state the fearful patient's dilemma against a counterrhythm as sure (and as fragile) as that of the heart. Britten's priorities in the setting gradually emerge in the subsequent measures. By melodic intervals that convey an insecurity of key, Britten establishes a persistent analogy for the physical and spiritual dis-ease that informs the poem. By sharply limiting melodic material in the setting, Britten conveys the narrow compass of the invalid's desperate ingenuity. And by setting a countermelody in the bass at the midpoint of the poem's sixth line ("Wisheth himselfe deliverd from prison"), Britten introduces an impression of critical commentary beneath the clever simile making.

A keen ear for intervals will detect such meaningful subtleties in the setting as the once-feared *diabolus in musica* interval, the diminished fifth, at the first instance of the word *damn'd* in the poem's seventh line and the resolution of that interval in the poem's final line (Illus. 5). One commentator describes it as "a clear analogy to the salvation being promised in the text."[12] Even an untrained ear, if attentive, will recognize Britten's emphasis on the assertion of faith with which the poem concludes. The voice rises to its affirmation as the uneasy tritone beneath relaxes and supports it.

damn'd ...   it dyes red soules to white....

Illus. 5.

"Batter my heart," the second setting of Britten's sequence, makes clear his intention to emphasize the contrasts apparent in the uneasy progress of Donne's pilgrim toward redemption. It is obvious at once, as the sharp staccato triplets in the piano drive the voice furiously ahead, that Britten finds in this sonnet a mood far different from that in "Oh my blacke Soule" (Illus. 6). The weary perseverance of the sick penitent yields now to frantic ingenuity rising from a passionate longing for violent correction.

12. Rembert Bryce Herbert, "An Analysis of Nine Holy Sonnets of John Donne Set to Music by Benjamin Britten," Ph. D. diss., American University, 1974, pp. 20–21.

Illus. 6.

Just as Donne challenges the reader with virtuoso wit as he presses against conventional ideas of decorum, so Britten challenges the listener with a virtuoso setting as he presses singer and accompanist against the limits of their respective instruments. The repetitive, inexorable accompaniment rises and falls by its own logic as the voice interposes the sonnet's hard monosyllables in dissonant bursts. The resources and experimental opportunities available to the modern composer appear to advantage, then, as Britten combines forces with Donne in a complex but expressive interpretation.

Such a setting can raise the issue of accessibility, to be sure. One critic cites this setting in particular to support her complaint about Britten's cycle as a whole: "These sonnets are almost unintelligible as songs to one who is not already familiar with them as poems." As a result, "the songs are less satisfying in performance than the poems alone are."[13] But to presume that serious audiences need not be required to have some acquaintance with the texts set as songs is to limit sharply the possibilities modern composers enjoy for setting complex texts adequately. For the listener who does know this sonnet, no other setting available will be likely to seem more responsive to its particular wit and energy. And that is surely the issue. Like any other modern artist, the serious composer should be able to assume that the most responsive part of his audience will be reasonably well informed, attentive, and judicious. Britten tests the resourcefulness of his listeners as he exercises his own, but his priorities in "Batter my heart" are, after all, clear. With his setting, he establishes the strongest possible con-

13. Patricia Samson, "Words for Music," *Southern Review* (Australia) 1 (1963), 46–47.

trast with the preceding setting and so defines at once the polarities between which his penitent will move.

"O might those sighes and teares," the third song in Britten's sequence, reaches for a mean between the extremes represented by the first two settings. Suggestive in some ways of lutesong, as the accompaniment at points seems to follow and comment on the vocal line, it is also suggestive, by its careful declamation, of Purcell. Yet its balance remains charged with tension. "To (poore) me is allow'd / No ease" (12–13), Donne's speaker says; thus, Britten allows a respite from the energy of "Batter my heart" without relaxing its sense of constraint. The single intimation of high feeling in the song at its *poco animato* expresses well the penitent's vexation that he cannot share the sensualist's consolation in remembered pleasures:

> Th'hydroptique drunkard, and night-scouting thiefe,
> The itchy Lecher, and selfe tickling proud
> Have the remembrance of past joyes, for reliefe
> Of comming ills. (9–12)

But after this moment of resentment, the venting of a safety valve, the setting slows again (*rilassando*) as the penitent recovers his hard discipline of self-knowledge.

"Oh, to vex me," next in the sequence, again allows the frantic, high spirits of Donne's supplicant to break through. Hardly "a lighthearted and witty spoof on all that has gone before,"[14] this setting provides suggestions of frivolity both to convey the inconstancy of the supplicant's spirit and to underscore his resulting anxiety: "So my devout fitts come and go away / Like a fantastique Ague" (12–13).

In the fifth sonnet of Britten's sequence, "What if this present," we once again hear the composer exploiting the twentieth-century idiom in order to provide an appropriate setting for a state of spiritual change. The accompaniment leaps about frantically for two measures before the singer enters to voice the sonnet's fearful opening question. Arpeggios and trills provide the most obvious means of scene painting (Illus. 7). Once the question has been voiced, it reverberates through the equivalent of another two measures in the piano alone. But as fear in the sonnet yields to restorative colloquy through the contemplation of "The picture of Christ crucified" (3), the character of the accompaniment changes. Trills in the right hand persist for a time; the trembling does not stop at once, but diminishes slowly. The left hand stalks in an irregular dirge, disturbing the act of contrition, before stabilizing with the development of the final comforting counsel:

> so I say to thee,
> To wicked spirits are horrid shapes assign'd,
> This beauteous forme assures a pitious minde. (12–14)

For these conclusive lines, the piano sustains simple supportive chords, anticipating

14. Herbert, "An Analysis of Nine Holy Sonnets," p. 26.

Illus. 7.

the whole note, a G_1 (two and one-half octaves below middle C), which resounds alone as the setting ends.

Britten's setting of this sonnet emphasizes the gradual shift from terror to confidence. Its critical moment, then, is the soul's contemplation of the crucified Christ. This moment in Britten's interpretation is one of anguish (Illus. 8). From such anguish arises the strength that makes possible the final recognition.

Illus. 8.

"Since she whom I loved," the most melodic and accessible of Britten's Holy Sonnets settings, discourages analysis. As Michael Kennedy has pointed out, the setting is "economical in actual notes" even as it gives an impression of "endless melody."[15] Peter Pears, who has performed all the Britten settings, speaks of this one as "a highly impassioned utterance, which is yet so surely balanced and logical in structure."[16] Just how the accompaniment and vocal line create this impression of great beauty out of such carefully limited means defies explanation, though Brian Morris provides a perceptive suggestion: "Oddly, and probably accidentally, Britten's direction 'Adagio multo rubato' sets the tone for Donne's celebration of the effects of God's 'robbery' of Anne Donne, and the steady $\frac{3}{4}$ movement of the vocal line against the triplets of the ac-

15. Michael Kennedy, *Britten* (London: Dent, 1981), p. 178.
16. Peter Pears, "The Vocal Music," in *Benjamin Britten*, ed. Donald Mitchell and Hans Keller (London: Rockliff, 1952), p. 70.

companiment encourages the singer to make his own emphases and climaxes."[17] What is clear is that the simplicity of the melody and the regular, harmonically pleasing pulse of the accompaniment help to relax momentarily some of the tension the cycle has generated, as Britten's imagination, brilliant even when at work with a small palette, prevents any lapse into the sentimental.

Rembert Bryce Herbert correctly perceives that the resolution of this setting, with its "assurance and lyrical power," prepares us for the opening of the next. "Since she whom I loved" concludes as "At the round earth's imagined corners" begins, *largamente*. From this point on in Britten's cycle, as Herbert observes, the relationship between God and the supplicant grows more and more straightforward, and the voice we hear in Britten's settings grows more and more confident. Harmonic and rhythmic patterns, which at first sound complex but later "dissolve" toward simplicity, support this process.[18]

As the cycle moves toward its conclusion, the exuberant *moto perpetua* of "Thou hast made me" seems to be a release in several senses. Scene painting is so obvious and flamboyant that it becomes comic (Illus. 9). Both piano and voice have the opportunity to compete in exhibitions of athletic prowess, as Britten allows himself the full play of his inventive wit. Of course, the sonnet is itself witty:

> But our old subtle foe so tempteth me,
> That not one houre I can my selfe, sustaine;
> Thy Grace may wing me to prevent his art
> And thou like Adamant draw mine iron heart. (11–14)

For his own dramatic ends, Britten has placed this sonnet wisely and given himself some creative liberties at the right time. The lightening we find in this penultimate setting enables us to respond more directly to the grand seriousness of Britten's conclusive interpretation.

The setting of "Death, be not proud" develops in three broad sections. The first and third represent proud assertion of the confident redeemed man against death, the

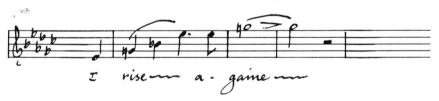

Illus. 9.

17. Morris, "Not, Siren-like" in *Essays in Celebration*, ed. Smith, pp. 246, 248.
18. Herbert, "An Analysis of Nine Holy Sonnets," p. 31.

second, a somewhat less forceful exposition of the means and universality of death. In the assertive sections, the vocal line assumes full authority; the bass line in the accompaniment gently supports, and in places follows, the voice. At no point does the calm passacaglia compete with or provide a critical commentary on the vocal line (Illus. 10).

Illus. 10.

The general impression of Britten's setting is one of assurance, an impression that seems consistent with most readings of Donne's poem. But Britten finds in lines 5–12 a subtle nervousness. With the recognition that "our best men" go with Death, that the means of death are many, and that "poppie,' or charmes" can simulate Death's sleep, Britten's vocal line conveys a strident insistence, rather than a calm assurance. "Britten sometimes seems unsure how to get all the words out," Herbert observes.[19] By Britten's interpretation, Donne's speaker is eager to get the words out, to anatomize and disenfranchise Death so that the conclusive threat will seem justified.

But no matter. Dealing with Death may still prove unpleasant, but assurance of victory remains firm. At the end of the long and complex cycle, the voice breaks away

19. Ibid., p. 32.

from its accompaniment and, in Pears's words, "can flower in its own way."[20] The singer addresses death on a strong F-sharp for two measures, then drops an octave—"thou shalt"—and concludes triumphantly on the tonic B, "die."

From an initial anxiety, fueled by an acute illness, regarding the blackness of the soul, the voice in Britten's cycle has moved through different and unpredictable stages in the life of faith to achieve at the last a sense of firm confidence in the soul's immortality. On the dramatic framework he obtains by careful arrangement of the sonnets he chooses to set, Britten sustains a musical structure that, no less than the poems themselves, manages to convey both the dynamic variety of the spiritual life and its essential coherence as a process leading toward assurance. Prepared to respond to the subtle shifts of mood and argumentative strategy in Donne, Britten creates songs that, while responsive to Donne's texts, represent a lively, fresh interpretive tradition.

But in addition to their intrinsic importance, Britten's settings of Donne are important also in that they show how texts by Donne—and, by extension, perhaps by other Metaphysical poets as well—invite striking interpretations in contemporary musical idioms. The very shifts of modality in the poems, which John Hollander rightly describes as an insuperable problem for composers in Donne's day, should recommend these poems to composers of today. The intellectual agility of Metaphysical poetry, together with its resistance to sustained dogmatism and its relative freedom from sentimental posturing, should make it attractive to a generation of composers exploiting the agility, objectivity, and hard-won experimental freedom of its own art. Several composers have already accepted this challenge, Britten most successfully. Others will follow. Donne would surely approve.

20. Pears, "The Vocal Music," p. 70.

NOTES ON THE CONTRIBUTORS

ILONA BELL has written on Herbert, Jonson, and Donne. A recent recipient of an ACLS research grant, she has taught at Smith College and at the Massachusetts Institute of Technology and is currently Assistant Professor of English at Williams College.

JAMES S. BAUMLIN recently completed his Ph.D. at Brown University, where he studied with Barbara Lewalski. He teaches history of rhetoric and Renaissance literature at Texas Christian University. His current research focuses on the interconnections among genre, rhetoric, and imitation in Donne's poetry.

WALTER R. DAVIS is Professor of English at Brown University. He is author of *Idea and Act in Elizabethan Fiction, A Map of Arcadia*, and numerous articles on Surrey, More, Sidney, Spenser, Drayton, Jonson, and Bacon, and is editor of *The Works of Thomas Campion*.

HEATHER DUBROW, Associate Professor of English at Carleton College, is author of *Genre* and of several essays on sixteenth- and seventeenth-century literature. She has recently completed a book on Shakespeare's nondramatic poetry.

DENNIS FLYNN is Associate Professor of English at Bentley College, Waltham, Mass. He is author of several essays on Donne and is currently working on a biography of Donne.

PAUL L. GASTON, Professor of English at Southern Illinois University, Edwardsville, has published books on W. D. Snodgrass and Joseph Conrad and articles on Jonson, sixteenth-century miniature painting, and Walker Percy. He is the author of several opera libretti, including one based on Jonson's *Bartholomew Fayre*.

JUDITH SCHERER HERZ is Professor of English at Concordia University, Montreal. She has written articles on Chaucer, Shakespeare, Milton, Marvell, E. M. Forster, and literary biography and has co-edited *E. M. Forster: Centenary Revaluations*. Her current projects include a book, *A Study of E. M. Forster's Short Narratives: Stories and Essays*, and an essay on conversation in *Paradise Lost*.

M. THOMAS HESTER, Associate Professor of English at North Carolina State University, is author of *Kinde Pitty and Brave Scorn: John Donne's Satyres* and of articles on Donne, More, classical satire, and Guilpin. He is co-editor of *John Donne Journal: Studies in the Age of Donne* and of *Renaissance Studies*. He is currently working on a book about genre and metaphor in Donne's poetry and co-editing the commentary of the satires volume of *The Variorum Edition of the Poetry of John Donne*.

KATHLEEN KELLY is Assistant Professor of English at Babson College, Wellesley, Mass., where she coordinates the writing program. She has written papers and articles on the teaching of writing; this is her first essay on English Renaissance poetry.

ANNA K. NARDO is Associate Professor of English at Louisiana State University. She is author of *Milton's Sonnets and the Ideal Community* and of articles on Shakespeare, Jonson, Milton,

Browne, Walton, and fantasy literature. Currently, she is working on a study of the ludic self in seventeenth-century literature.

PATRICK F. O'CONNELL teaches theology and humanities at St. Anselm College, Manchester, N.H. He has published essays on Donne, Thoreau, Dickinson, and various medieval devotional works. He is currently editing the fifth volume of *Journal* for the Princeton edition of *The Writings of Henry D. Thoreau*.

MICHAEL P. PARKER, Associate Professor of English at the United States Naval Academy, has published essays on Carew, Suckling, Waller, and Davenant and is co-author of an architectural guide to Annapolis. He is currently working on a book-length study of Carew's poetry.

TED-LARRY PEBWORTH is Professor of English at the University of Michigan–Dearborn. He is author of *Owen Felltham*, co-author of *Ben Jonson*, and co-editor of *The Poems of Owen Felltham*, *"Too Rich to Clothe the Sunne": Essays on George Herbert* and *Classic and Cavalier: Essays on Jonson and the Sons of Ben*. He is currently editing *The Poems of Sir Henry Wotton* (forthcoming). A member of the Advisory Board and a textual editor of *The Variorum Edition of the Poetry of John Donne*, he has published critical and bibliographical essays on numerous seventeenth-century figures and subjects.

STELLA P. REVARD is Professor of English at Southern Illinois University at Edwardsville. She is author of *The War in Heaven: "Paradise Lost" and the Tradition of Satan's Rebellion* and of articles on Milton, Yeats, Jonson, Drayton, and Shelley. She is currently at work on a book on Pindar and English Renaissance poetry.

ROGER B. ROLLIN, William James Lemon Professor of Literature at Clemson University, is author of *Robert Herrick*, editor of *Hero/Anti-Hero*, and co-editor of *"Trust to Good Verses": Herrick Tercentenary Essays*. He has also published essays on Milton, Herbert, and Jonson and on topics in popular culture ranging from television and movies to popular culture aesthetics. His interest in the applications of psychology and psychoanalysis to the study of the arts has most recently led him to an experiment to obtain empirical data concerning readers' responses to seventeenth-century poems.

JOHN T. SHAWCROSS, Professor of English at the University of Kentucky, has published widely on seventeenth- and twentieth-century literature. Editor of *The Complete Poetry of John Donne* and *The Complete Poetry of John Milton*, he is a member of the Advisory Board and chief textual editor of *The Variorum Edition of the Poetry of John Donne*. Author of *With Mortal Voice: The Creation of "Paradise Lost"* and compiler of *Milton: A Bibliography for the Years 1624–1700*, he has in progress a biography of Milton and a critical book on Donne's poetry and prose.

CLAUDE J. SUMMERS, Professor of English at the University of Michigan–Dearborn, is author of books on E. M. Forster, Christopher Isherwood, and Christopher Marlowe, co-author of *Ben Jonson*, and co-editor of *Classic and Cavalier: Essays on Jonson and the Sons of Ben*, *"Too Rich to Clothe the Sunne": Essays on George Herbert*, and *The Poems of Owen Felltham*. He is an associate editor of *Seventeenth-Century News*. His essays include studies of Marlowe, Shakespeare, Donne, Herbert, Herrick, Vaughan, Isherwood, Auden, and others.

INDEX TO WORKS CITED

This index includes only primary works. The individual Donne elegies and Holy Sonnets are cited by their initial phrases.